Laptop Basics for the Over 50s

Prentice Hall
is an imprint of

Harlow, England • London • New York • Boston • San Francisco • Toronto • Sydney • Singa
Tokyo • Seoul • Taipei • New Delhi • Cape Town • Madrid • Mexico City • Amsterdam • Mu

PEARSON EDUCATION LIMITED

Edinburgh Gate
Harlow CM20 2JE
Tel: +44 (0)1279 623623
Fax: +44 (0)1279 431059
Website: www.pearsoned.co.uk

First published in Great Britain in 2010

ISBN: 978-0-273-72912-9

British Library Cataloguing-in-Publication Data
A catalogue record for this book is available from the British Library

Library of Congress Cataloging-in-Publication Data
Holden, Greg.
Laptop basics for the over 50s in simple steps / Greg Holden.
p. cm.
ISBN 978-0-273-72912-9 (pbk.)
1. Laptop computers. 2. Computers and older people. I. Title.
QA76.5.H6287 2010
004.16--dc22
2009037706

10 9 8 7 6 5 4 3 2 1
13 12 11 10 09

Designed by pentacorbig, High Wycombe
Typeset in 11/14 pt ITC Stone Sans by 3
Printed and bound by Rotolito Lombarda, Italy

The publisher's policy is to use paper manufactured from sustainable forests.

Laptop Basics for the Over 50s

Greg Holden

Use your computer with confidence

Get to grips with practical computing tasks with minimal time, fuss and bother.

In Simple Steps guides guarantee immediate results. They tell you everything you need to know on a specific application; from the most essential tasks to master, to every activity you'll want to accomplish, through to solving the most common problems you'll encounter.

Helpful features

To build your confidence and help you to get the most out of your computer, practical hints, tips and shortcuts feature on every page:

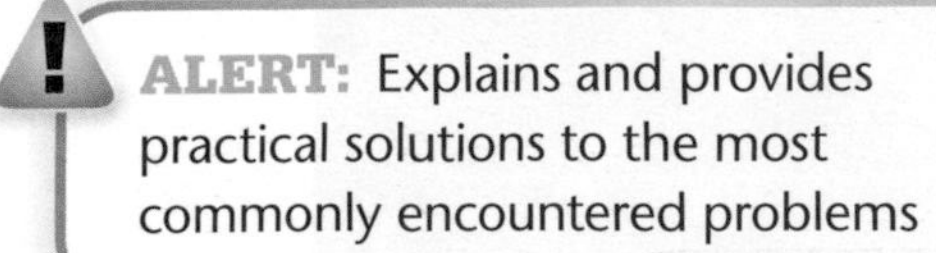

ALERT: Explains and provides practical solutions to the most commonly encountered problems

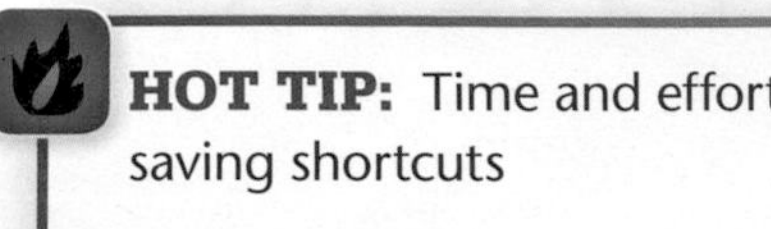

HOT TIP: Time and effort saving shortcuts

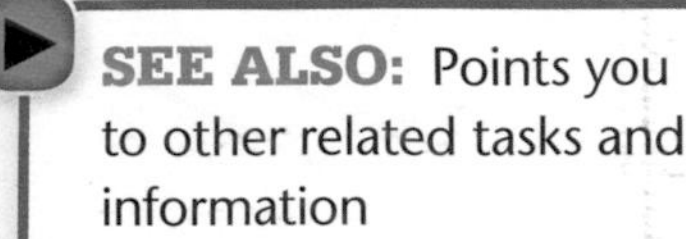

SEE ALSO: Points you to other related tasks and information

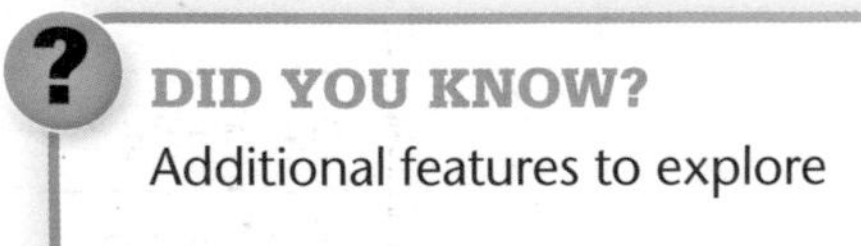

DID YOU KNOW? Additional features to explore

WHAT DOES THIS MEAN?

Jargon and technical terms explained in plain English

Practical. Simple. Fast.

Dedication:

To my teacher, Gelek Rimpoche.

Author's acknowledgements:

Two people continue to support and encourage me through many changes in my life. I am grateful to acknowledge my agent, Neil Salkind, and my assistant and friend, Ann Lindner. In addition, the staff of Studio B Productions have provided invaluable assistance. And last but not least I thank the staff at Pearson, especially Steve Temblett and Katy Robinson, who are working hard to bring computers well within the reach of those of us entering the best years of our lives.

Contents at a glance

Contents

Top 10 Laptop Tips

1 Finding the right laptop

2 Starting to use your laptop

3 Getting online/ connecting to the Web

4 Getting to know Windows

5 Keeping in touch with friends

6 Working with text, music, videos and more

7 Taking your laptop on the road

8 Keeping your laptop running smoothly

9 Networking and creating user accounts

10 Managing files and disk drives

Top 10 Laptop Problems Solved

Top 10 Laptop Tips

Tip 1: Choose the right variety of laptop

Whether you walk into a computer store or shop online, you'll be confronted with signs and labels that call the available devices by different names. They're all laptops because they are portable and can sit on your lap while you use them. But their size and functions vary, so merchants give them a variety of labels. Knowing what they are beforehand will prevent you from being confused.

1. Decide what you want to do with your laptop. If you only want to check email and the occasional weather report online, choose a netbook.

DID YOU KNOW?

If you only want a machine to watch DVDs from any room in your house, a computer may be more than you need. Look for a portable DVD player, which can be as small as a netbook and less expensive than most laptops.

2 If netbooks seem too small in size, look for a slightly larger notebook.

3 Take games and other technical needs into consideration. If you want to play games and do some work on your laptop, go for a full-featured gaming laptop.

WHAT DOES THIS MEAN?

Netbooks: stripped-down, low-price laptops designed primarily for web surfing and email. They have less memory than laptops so can only run a limited number of applications.

Notebook: a small laptop; it has the same memory and features as a regular laptop, the only difference is the size.

Basic laptop: a moderate size laptop with adequate memory and storage that is not as small as a notebook or netbook.

Gaming laptop: a laptop loaded with memory, dual processors and other bells and whistles to handle any technical task.

Tablet PC: a laptop that acts as a tablet on which you write or tap with a special pen rather than using a mouse or touchpad.

Tip 2: Explore the Mobility Center

One of the first features you should explore is the Windows Mobility Center. It contains a variety of settings that makes your computer easier to use. Whenever you want to make your display bright, adjust the sound or change other features, visit the centre by following these steps.

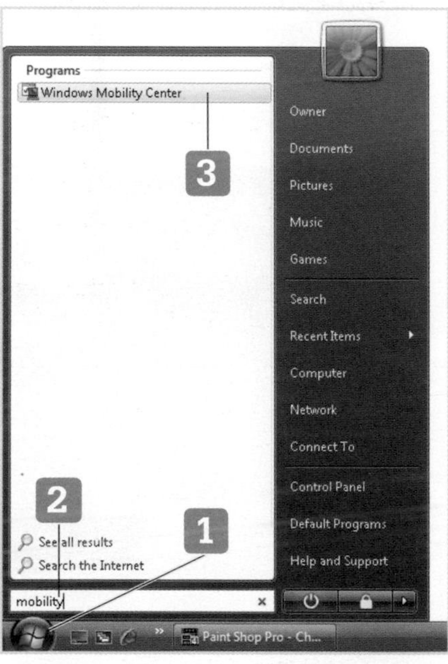

1. Click the Start button.
2. Type mobility.
3. Under Programs, in the results, click Windows Mobility Center.
4. Click one of the options for changing your laptop's visual, audio, or other settings.
5. When you're done, click the red X (the Close button) to close the window.

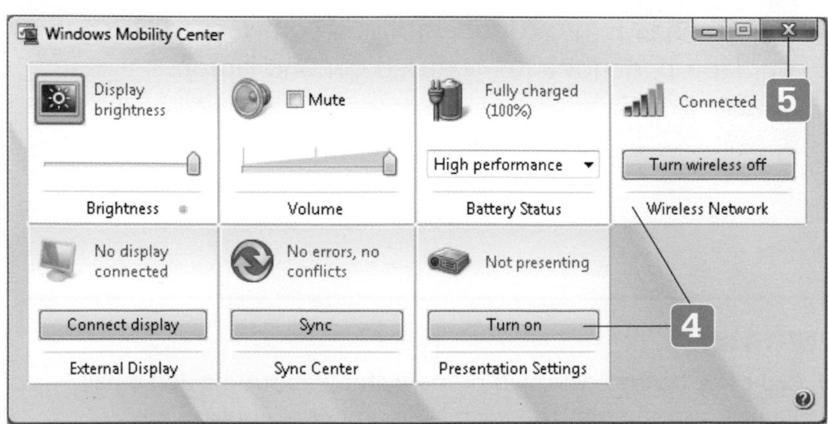

DID YOU KNOW?
Windows Mobility Center is available only on mobile PCs (e.g. laptops, notebooks, smart PCs, tablet PCs).

HOT TIP: Windows Mobility Center offers a blue question mark at the bottom of its interface. Click it to access the Help and Support articles made available.

Tip 3: Navigate to a website

Once you are connected to the Internet, either wirelessly or via a wired Ethernet connection, you can start browsing websites. Windows comes with Microsoft's own web browser, Internet Explorer, built in so you can start using it right away.

1. Click the Internet Explorer icon just to the right of the Start button on the taskbar (it looks like a blue letter 'e').
2. Click once in the Address bar to highlight the current webpage's address (also called a URL or Uniform Resource Locator).
3. Type a new address and press Enter to go to a new webpage.

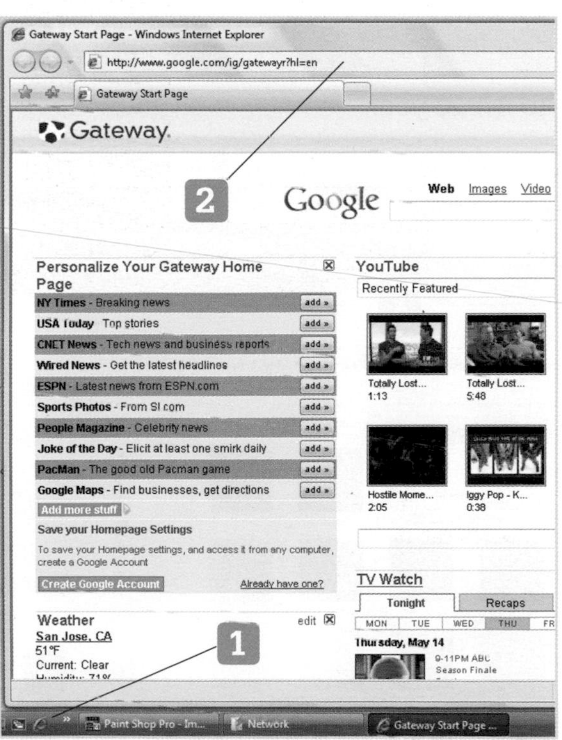

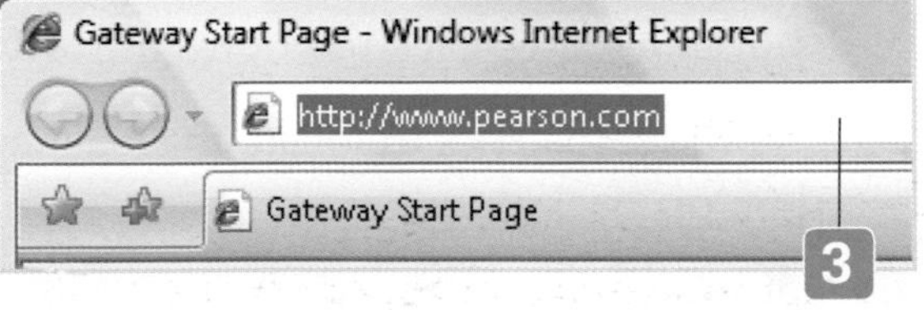

SEE ALSO: When Internet Explorer first opens, it displays the default start-up page – probably one configured by your computer manufacturer. You can change this to your own start-up page as described in Change your browser's home page in Chapter 3.

DID YOU KNOW?

Internet Explorer is not the only web browser around. Many users (including me) prefer a free web browser called Firefox, which you can download and install from www.mozilla.org.

Tip 4: Change the background

The picture on the desktop, which is called the background, can tell the world who you are … like the ring tone on your phone. Unlike a screen saver, which only appears after your laptop has been idle for a period of time, the background is always there, while you're working.

1. Right-click an empty area of the desktop.
2. Click Personalize.

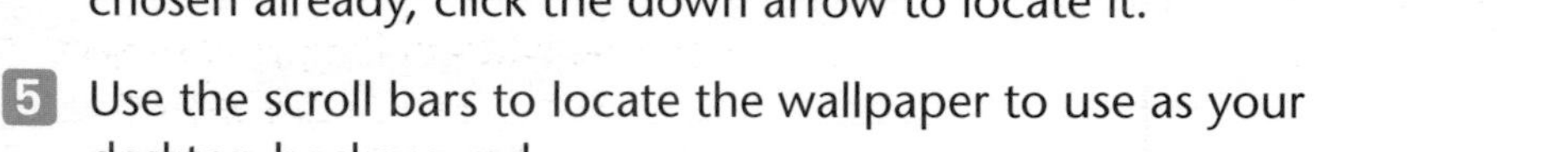

3. Click Desktop Background.

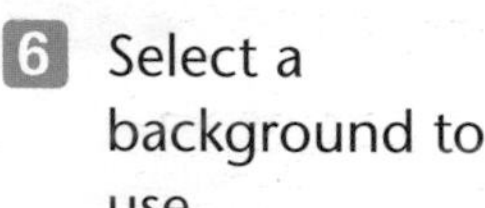

4. For Location, select Windows Wallpapers. If it is not chosen already, click the down arrow to locate it.
5. Use the scroll bars to locate the wallpaper to use as your desktop background.
6. Select a background to use.
7. Select a positioning option (the default is the most common).
8. Click OK.

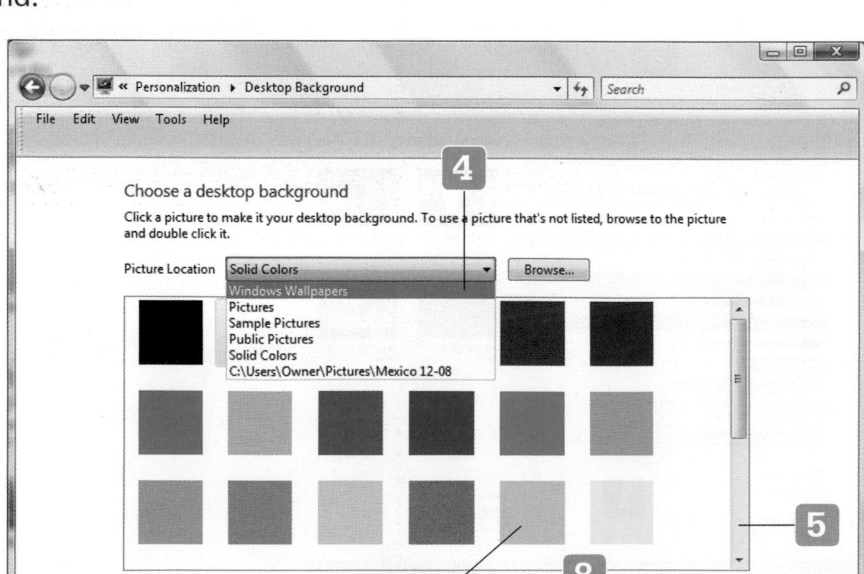

HOT TIP: Click Browse and navigate to another location if the image you want is not in your My Pictures folder.

DID YOU KNOW?

Screen savers and backgrounds used to be needed to save your screen from burn-in, but that is no longer the case.

Tip 5: Compose and send a new message

Much of the time, rather than responding to someone else's message, you'll be composing one from scratch. The process is almost the same as for responding to a message. But you need to make sure you have the correct email address for your recipient(s).

1. Click Create Mail.
2. In the To field, type the recipient's email address.
3. Type a subject in the Subject field.
4. Type the message in the body pane.
5. Click Send.

DID YOU KNOW?
Be precise when writing your subject line so your recipients can easily recall what the email was about.

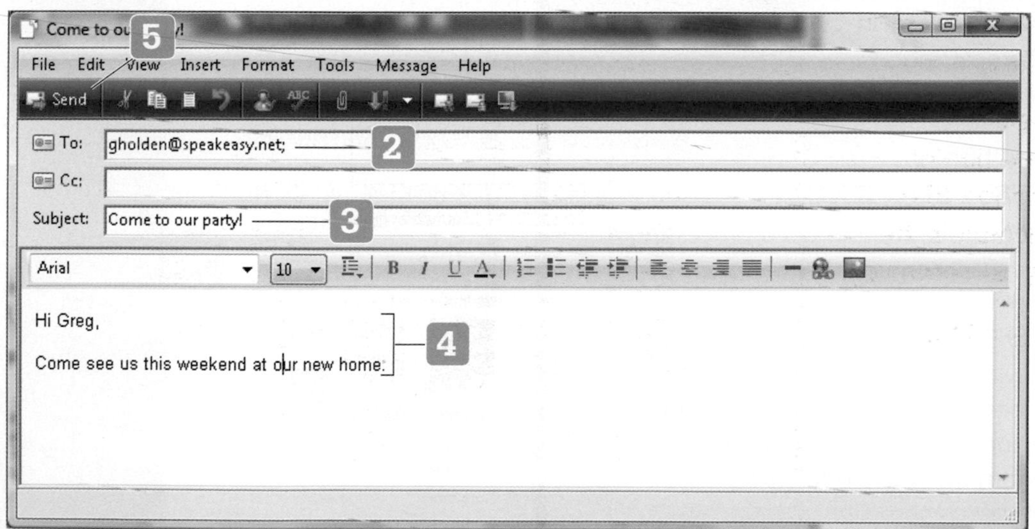

HOT TIP: If you are sending your email to more than one recipient, separate each email address with a semicolon. The easy way to do this is to close Tools and then click Select Recipients to quickly add recipients from your Contacts list.

DID YOU KNOW?
If you want to let someone know what's in the email but don't expect them to respond, you can put them in the Cc line. If you don't want others to know that you sent the email to someone, you can put them in the Bcc line.

Tip 6: Write a letter

You can always write personal letters by hand, but when it comes to business communications or group messages, typing a letter on your computer is by far the most convenient option. Here's how to get started with Windows' built-in application, WordPad.

1. Click Start.
2. Select All Programs.
3. Click Accessories.
4. Click WordPad.

DID YOU KNOW?
WordPad, which is a built-in word processor that comes with Windows, is perfect for straightforward word processing.

DID YOU KNOW?
You'll see another word processing application under Accessories: Notepad. This application is for creating plain-text documents with virtually no formatting. It's best suited for creating webpages and computer programs, not formatted text documents.

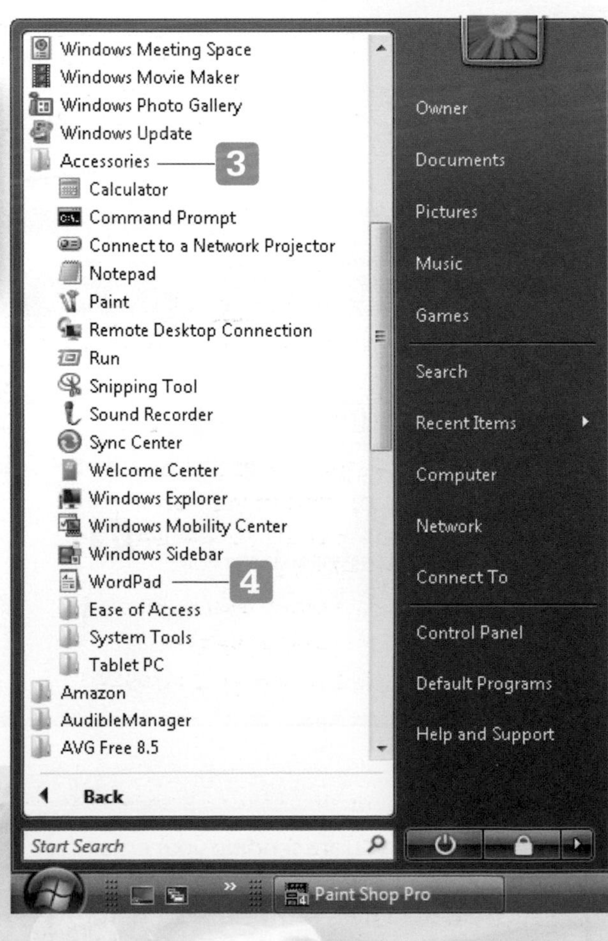

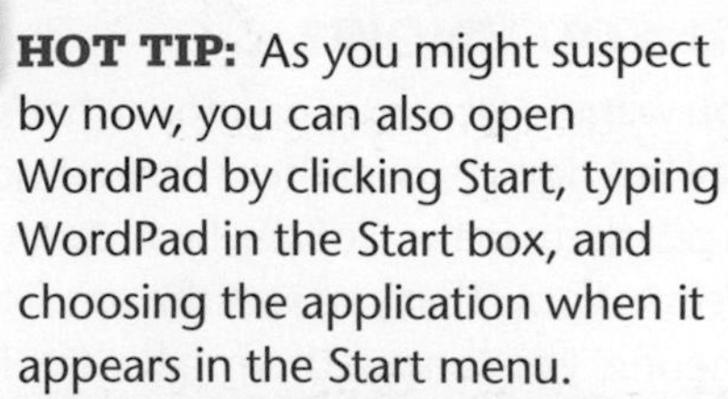

HOT TIP: As you might suspect by now, you can also open WordPad by clicking Start, typing WordPad in the Start box, and choosing the application when it appears in the Start menu.

5 Notice the text cursor, which is positioned so you can start typing. Type your message; press Enter to break a line when needed.

6 Click Center to centre a paragraph.

7 When you are done, click Save.

8 Give your file a name and press Save to save it on your laptop.

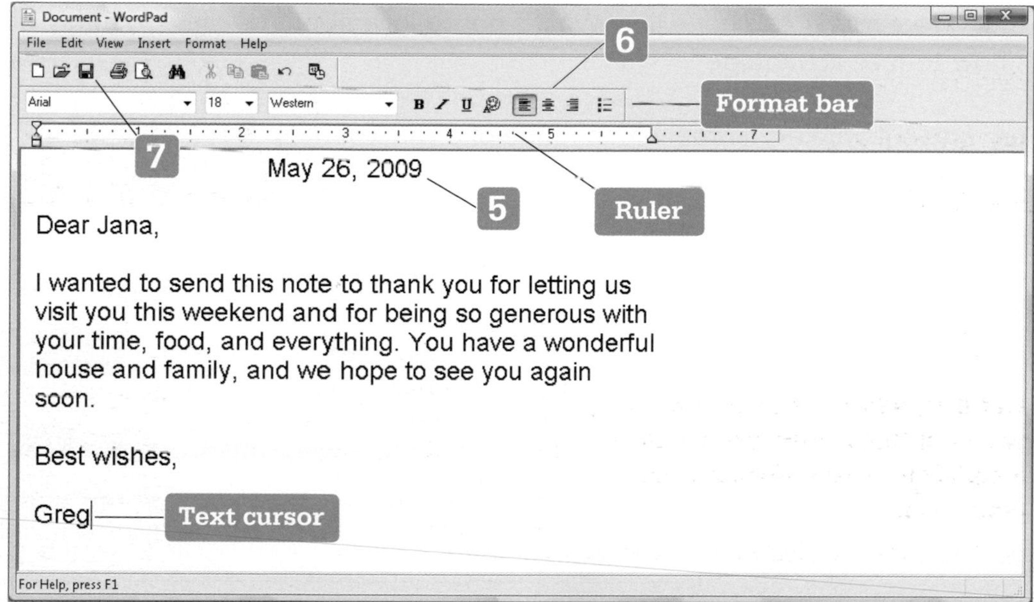

HOT TIP: The bar just above the ruler provides options so you can select font type and size (to the left) and buttons to add bold, italics, underlining, text colour, alignment, and bullet points (to the right).

HOT TIP: To print your letter, click the Print icon (just right of the Save icon in the toolbar).

ALERT: Only press Enter when you want to force a line break. Otherwise, let the word processing program automatically break lines for you.

WHAT DOES THIS MEAN?

.RTF: stands for Rich Text Format, a file format commonly used by word processing applications.

.TXT: stands for Plain Text Format.

.DOC: used to signify a Microsoft Word document.

Tip 7: Connect to a Wi-Fi hotspot

'Free' is one of my favourite words, so my eyes are always scanning billboards and travel brochures for places to stay, eat and just hang out that provide free Wi-Fi hotspots. If your laptop has wireless capabilities, you can access the Internet without physically connecting to a router or phone line. What's not to love about one less monthly bill? Here's how to take advantage.

1. Turn on your wireless laptop within range of a wireless network.
2. Look for your prompt from the Notification area that wireless networks are available.
3. Right-click the network icon (which looks like two computers next to each other) and click Connect to a network.
4. Click a network.
5. Click Connect.

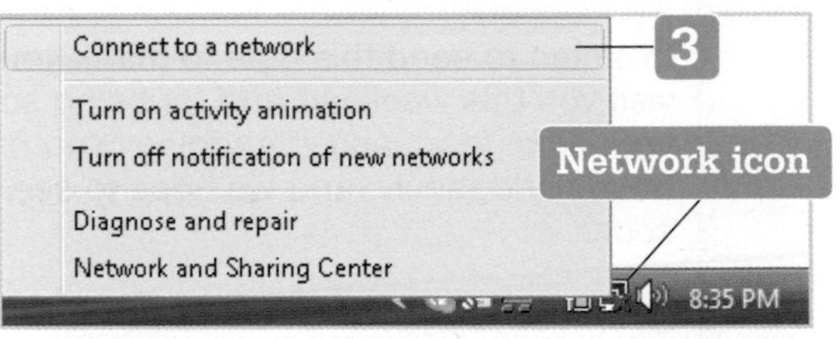

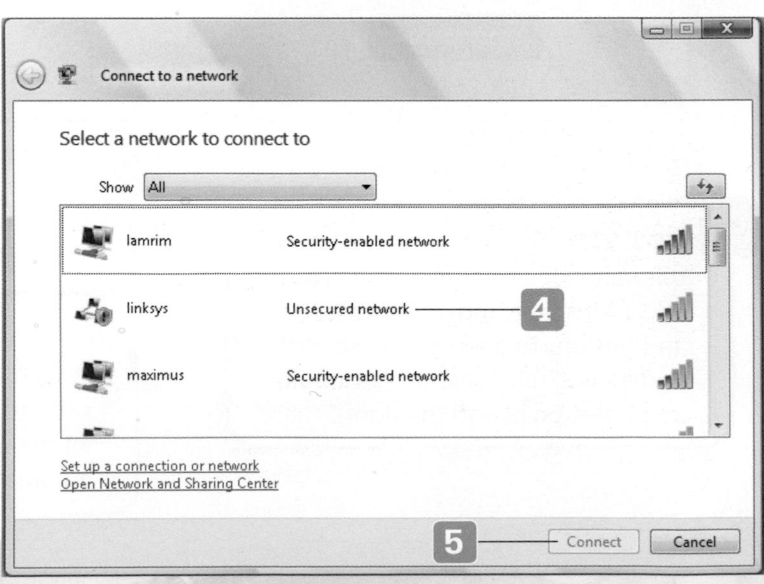

HOT TIP: If you don't see a pop-up, click Start and click Connect To. If prompted, choose Public network. Of the wireless options available, choose the one with the most green bars. The more green bars you have, the stronger the signal.

DID YOU KNOW?
If the Wi-Fi hotspot has a patio, you may be able to sit close to the door and still get access. Otherwise, you may have to actually be in the building itself.

Tip 8: Manage battery power use

In Chapter 8 you will learn how to conserve battery power. Your laptop also has battery power routines that you can adjust. Preconfigured power schemes will help you manage your battery life.

1. Click Start.
2. Click Control Panel.
3. Click Hardware and Sound.
4. Click Power Options.

3
Hardware and Sound
Play CDs or other media automatically
Printer
Mouse

4
Power Options
Change battery settings | Change what the power buttons do |
Require a password when the computer wakes | Change when the computer sleeps

5. Click one of the power schemes, such as Power saver, which will maximise battery life.

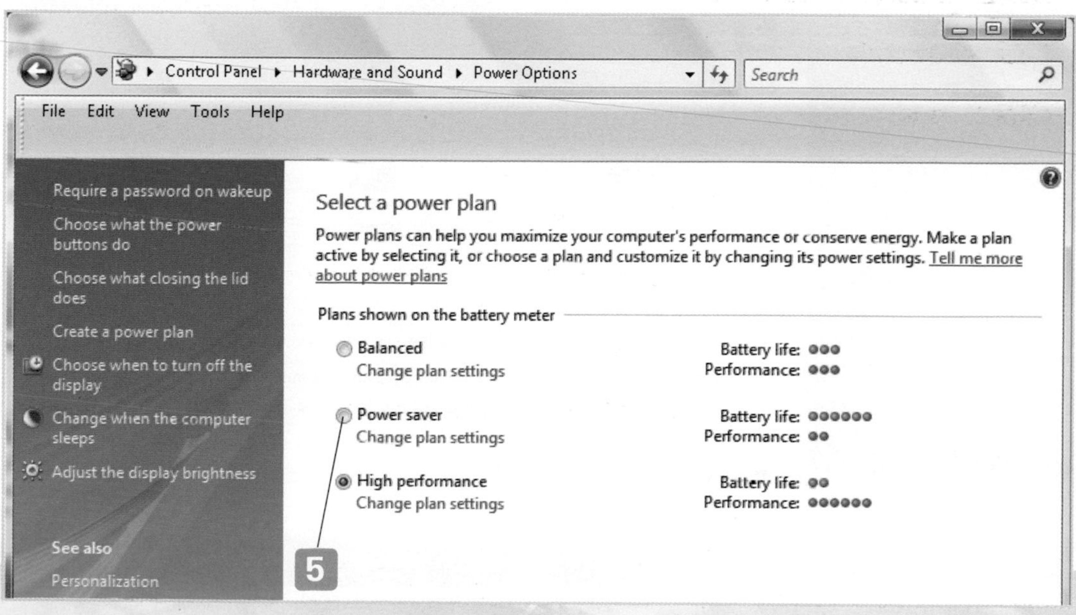

ALERT: Keep in mind that there are trade-offs with power schemes – the routine that gives you the longest battery life will also cause your laptop to go to sleep the quickest when you're not using it.

Tip 9: View networked computers

It seems like magic. From one computer to the other, you can look at anything from photos to documents – as long as the computer's owner has decided to share those resources with you. Here's how to view the contents of a computer that can be shared over a network.

1. Open Network and Sharing Center.
2. Click View computers and devices.
3. All computers and devices connected to the network are displayed.
4. Select the computer you want to use and double-click it to view available items.

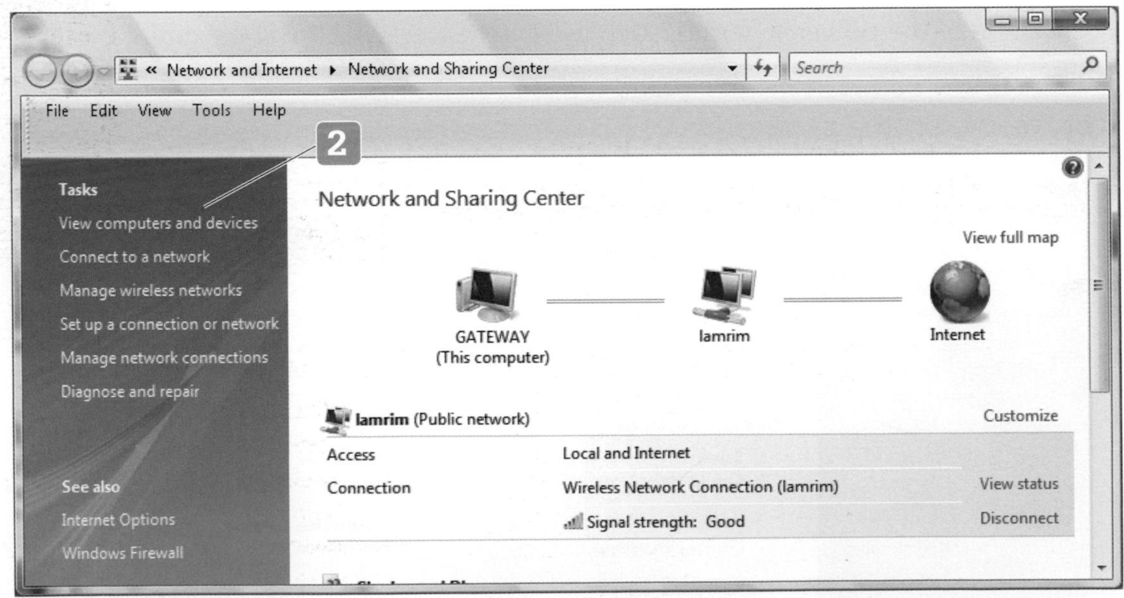

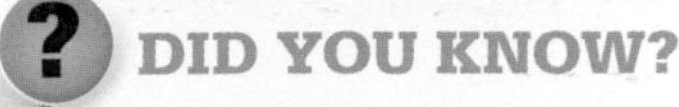

DID YOU KNOW?

In order to see resources such as folders or printers, you need to have file sharing activated. You also must have a resource that you have designated as shared.

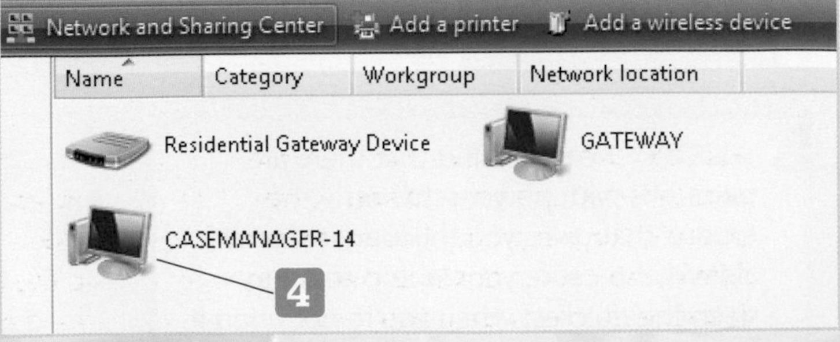

Tip 10: Explore drive or folder contents with Windows Explorer

Before we get into what to do with your files and folders, you simply need to determine what's there in the first place. Here's how to get started by exploring the contents of your drive or folder with Windows Explorer.

1. Click Start.
2. Type windows explorer and press Enter, or click Windows Explorer in the Start menu.
3. Click the folder you want to explore.
4. If needed, click the arrow to expand a folder.
5. Double-click the folder or files you want to explore.

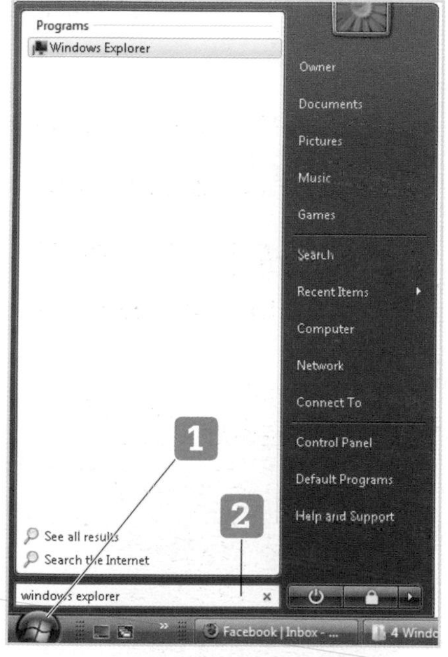

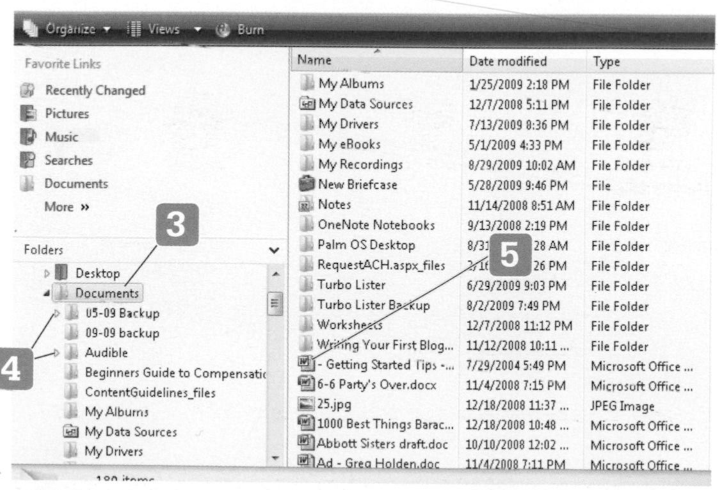

DID YOU KNOW?

Windows Explorer and My Computer (which you access by clicking Start and choosing Computer) look virtually identical. The difference is that Explorer starts by opening your Documents folder, while My Computer starts at the disk drive level.

DID YOU KNOW?

You can have more than one Explorer window open at a time. Doing so can be useful for comparing the contents of different folders or drives and assisting in transferring files back and forth.

ALERT: Don't experiment too boldly with the contents of the Windows and Programs folders. They contain files that are essential to the functioning of your laptop. If you don't know what something contains, you might want to leave well enough alone!

1 Finding the right laptop

Introduction

You say you've never used a laptop? You're not familiar with computers at all, let alone the portable variety? No worries: you've come to the right place. This chapter will get you started from square one. It assumes you want a laptop and need to know what all the computer mumbo-jumbo means. It describes the most important features to look for and how to get comfortable with using and carrying your laptop.

Luckily for you, there are more varieties of laptop than ever before. Many are just as fast and powerful as their larger desktop cousins. You're sure to find one that fits your needs – not necessarily the biggest or most powerful laptop ever created, but the one that is best suited to you.

Choose the right size and weight

Bigger is not necessarily better when it comes to laptops: neither is smaller. Think Goldilocks, and find one that's 'just right'. One of my own laptops, a Sony Vaio, has a big and bright screen but is heavy and makes my shoulder sore when I lug it around in its carrying case. On the other hand, laptops called netbooks are available that are only the size of a hardcover book. Consider these factors when looking for a laptop that's just the right size.

1. Find a laptop that is small and easy to carry. A laptop like the one on the left has a big screen but weighs more than 3 kg. Newer ones like the one on the right are much thinner and only weigh about 1 kg.
2. Ask the salesperson to put the computer in a shoulder bag, if possible, and place it on your shoulder to see how heavy it feels.
3. Check monitor size and view some webpages or other files on the monitor before you buy it.

HOT TIP: If type seems too small on a monitor, the screen resolution may be too fine. You can adjust the resolution to make type appear larger. See Chapter 2 for more information.

DID YOU KNOW?
When you use your laptop at home, you can connect it to an external monitor so type and images are easier to read.

Get enough memory and speed

As you probably know already, memory is an issue the older you get. Computers have memory too, but it performs different functions than simply 'remembering' past files or actions. When shopping for a laptop or other computer, make sure you get the most memory and the fastest processing speeds you can. That way you'll maximise the number of programs you can run, the number of files you can store and the speed with which processes are completed.

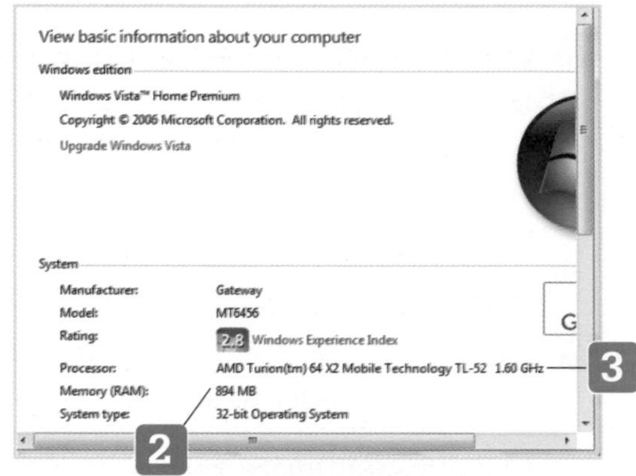

1 Pay attention to Random Access Memory (RAM), which enables programs to run. RAM is measured in either megabytes (MB) or gigabytes (GB). The higher the number, the more RAM you have available.

2 Compare hard disk storage memory, which allows you to keep files ranging from simple text documents to entire movies on your computer. Click Start, choose Computer and click System properties to view the RAM available.

3 Ask about processor speed, which controls how fast your computer copies files or performs calculations.

4 Some laptops have dual processors (shown here as 'Intel Core 2 Duo processor'), which enable them to perform multiple functions.

TOSHIBA SATELLITE A355-S6935 NOTEBOOK

- Huge 400GB storage capacity
- Intel Core 2 Duo processor T6400 — 4
- 400GB hard drive, 4GB memory
- Wireless-N networking
- Reads & writes DVDs & CDs plus
- Labelflash
- 16" TruBrite LCD, 1366 x 768
- Weight: 6.48 lb
- Vista Home Premium 64-bit w/SP1
- 5-in-1 memory card reader

DID YOU KNOW?

Every computer is able to perform multiple functions at once, which is an activity called *multitasking*. You only need dual processors if you perform complex mathematical calculations or other scientific functions. For everyday use, a single processor is adequate.

WHAT DOES THIS MEAN?

GB: gigabytes (1 GB = 1000 MB).

MB: megabytes (1 MB = 1000 bytes).

DRAM: Dynamic Random Access Memory.

SDRAM: synchronous DRAM, a type of DRAM.

SIMM: single inline memory module, an object inserted into the computer to add memory to it.

Hard disk: memory used for file storage, in the form of a round disk that spins in an enclosed case.

Choose the right type of laptop

Whether you walk into a computer store or shop online, you'll be confronted with signs and labels that call the available devices by different names. They're all laptops because they are portable and can sit on your lap while you use them. But their size and functions vary, so merchants give them a variety of labels. Knowing what they are beforehand will prevent you from being confused.

1. Decide what you want to do with your laptop. If you only want to check email and the occasional weather report online, choose a netbook.
2. If netbooks seem too small in size, look for a slightly larger notebook.
3. Take games and other technical needs into consideration. If you want to play games and do some work on your laptop, go for a full-featured gaming laptop.

? DID YOU KNOW?

If you only want a machine to watch DVDs, a computer may be more than you need. Look for a portable DVD player, which can be as small as a netbook and less expensive than most laptops.

WHAT DOES THIS MEAN?

Netbooks: stripped-down, low price laptops designed primarily for web surfing and email. They have less memory than laptops so only run a limited number of applications.

Notebook: a small laptop; it has the same memory and features as a regular laptop, the only difference is the size.

Basic laptop: a moderate size laptop with adequate memory and storage that is not as small as a notebook or netbook.

Gaming laptop: a laptop loaded with memory, dual processors and other bells and whistles to handle any technical task.

Tablet PC: a laptop that acts as a tablet on which you write or tap with a special pen rather than a mouse or touchpad.

Choose between mouse, touchpad, pen or wand

How do you choose menu items and click on links? You do so with an input device – a device you move with your hand to make selections. The choice is important: you don't want to purchase a laptop only to find that you are unable to use it or dislike using it.

1. Try the touchpad. Most laptops come with touchpads – pads just below the keyboard where you move your finger to move a pointer around your computer screen.
2. If you find the touchpad hard to use, look at a tablet PC, which uses a special pen for tapping and writing on screen.
3. A few laptops also come with a wand you wiggle to move the cursor on screen.
4. If none of these options seems comfortable, consider purchasing an external mouse.

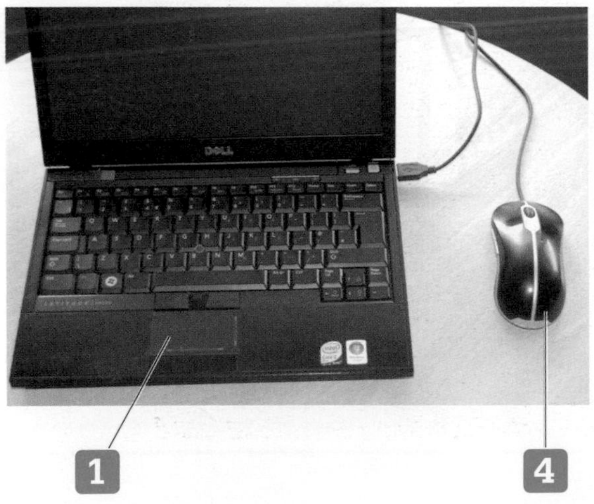

DID YOU KNOW?
Some 'miniature' mice are available especially for laptops. Their small size makes them easy to fit in a laptop case.

DID YOU KNOW?
Tablet PCs are especially good because they have a handwriting recognition feature. But it's not perfect, and your handwriting has to be neat for it to work well. Try it out before you purchase such a device.

Try out the keyboard

Laptop keyboards are small and compressed. The keys are much closer together than on a standalone keyboard. Function, Page Up, Page Down and other special keys are in different places than on a regular keyboard too. Try before you buy.

1. Before you buy, place your hands on the keyboard and try typing to make sure it's comfortable.
2. Make note of the space where your hands rest while you type: is it big enough?
3. Type a short note and make sure the keys aren't too small or close together.
4. Move your thumb or finger down to the touchpad and click the button on the left. Is it easy to make a selection?

HOT TIP: Just as you can buy an external mouse for use with your keyboard, you can purchase an external keyboard as well. External keyboards, like external mice, come in two varieties: wired and wireless. The wired variety plugs into a standard port available in nearly all laptops called a USB port. But make sure the keyboard fits in your laptop carrying case – or if it does not, make sure you are only going to use it at home.

DID YOU KNOW?

Some keyboards are spill resistant. This is one factor that you may want in a keyboard if, like me, you tend to keep a cup of coffee nearby.

Listen to your laptop

If you plan to watch movies or talk to your family using an online conferencing service such as Skype, sound is a consideration. Some laptops have excellent built-in sound. But many have built-in speakers that don't put out a lot of volume. Test your laptop's volume and sound quality before you make a choice.

1. Ask the salesperson where the speakers are. On some laptops, they are on the front edge of the computer so the laptop can play audio while the top is closed.
2. Speakers that are near the keyboard will be covered up and hard to hear if the top is down.
3. Have the salesperson insert a CD so you can listen to audio.
4. Turn up the volume in the system tray so you can test the maximum loudness.

HOT TIP: The volume control in the system tray isn't the only setting for controlling audio. Double-click the volume icon to view a more detailed set of volume controls. Click Start, choose Control Panel, choose Hardware and Sound, and click Manage audio devices under Sound, click Speakers, click Properties, and click the Levels tab to access other sound controls.

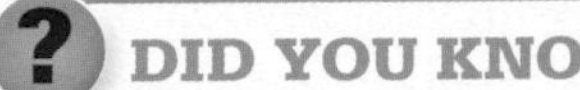

DID YOU KNOW?

You may want to purchase external speakers for your laptop, especially if you plan to watch movies with others. Flat, compact speakers are available that fit easily in laptop cases. At the time of writing, Amazon.co.uk offered the Logitech V10 speakers for under £30, for instance.

Carry your laptop

Laptops are made to be carried from one place to another. But you might find some of them uncomfortable to carry for a long walk. You don't want to strain your shoulder. Salespeople will be happy to help you try out a laptop in a carrying case, and you should take advantage of this. Also keep in mind some good practices for travelling with your laptop.

1. Put the laptop you like in a carrying case and walk around with it.
2. Move the laptop from one side to another if it feels too heavy.
3. Make sure the power cable and other accessories are in the case so your test is realistic.

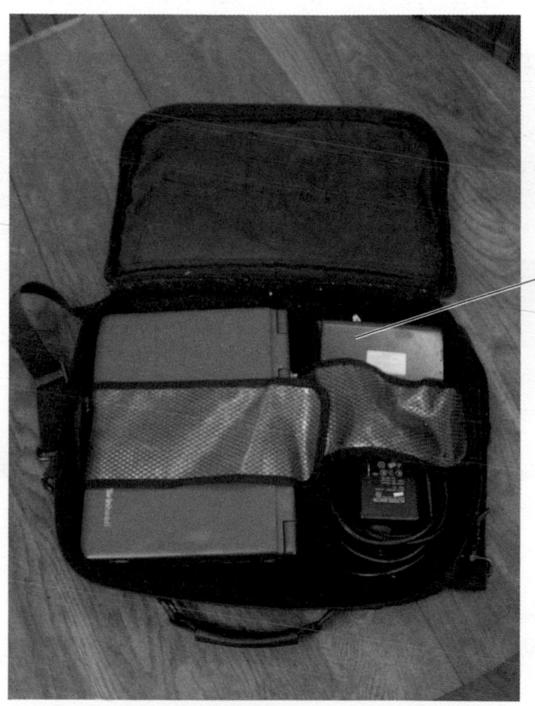

ALERT: If you feel pain while carrying your laptop on your shoulder, switch shoulders or carry it in your hand. Or take breaks so you don't cause a strain or muscle injury.

HOT TIP: Look for a carrying case that has a well-padded shoulder strap to minimise discomfort.

Adjust the monitor

While you are shopping for laptops, make sure you inspect the monitor carefully. Not all monitors are created equal. A 15-inch monitor is considered standard. But if you don't find this big enough, some models come with 17-inch screens. And 19-inch and 20-inch models are available. But the bigger the screen, the heavier the laptop.

1. Ask where the control is to open the laptop monitor. Make sure it is easy to move.
2. Read some webpage text or other contents to make sure they are clear.
3. Point the screen at some bright lights to see how bad the glare is – make sure you can read text even in bright light.

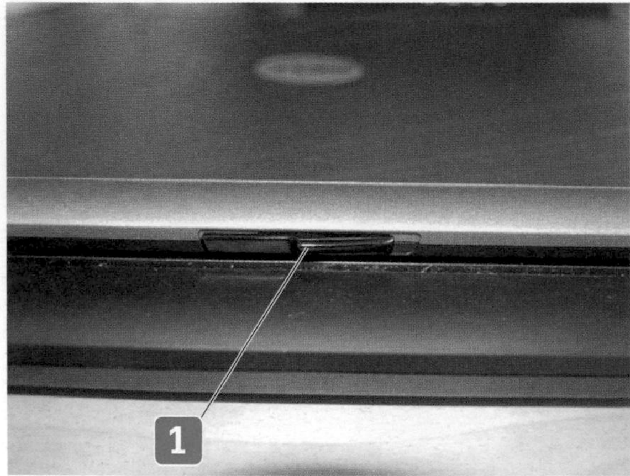

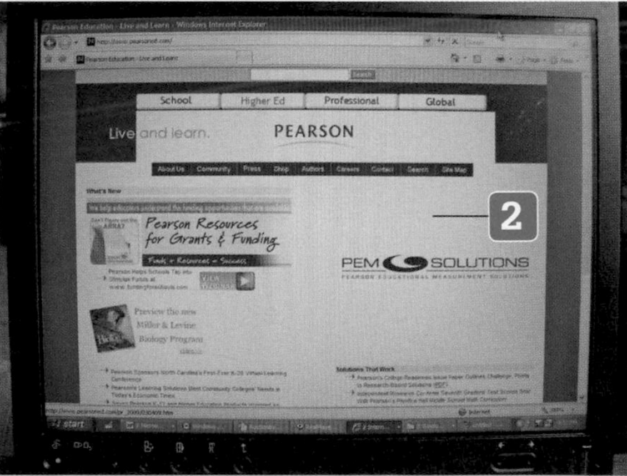

DID YOU KNOW?
The monitor size isn't the only factor that affects whether icons and other objects are easy to read. Another is the resolution – literally, the number of pixels the monitor is set to display. A pixel is a tiny rectangular unit; all computer images are made up of thousands or even millions of pixels. You can change the screen resolution so that screen contents appear larger; see Make your display more readable in Chapter 2.

HOT TIP: All laptop monitors are adjustable. You can move them up and down to reduce glare. Some even swivel to the right or left as well. Get used to adjusting monitors to fit your surroundings.

Make sure you have enough ports and slots

Around the edges and in back of your laptop, you find may holes, buttons and slots of different kinds. Either ask your salesperson or read your manual so you understand what they all do. When you need to add media such as CDs, flash drives, external keyboards or other devices, you'll need to use them.

1. Know where the USB ports are. (There may be some on either side of the laptop.)
2. Know where to plug in your power cable.
3. Know how to open and close the CD drive.
4. SD drives work with SD cards, which are common on phones and other devices.
5. The Ethernet cable connects you to the Internet and is usually next to the phone port.

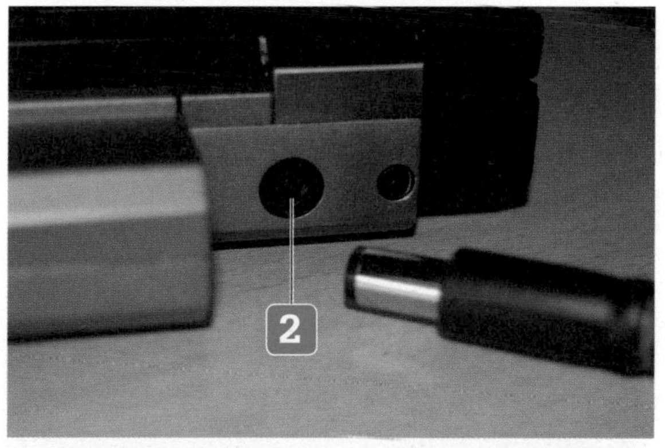

The USB symbol

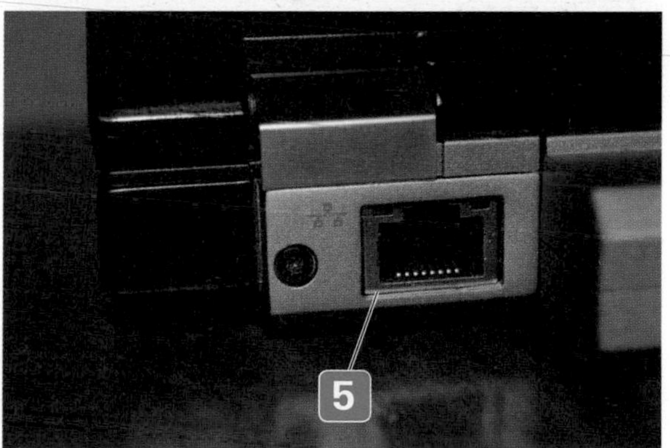

HOT TIP: Knowing where your USB ports are is most important because you're likely to use them most often. They are marked with the USB symbol.

DID YOU KNOW?

Usually there are two audio ports, one for a set of headphones or external speakers, and one for a microphone. They are typically next to one another. A video port connects to an external monitor.

Find a comfortable sitting position

Laptops are intended to work in more than one location. You won't necessarily be using your laptop at a desk. You can sit on a couch, on your patio or on your front steps. Because the keyboard and monitor are so close to one another and cannot be positioned separately as with a desktop, you need to find a comfortable position. Otherwise you might get tired and could feel discomfort, particularly in your back or wrists.

1. Make sure your back is well supported.
2. Make sure the keyboard can be reached easily; don't stretch for the keys, and make sure your wrists are supported.
3. Try to use an office chair or a chair with a straight back and that can be adjusted.

HOT TIP: Try to position the keyboard so your arms are level and you do not have to stretch to make your fingers reach the keys. If the keyboard is too low you'll have to bend down and possibly strain your back to reach it. If it is too high, your wrists and arms will stretch.

HOT TIP: Actually putting the laptop on your lap for any length of time can be problematic. Most laptops emit heat, and you're likely to feel this after a while. Try to place the laptop on a table or flat surface if possible.

Buy a laptop desk

Special portable desks are available that help solve some of the problems associated with positioning your laptop. They provide a flat surface for your computer; they allow you to get the laptop close to you while cushioning your legs; and they are easily carried around, like the laptop itself.

1. Look for a laptop desk that has cushioning on the bottom and a carrying handle.
2. Place your laptop desk on your lap while making sure your back has adequate support.

ALERT: Don't overload your laptop desk with drinks or too many other accessories. They're not intended to hold much more than the laptop itself, and liquid spills can damage your computer.

DID YOU KNOW?

At the time of writing, CDiscount.co.uk was offering the Targus laptop desk at a reduced price of £15.99. Search Google (http://www.google.co.uk) for 'laptop desk' to find more options.

Choose a laptop case

The first and most important accessory you need to buy for your laptop is a carrying case. If your laptop is small enough (for instance, a netbook) it will fit in nearly any shoulder bag or briefcase. But it will be jostled around with your other possessions and could be damaged. A good laptop case offers several advantages.

1 Look for a case that is well padded so the laptop has some protection.

2 Most cases are divided into several sections – one for the laptop, one for the power cord and another for other accessories.

3 Look for a case with dividers that can be removed for more flexibility.

4 Many cases include a handle as well as a shoulder strap. The shoulder strap can also be removed if you prefer to carry by hand.

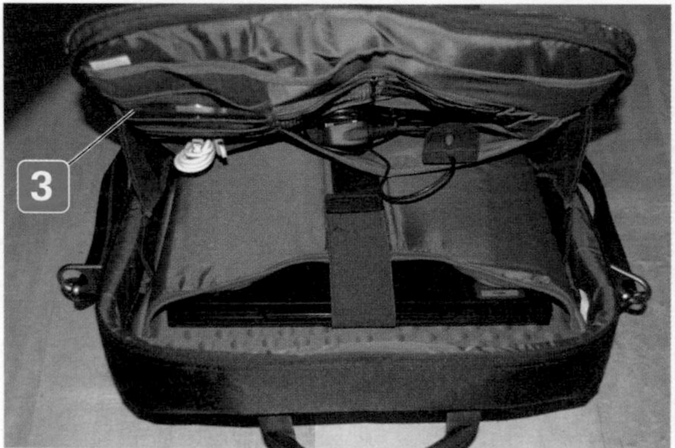

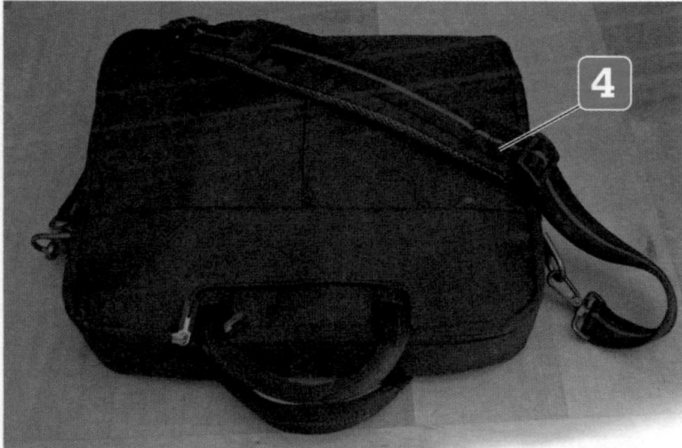

? DID YOU KNOW?

Some laptop bags are specially designed for women; they look more like tote bags than traditional briefcase-style computer cases. They are colourful and have plenty of room for things other than your laptop, too. You'll find descriptions and photos at http://mobileoffice.about.com/od/packingyourmobilegear/tp/womensbags.htm.

HOT TIP: Laptop backpacks are available; they provide good alternatives to the usual shoulder bag. If you plan to travel frequently with your laptop, you might also consider a rolling laptop case, which works like a suitcase with wheels and a long handle so you can pull it behind you.

Add an external mouse

Perhaps the single feature that newcomers to laptops find most difficult to use is the touchpad, wand or other input device. Once you are used to using a mouse with a desktop computer, you might find it jarring and difficult to make the switch. For a nominal expense, you can purchase a mouse that you can carry along with your laptop to make it easier to use.

1. Consider a miniature mouse that will be easy to carry, especially with a netbook. The image here shows a standard mouse and a laptop-sized mouse on the right.

2. Connect your mouse and wait for Windows to detect it.
3. Wait for Windows to automatically install the required software for the mouse (called a driver).
4. If Windows is not able to find the driver, you'll be prompted to install it from a CD.

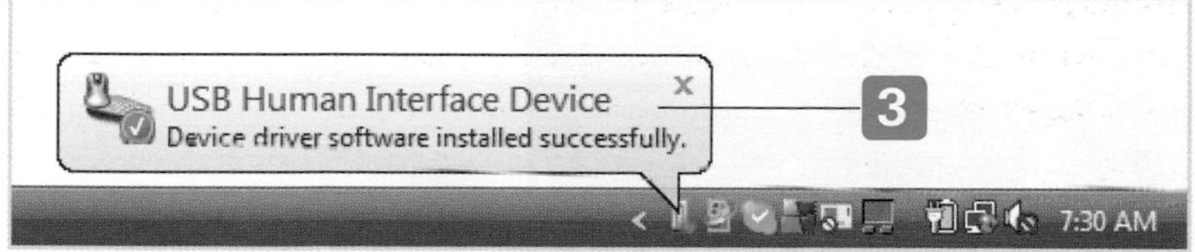

DID YOU KNOW?

If you buy a wireless mouse, you'll still need to connect a wireless adapter to your laptop, and Windows will either have to detect it and install the required driver, or you'll have to install the driver from a CD.

Plug in a bigger monitor

Chances are you'll carry your laptop from place to place and use its built-in monitor with no problems – especially if you have taken the time to choose your monitor carefully, as described earlier in this chapter. But when you're at home, you might find an external monitor such as a conventional CRT monitor or flat-panel display useful. This applies particularly if it is bigger than your laptop screen and you want to watch TV, movies or other content with friends or family. In that case it's easy to connect a second, larger monitor to your laptop.

1. Plug the monitor's video plug into the 15-pin video plug on your laptop. Make sure the broader sides of the plugs match – the plugs are not rectangles and the broader side should go at the top.
2. Press and hold down the Function (Fn) key and then press the video key on your keyboard – the one with the video screen on it.
3. The contents of your laptop monitor should appear on the external monitor at the same time.

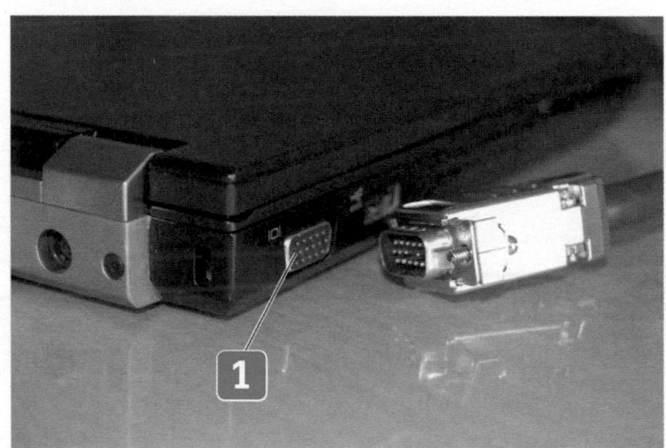

HOT TIP: You don't have to turn off your monitor or laptop before you connect the monitor.

DID YOU KNOW?

Flat screen monitors are available that are easy to carry around your house. They can move with your laptop if you wish and are becoming less and less expensive. Check out the 22-inch laptop monitor offered by Acer through Laptopsdirect.co.uk for £205.96 at the time of writing.

2 Starting to use your laptop

Introduction

Now that you've purchased your new pride and joy, it's time to take it for a test drive. Like most relationships, the trick is to take it nice and easy at first. Even if you're the kind of person who likes to read the last chapter of a book first, it will work out best to read this chapter all the way through before you jump in. Just follow the steps in order, and you'll get your big reward at the end: a machine that's nicely humming with no unplanned stalls by the side of the road.

Find your laptop's power port

Once you bring your new laptop home, you might not actually need to plug it into a power outlet in order to start it up. That depends on whether the laptop's battery has been charged. It's a good idea to plug in your laptop though, because doing so charges the battery. To hook up the juice of your new laptop, just do the following:

1. Find the round power port on your laptop. Some are on the side; some are in the back. Look for the plus sign (+) near the port.
2. Plug the small round end of your power cable into it. Make sure it is seated firmly.

SEE ALSO: All laptops come with one built-in battery; that is what makes them portable. You'll learn more about maintaining your laptop battery later in this chapter.

HOT TIP: Take care when you plug in your power cord that the cable isn't bent too severely. Over months or years, repeated bending can cause the cable to get frayed, and you'll have to replace it. (This has happened to me at least twice.)

Connect your power supply

Once your laptop is plugged into the computer, you can plug it into the power mains – or better still into a surge suppressor, a device that prevents electrical damage from sudden variations in power. Such items often have several power outlets built in, so they can accommodate many other appliances too.

1. Make sure the power cord is plugged firmly into the transformer – the large plastic box that comes with the power cord.
2. Plug the cord into the wall socket or power strip.

HOT TIP: Make sure you plug your laptop into an outlet that has three plugs rather than an older two-prong variety. The third plug provides a ground and helps prevent electrical shorts that can damage a computer.

DID YOU KNOW?

It's a good idea to keep your laptop plugged in when you're not using it (even if the lid is closed and it is off or 'hibernating'), as this keeps the battery charged up. When you want to use the laptop elsewhere, you can then disconnect it from the power cord and it will be ready to go.

Connect external devices

Before you turn on your laptop, it's a good idea to connect any external devices you plan to use. These might include an external mouse or a portable hard disk called a flash drive or 'pen drive'. For virtually all laptops, these connect by means of USB ports.

1. Plug the device securely into the USB port.
2. Make sure the USB design shows on top so the connector is right side up.
3. Once your computer has started up, look for the device by clicking Start and choosing Computer.
4. Your pen drive should appear in Computer under the category Devices with Removable Storage.

HOT TIP: Many computer users wear their pen drives on a strap around their necks or on a keychain so they won't get lost. Consider doing this, particularly if you store important information on your drive.

DID YOU KNOW?
You don't have to 'turn on' your USB port or your USB device to use it.

Open your laptop

Laptops are designed to be safe and secure. The usual 'clamshell' design ensures that the screen remains undamaged when you carry it around. Release the monitor from the bottom of the laptop and open it up so you can start using it.

1. Find the release mechanism.
2. Open your laptop's lid.
3. Position the monitor so it is ready for use.

HOT TIP: When you first open your laptop, you might not see anything on screen. You might have to tap the power button lightly to turn it on or to 'awaken' it if it was previously placed in hibernation mode.

ALERT: You need to close the lid gently and avoid slamming it shut so you don't damage the latch. And don't carry your laptop around with the lid up or you might bump or scratch the monitor.

Switch on your laptop

Once you have your laptop plugged in (if necessary) and any external devices connected, you can turn it on. The location of the power button varies from one laptop to the next; refer to the manual that came with it to find it.

1. Locate the Power button, which is usually above the keyboard in the centre or off to one side.
2. The button itself or other lights should light up to let you know your laptop is on.
3. If it takes a minute or two for the computer to boot up, that's not unusual. Relax and be patient.

DID YOU KNOW?
The on–off control on most laptops takes the form of a button rather than a switch you flip back and forth.

ALERT: Get in the habit of pressing the power switch only for a second or so and then releasing it. If you hold it for several seconds, you might well turn your laptop off. Many laptops are configured to turn off if you hold the power button down for a length of time.

Tour your desktop

Whenever you start up your laptop, you'll see at least two things: a logon screen and your desktop. The logon screen is where you enter a protective password if you have created one. The desktop is where you locate applications, find files and switch from one program or document to another.

1. Click the logon icon to access your desktop.
2. When your desktop appears, check the program icons. Double-click any icon to start it up.
3. Check your System Tray and the clock and make sure the time is accurate.
4. Know where the Start button is.

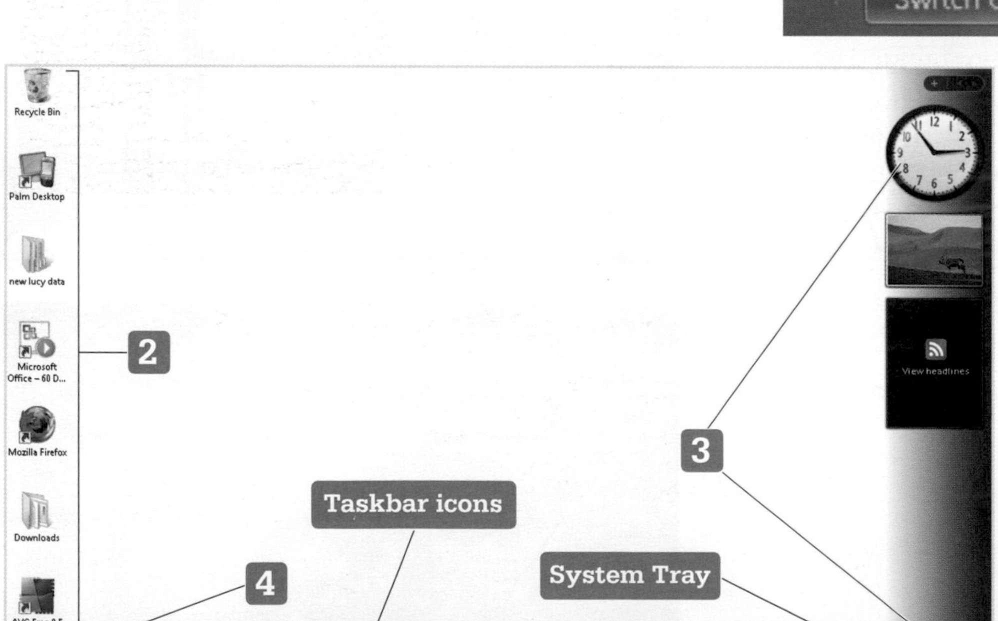

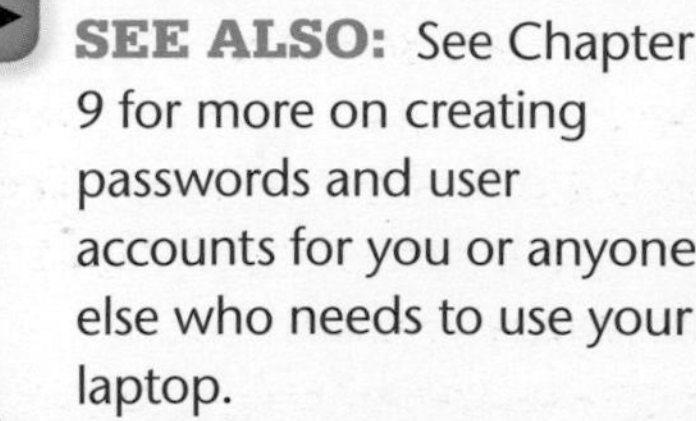

SEE ALSO: See Chapter 9 for more on creating passwords and user accounts for you or anyone else who needs to use your laptop.

DID YOU KNOW?
When the taskbar first appears, it's empty except for the Start button. But each time you start a program, such as the web browser Internet Explorer, it appears as a button on the taskbar so you can open or close a window or switch from one program to another.

Explore the Mobility Center

One of the first features you should explore is the Windows Mobility Center. It contains a variety of settings that makes your computer easier to use. Whenever you want to make your display bright, adjust the sound, or change other features, visit the centre by following these steps.

1. Click the Start button.
2. Type mobility.
3. Under Programs, in the results, click Windows Mobility Center.
4. Click one of the options for changing your laptop's visual, audio or other settings.
5. When you're done, click the red X [the Close button] to close the window.

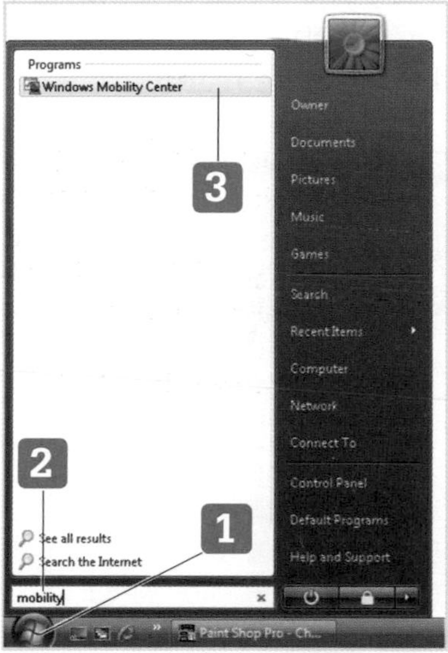

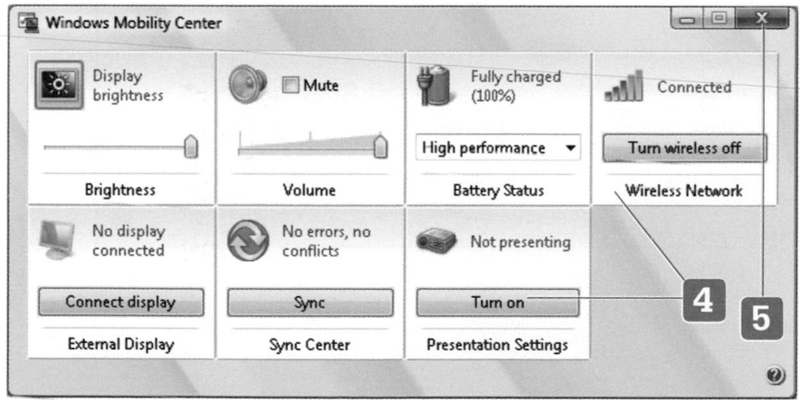

DID YOU KNOW?
Windows Mobility Center is available only on mobile PCs (e.g. laptops, notebooks, smart PCs, tablet PCs).

HOT TIP: Windows Mobility Center offers a blue question mark at the bottom of its interface. Click it to access the Help and Support articles made available.

Make your display more readable

What you see isn't necessarily what you're stuck with. If you're starting to squint like me when you try to focus (or if your arms are getting too short to make reading a menu comfortable), you have a friend in your laptop. Follow the steps below to make your display more readable:

1. Open the Mobility Center as described in the preceding section.
2. Turn the brightness up by moving the slider to the right.
3. If you have an external display, click Connect display to connect it.

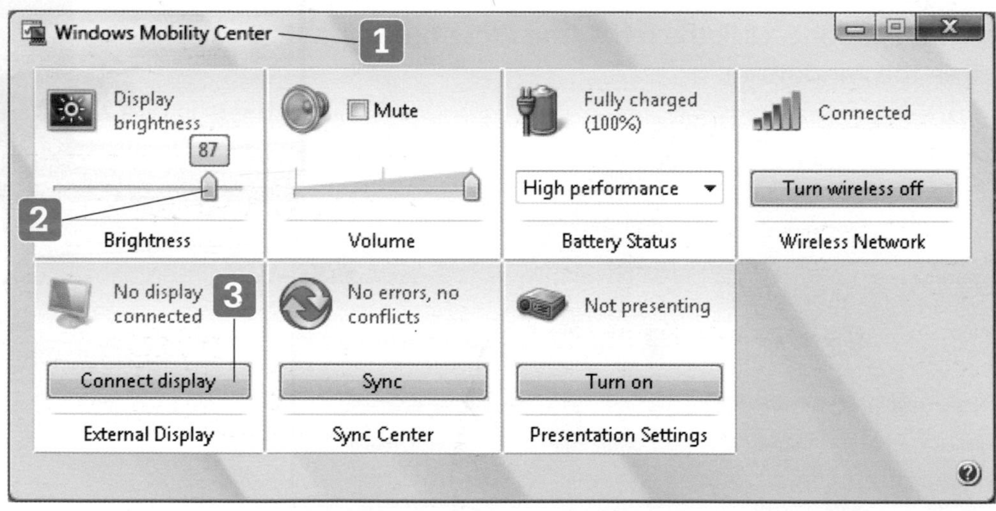

SEE ALSO: Plug in a bigger monitor in Chapter 1 for more information on where to connect an external monitor to your laptop.

DID YOU KNOW?

Some computer manufacturers may add additional options to the Mobility Center; the version you see may look slightly different to the one shown here.

Change resolution

The resolution of a computer monitor refers to the number of tiny rectangles called pixels that are contained within it. Most computer images are made up of pixels. Often the default resolution is similar to 1280 × 800 which causes millions of pixels to be displayed – but it makes icons and text small. By changing the resolution, screen contents appear larger.

1. Click Start and choose Control Panel.
2. Click Adjust screen resolution.
3. Move the Resolution slider to the left, towards Low.
4. Click Apply to change the resolution without closing Display Settings.
5. Click OK to change the resolution and close Display Settings.

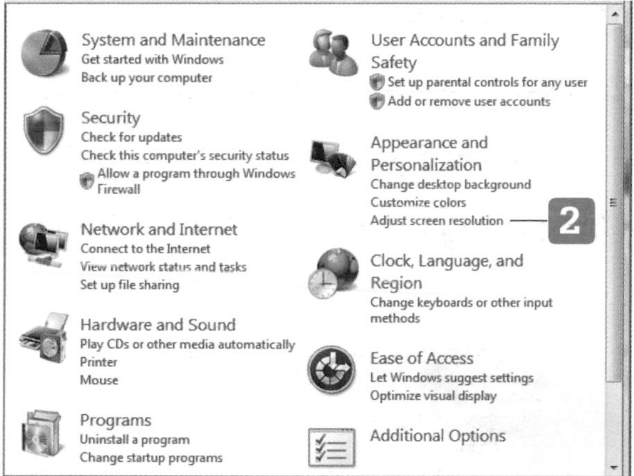

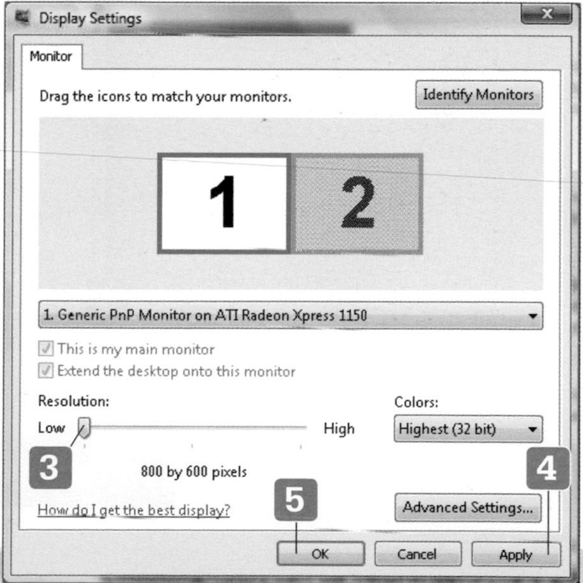

HOT TIP: Choosing Apply can be helpful because it allows you to change resolution quickly again if you don't like the first change you made. You don't have to re-open Display Settings.

DID YOU KNOW?

The Windows Control Panel comes in two versions. If you don't see Adjust screen resolution as an option, you're probably in 'Classic View'. Click Control Panel Home to see the Adjust screen resolution option.

Adjust the volume

Earlier in this chapter, you learned about the Mobility Center, which has a volume control for your laptop. But there's another volume control in your System Tray that's easier to access – and that's available to you all the time. Here's how to make adjustments:

1. Single-click the Volume control in the System Tray. It looks like a speaker icon.
2. Move the volume slider up to increase the volume, or move the volume slider down to decrease the volume.
3. Click Mute to mute the volume completely.

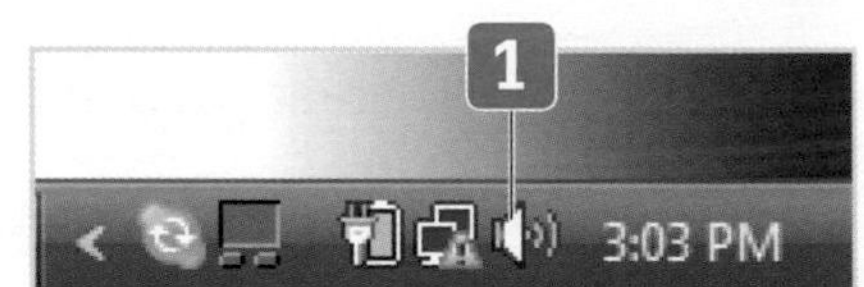

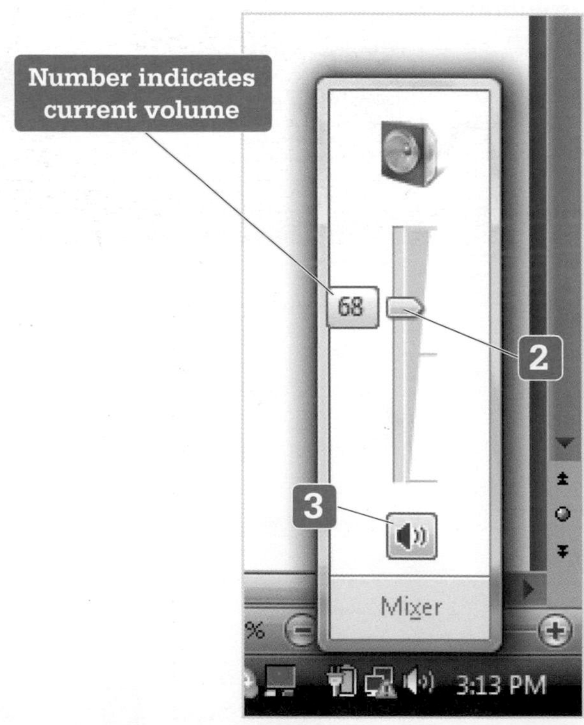

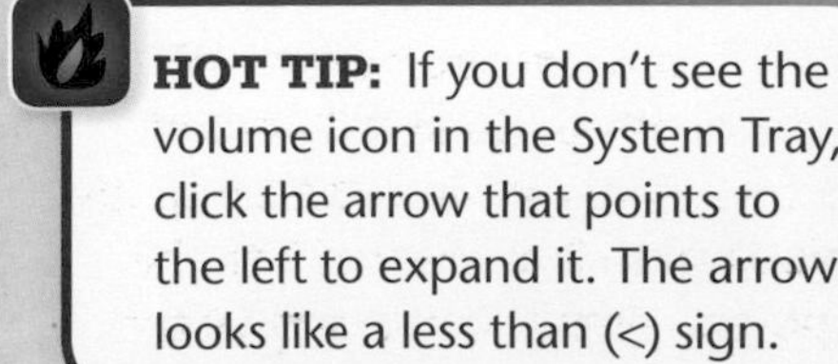

HOT TIP: If you don't see the volume icon in the System Tray, click the arrow that points to the left to expand it. The arrow looks like a less than (<) sign.

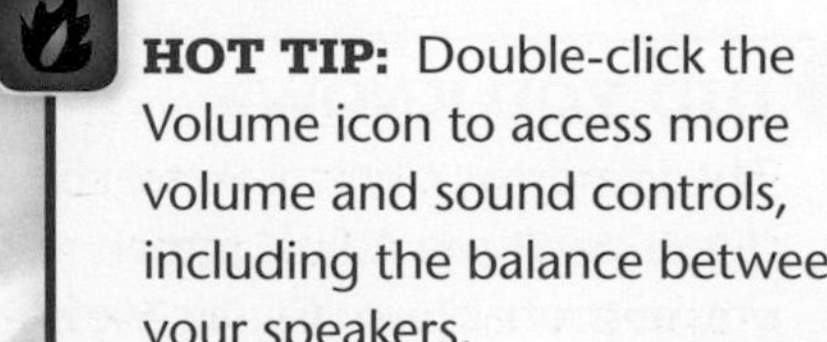

HOT TIP: Double-click the Volume icon to access more volume and sound controls, including the balance between your speakers.

Load a CD or DVD

Not only does your laptop allow you to work with printers and other devices to your heart's content but you've also got an entertainment centre as part of the package deal. You can use your laptop to play an audio CD or a video DVD, or load software you need to use external devices such as printers. Consult your owner's manual (or your laptop salesperson) to find the location of the button that opens your CD drive. Then follow these steps.

1. Press and release the button that opens the CD drive.
2. Gently place the CD or DVD face up on the circular disk holder.
3. Push the CD drive button again to close the tray.
4. When an AutoPlay dialogue box appears, choose one of the available options.

DID YOU KNOW?
There is no software instruction in Windows that allows you to open the CD drive. You do that by manually pressing a button. Usually the button is on the CD drive cover itself.

ALERT: You can also close the CD drive by gently pushing it. It should retract automatically into the computer. But don't push it all the way into the computer – simply start it and let the computer draw it inside.

Connect your printer

You're probably not going to want to take your printer with you when you tuck your laptop under your arm and head for the coffee shop. But eventually you'll want to introduce the two and make sure they can communicate smoothly. Just follow the steps here.

1. Plug in the printer and connect it to the PC using a USB cable.
2. Insert the CD for the device, if you have it.
3. If a pop-up message appears regarding the CD, click the X to close the window.
4. Turn on the printer and wait while the driver is installed.

DID YOU KNOW?
USB is a faster connection than a parallel port, but FireWire is faster than both.

HOT TIP: If there are specific instructions that came with your printer, follow them instead of the generic steps offered here. If the printer does not install properly, refer to the printer's user manual.

My laptop went blank!

Because laptops frequently operate on batteries, they have power-saving features. One of those features causes the display to go dark when you haven't used it for a time. If you close the computer lid and carry it to another location, when you open it again, the screen will be dark to save power also. Don't panic. Just follow these steps.

1. First, push one or two keys on the keyboard in case your screen is blank and your laptop hasn't gone to sleep yet.
2. If your desktop does not reappear, press the power button briefly and release.
3. When the logon screen appears, click the icon and enter your password if necessary.

SEE ALSO: You can intentionally put your laptop to sleep if you have finished using it and you don't want to turn it off completely. See Put your laptop to sleep or turn it off, later in this chapter.

ALERT: Make sure you only press your power button once, and for less than a second. If you press and hold it down for several seconds you'll force the computer to turn off completely. You may lose work you have not saved.

Adjust your power-saving settings

These days it's all about ecology. But conservation has a special benefit with regard to your laptop in allowing more time before you have to recharge. By adjusting your power-saving settings, you control how long your laptop will sit before it puts itself to sleep automatically. Here's how to be green while keeping your laptop available for work you need to do.

1. Click Start and choose Control Panel.
2. Click Hardware and Sound.
3. Click Power Options.

Hardware and Sound — 2
Play CDs or other media automatically
Printer
Mouse

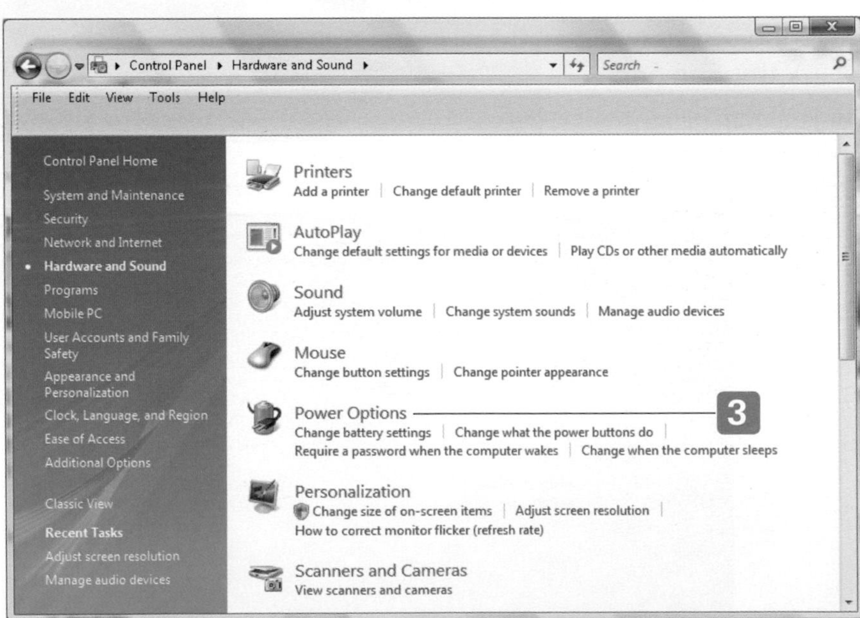

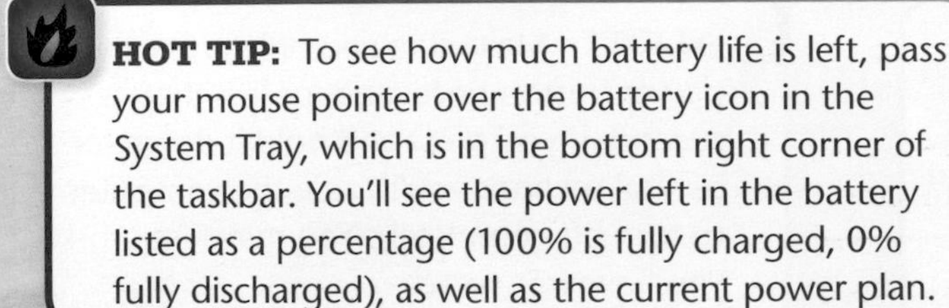

HOT TIP: To see how much battery life is left, pass your mouse pointer over the battery icon in the System Tray, which is in the bottom right corner of the taskbar. You'll see the power left in the battery listed as a percentage (100% is fully charged, 0% fully discharged), as well as the current power plan.

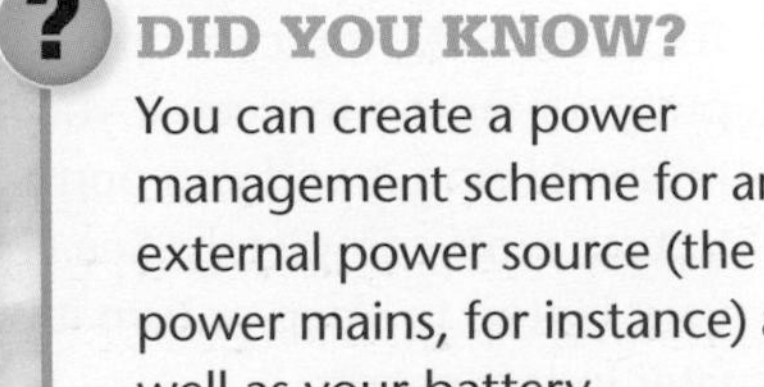

DID YOU KNOW?

You can create a power management scheme for an external power source (the power mains, for instance) as well as your battery.

Define your laptop's power controls

You can exercise control over what happens when you close your laptop's lid or press your power button. For each of these options you can choose Shut Down, Do nothing, Sleep, or Hibernate.

1. Open Power Options as described in the preceding section.
2. When the Power Options window opens, scan the options for balancing power usage with laptop performance.
3. Click one of the buttons to choose a power plan.
4. Click one of the links at the top of the left-hand column to control how the laptop goes to sleep or operates while it is asleep.

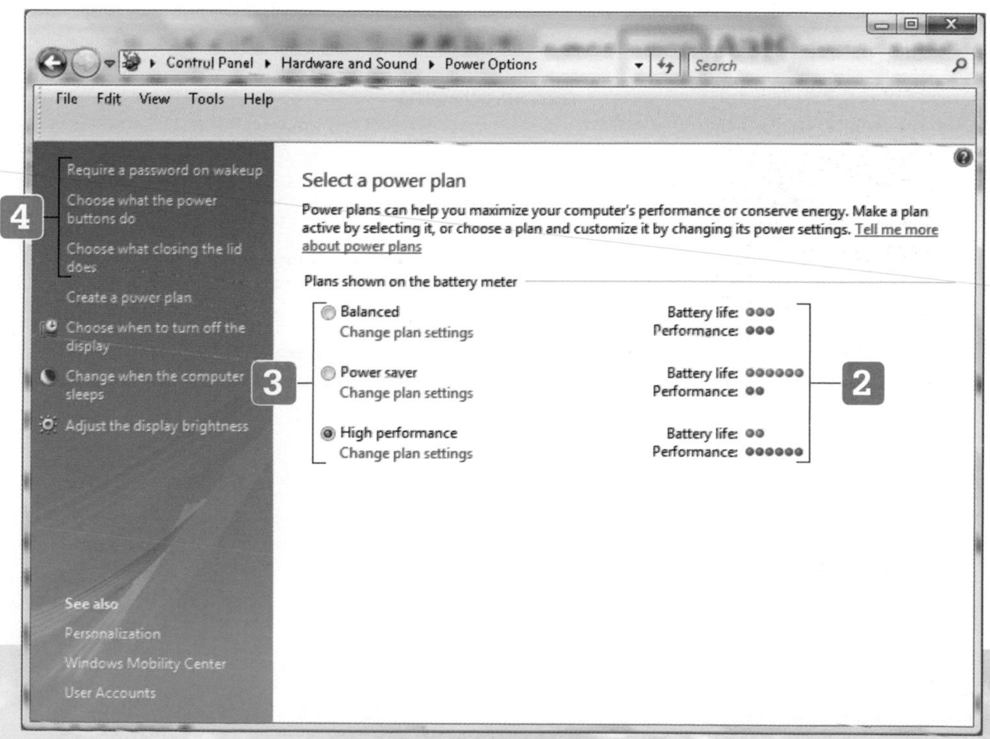

ALERT: If you do not require a password when your laptop 'wakes up', anyone can start using it. If you have email or other windows open, your privacy could easily be violated.

5 When the System Settings window appears, click the down arrow next to one of the options to choose a behaviour.

6 Click this button to require a password to access the laptop after it has been put to sleep.

7 Click Save changes.

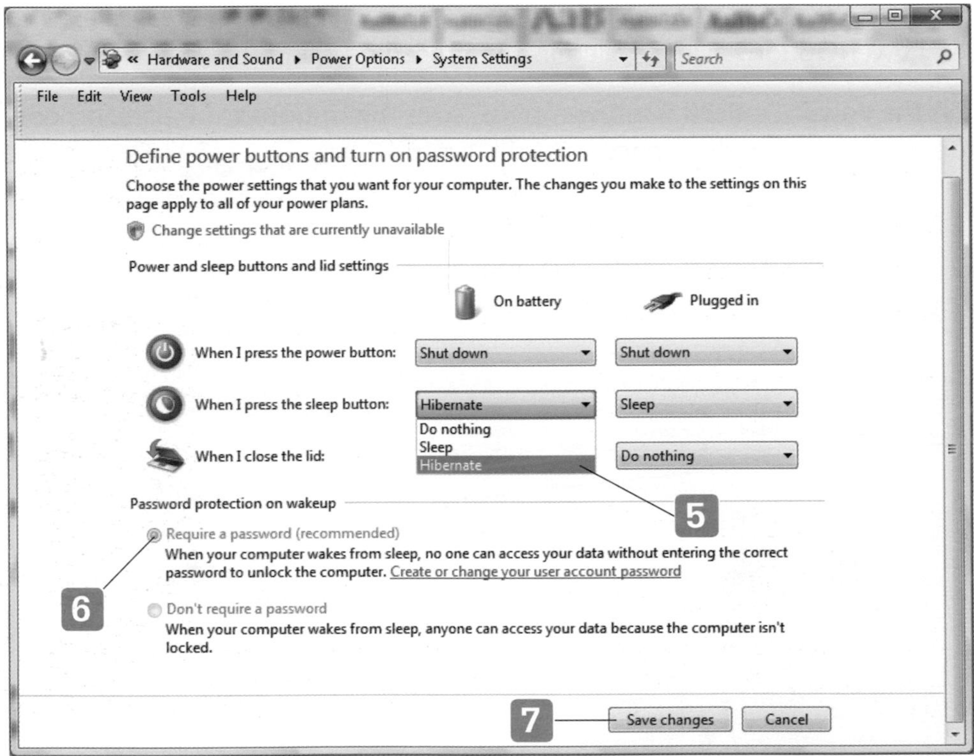

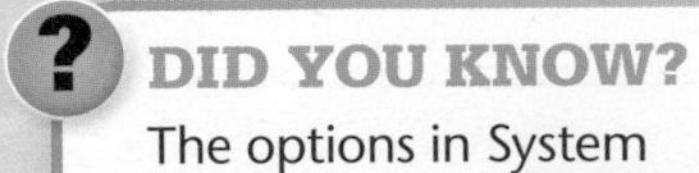

DID YOU KNOW?

The options in System Settings may differ from what you see here depending on the controls your laptop manufacturer makes available.

Put your laptop to sleep or turn it off

A catnap is one of life's pleasures, so don't deprive your laptop of this escape. It'll help your laptop save power and work longer on its battery as well. In addition, when you're done for the day you can shut your computer down.

1. Click Start.
2. Click here to put your laptop into Sleep mode.
3. Click here to access other options.
4. Click one of these options to put your laptop to sleep, cause it to hibernate or shut it down.

DID YOU KNOW?

Some laptops have different buttons for putting the laptop to sleep and turning the power off or on.

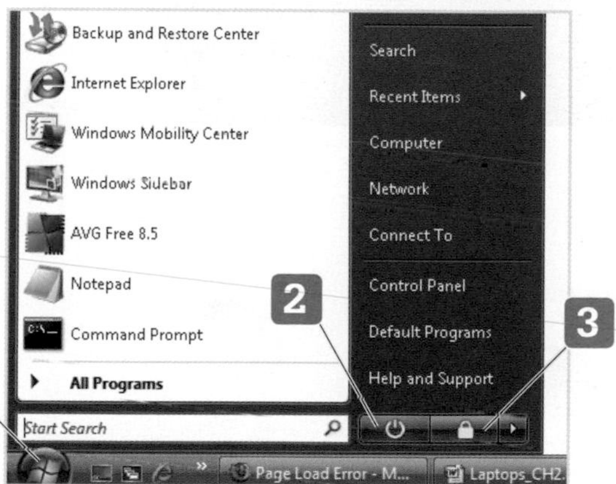

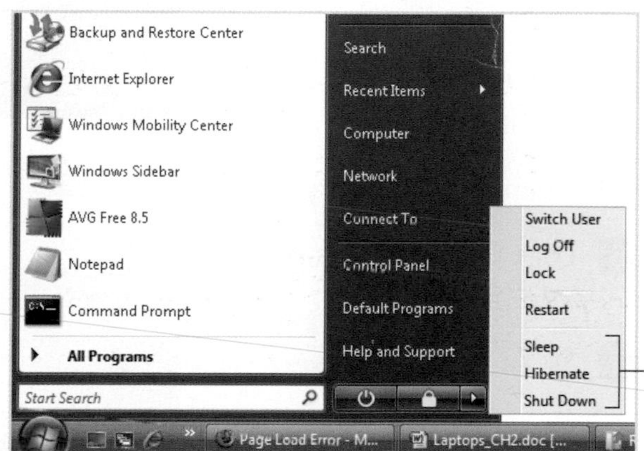

WHAT DOES THIS MEAN?

Windows gives you three modes for turning off your computer when you're not using it; Shut Down, Hibernate or Sleep. What's the difference between them?

Shut down: this means you turn your computer off completely, and that includes closing any open windows or applications. When you turn your computer on again after shutting it down, it goes through its complete start-up routine, and you start with a blank screen.

Hibernate: this means Windows saves any work you had under way before your computer goes blank. Open applications and files remain open and appear when you start your computer up again. Hibernate saves battery power.

Sleep: this mode should be used only when you are going to be away from your laptop for a short period of time. Your work isn't saved before the screen goes blank. Battery power isn't saved in sleep mode because your power isn't completely turned off.

Change the battery

Eventually a new battery will be needed. Like anything else, making the change is simple as long as you know how to do it. Just follow these steps:

1. Unplug the laptop from the wall outlet and remove the power cable. Set the power cable aside.
2. Carefully turn the laptop upside-down and place it on a desk or table.
3. Locate the battery bay and open it.
4. Unlatch the battery latch.
5. Change the battery.
6. Lock the new battery into place.
7. Secure the latch.

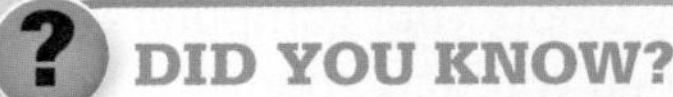

DID YOU KNOW?

Sometimes you have to use a screwdriver to get inside the battery bay. Other times you simply need to slide out the compartment door.

HOT TIP: There's a latch that holds the battery in place even after the battery bay's door has been opened. You'll need to release this latch to get to the battery.

Assign yourself a user name and password

Your first line of security is to assign yourself a user account, including a password, to keep unauthorised users from viewing your files without your permission.

1. Click Start and choose Control Panel.
2. Click User Accounts and Family Safety.
3. Click Change your Windows password.

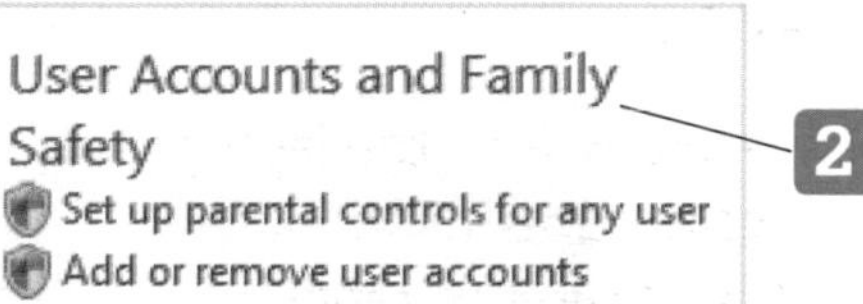

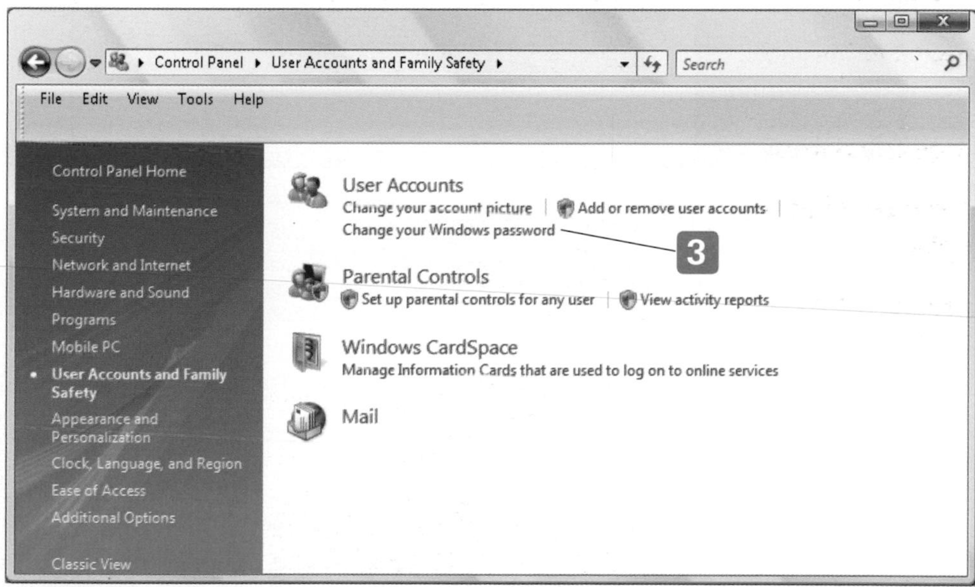

DID YOU KNOW?

You already have an account name. It is the one that appears when you first start your laptop. You can change this in the User Accounts section of the control panel.

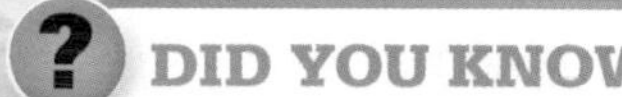

DID YOU KNOW?

It's a good idea to protect your laptop with a password, but be aware that you will have to enter it each time you start up your laptop or wake it up from sleep mode.

4. When the window appears with your account information, click Create a password for your account.
5. Enter your password once and then retype it to confirm it.
6. Enter a hint to remind you of your password in case you forget it.
7. Click Create password.

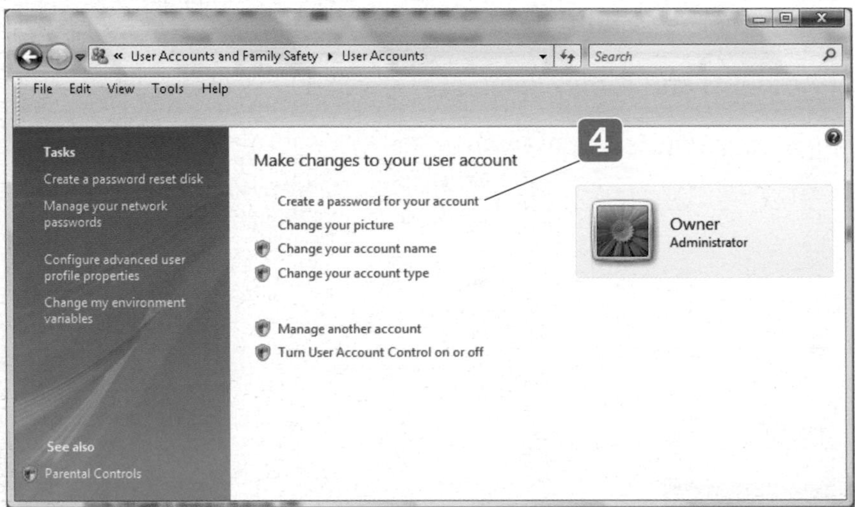

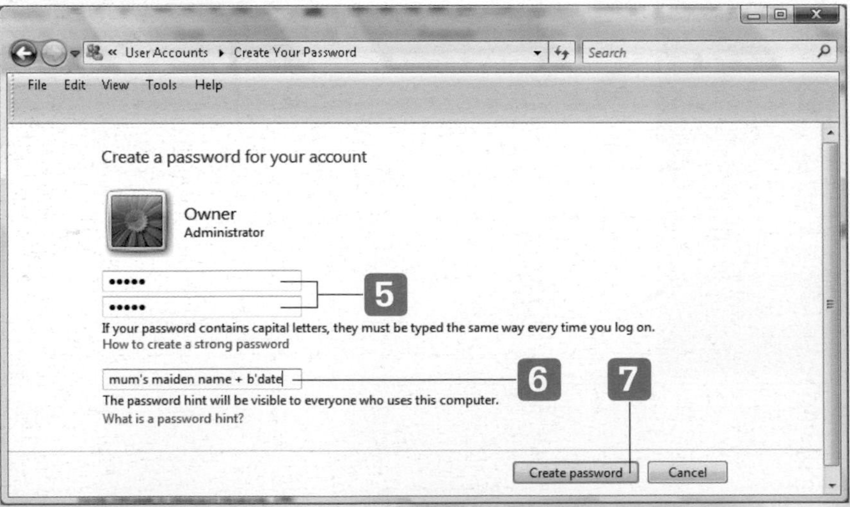

? DID YOU KNOW?

When you need to make a system-wide change, you have to be logged on as an administrator or type an administrator's user name and password.

HOT TIP: Create a password that contains upper- and lower-case letters and a few numbers. Write the password down on a piece of paper that you need to keep somewhere safe and out of sight. (But remember where you put it!)

3 Getting online/ connecting to the Web

Introduction

However you've used your computer in the past, you'll find that your laptop connects you to more possibilities than you've ever imagined. You'll be able to take it to research sites, libraries, coffee shops, meetings, family gatherings, hotel rooms and who knows where else. Some of the activities described in this chapter can happen with any old computer. But you may find that they are more convenient and fun on your laptop than your tabletop model. In either case, there are a few security precautions you should take, which are also discussed. Thanks to the super-charged atmosphere of the online information highway, you'll find more and more ways to tune in and turn on.

Choose an Internet Service Provider

If you have purchased a new laptop or obtained one that is relatively new, it almost certainly has a wireless card – hardware that lets you make a wireless connection to the Internet from a place like a Wi-Fi hotspot. You also have an Ethernet port, which enables you to make a 'wired' connection from a hotel, a library or from home. Where do you get your home connection? From an Internet Service Provider (ISP), a company that's in the business of getting people online. You need to choose a provider and subscribe to it by agreeing to pay a monthly fee. In return, you'll get an email service, the ability to browse the Internet and space to store files and create webpages.

1. If you have cable television service, ask your provider how much more per month Internet access would cost.
2. If you have a mobile phone service, ask your mobile provider if you can get online with your laptop using its mobile broadband service. You can get a wireless card for laptops that can get online from anywhere you have mobile coverage.
3. Visit a site like Broadband-Finder (www.broadband-finder.co.uk) to compare prices and services.

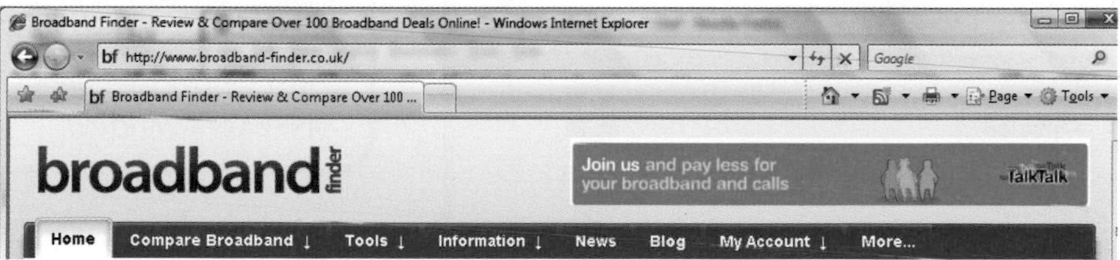

ALERT: Try to get a broadband (also called 'high-speed') Internet connection. If you don't, you'll be forced to get online with a slower dial-up connection.

HOT TIP: For the ultimate in freedom and the ability to connect from a train, bus or practically anywhere, consider a mobile phone or wireless satellite provider.

HOT TIP: One of the advantages of 'bundling' Internet service with existing satellite, mobile or cable service is cost: many providers offer multiple services for a rate that is lower than if you paid for them separately.

Create an Internet connection

Your Internet provider will give you the technical details you need to get online: the name of the server, your email user name and password, and so on. Once you have them and your provider has run the required cables or configured phone lines (for DSL service) you use Windows to set up your laptop's Internet connection.

1. Open Network and Sharing Center.
2. Under Tasks in the left-hand column, click Set up a connection or network.
3. Click Connect to the Internet and then click Next.
4. In the next screen, click Wireless, Broadband, or Dial-up, depending on the connection your ISP gives you. Click Next.
5. Enter the information from your ISP and enter a password.
6. Click Connect.

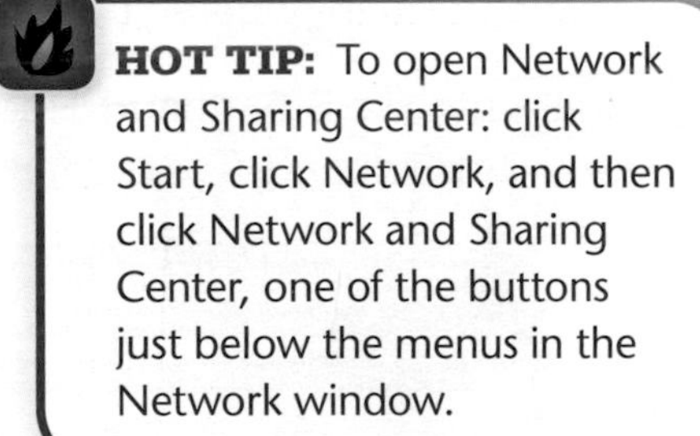

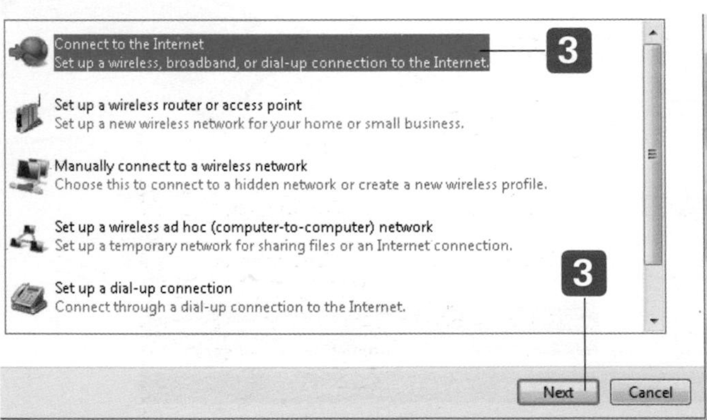

HOT TIP: To open Network and Sharing Center: click Start, click Network, and then click Network and Sharing Center, one of the buttons just below the menus in the Network window.

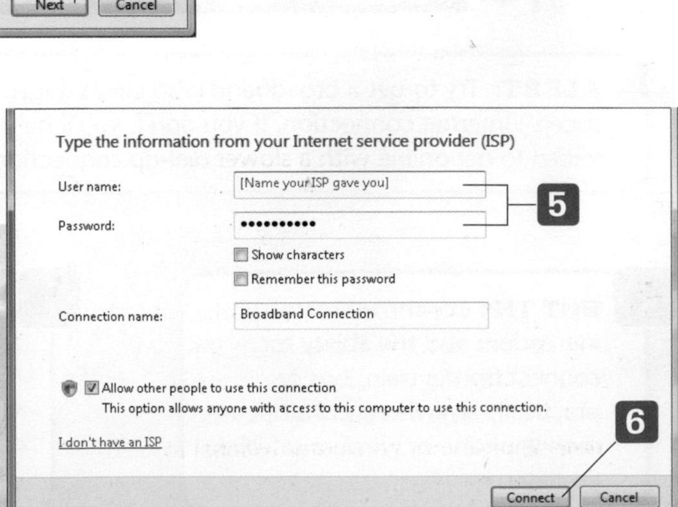

Turn your wireless function on or off

Most laptops are capable of wirelessly connecting to the Internet. They have a built-in antenna that searches for a signal from a wireless router. But to make use of this feature you need to turn wireless function on or off, and it may not be on by default. To hook up the wireless function on your new laptop, just do the following:

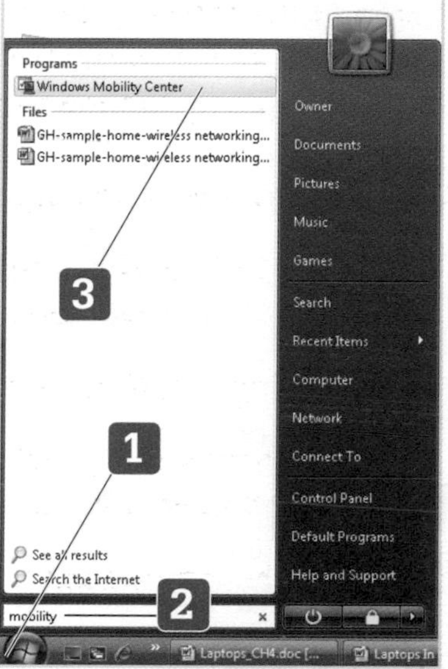

1. Click Start.
2. Type mobility.
3. Click Windows Mobility Center to open it.
4. Click Turn wireless off to disable Wi-Fi.
5. Click Turn wireless on to enable Wi-Fi.

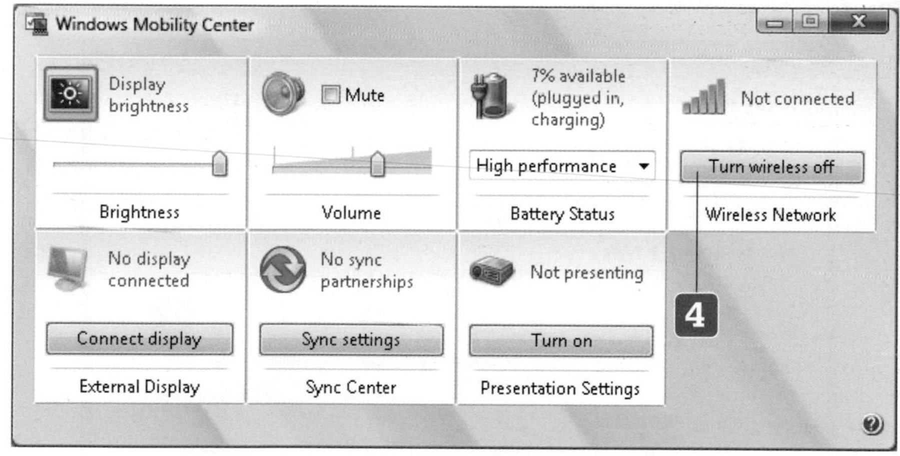

HOT TIP: One of my own laptops has a keyboard command that turns the wireless function on and off. I press Fn (the Function key) and F2 at the same time. Check your computer manual to see if you have a shortcut, too.

DID YOU KNOW?

Turning off wireless when you don't need it has a security benefit. Otherwise, if your laptop automatically connects to a wireless network in your vicinity any hackers who are on the same network can snoop on you and possibly use special software to track passwords you enter.

Plug your laptop into an Ethernet network

Not everyone has an Ethernet network at home, although you might. Ethernet is a network technology that transfers data at high speed. It's used to convey a high-speed Internet connection from a router to a computer. But when you travel you're likely to encounter Ethernet in your hotel. So you need to know how to plug in your laptop and get to work or play. Here's what to do.

1. Connect physically to a wired network by plugging your Ethernet cable into the Ethernet port on your laptop. Look for the symbol shown here.
2. Your computer should automatically connect to the network. In addition, when the Set Network Location window appears, select Public or Private (or you may see a screen with the options Home, Work, or Public location).
3. Click Next.
4. Click Close.

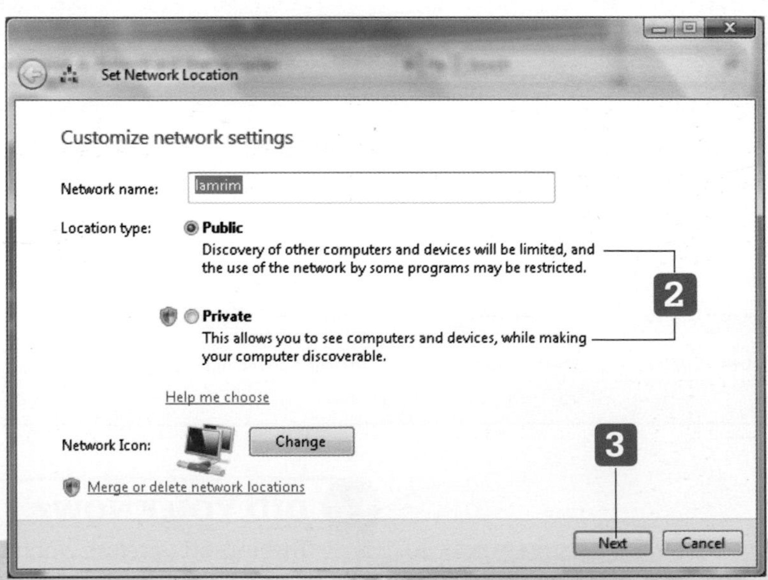

SEE ALSO: If your computer does not automatically connect to the network, you may need to enable network discovery, as described in the next task.

HOT TIP: If your computer does not automatically connect to the Internet, right-click the network connection icon (which looks like two computers close together) in the System Tray. Choose Diagnose and repair.

Enable network discovery

Network discovery is a way of telling Windows that you want your computer to detect and have the option of joining other networks. This enables your laptop to connect to a public network such as a Wi-Fi hotspot or a private network in your own home.

1. Open Network and Sharing Center.
2. Under Sharing and Discovery, click the down arrow next to Off, by Network discovery, so that it becomes an upwards arrow.
3. Click Turn on network discovery if necessary.
4. Click Apply.
5. Click the X to close the Network and Sharing Center.

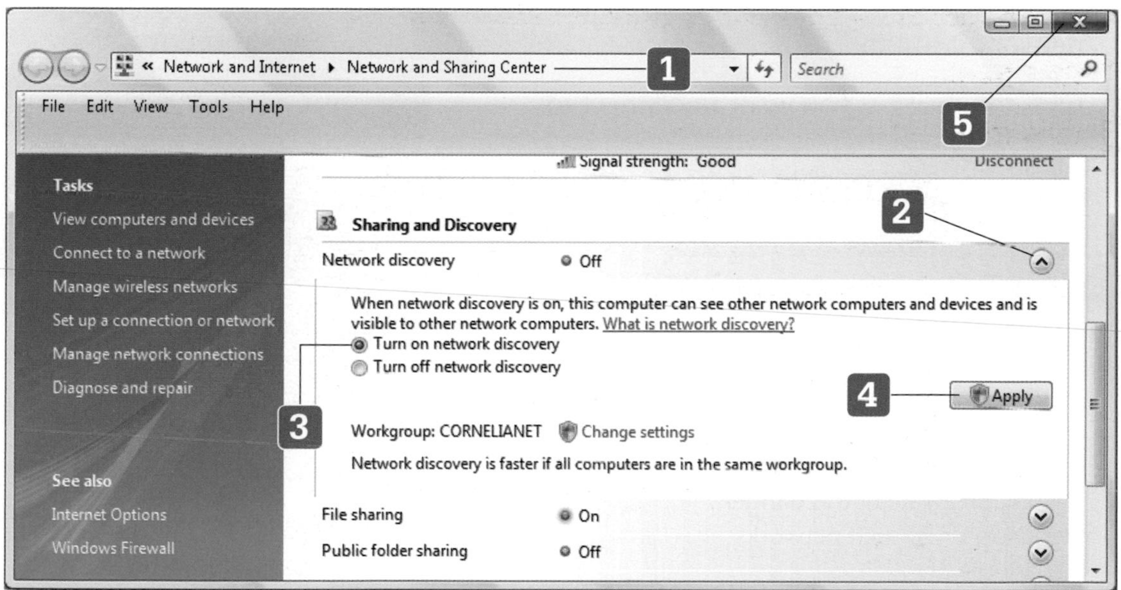

DID YOU KNOW?

Other options in the Network and Sharing Center let you set up file sharing, public folder sharing, printer sharing and other aspects of working with others on a computer network. Look here if you or others are having trouble accessing shared files, folders, printers or media.

DID YOU KNOW?

The Tasks pane in the Network and Sharing Center lets you manage wireless networks, manage network connections or view computers or other devices on your network.

Locate a wireless network

It's like your reading glasses. You had them a minute ago. They couldn't have gone far. But where can your wireless network be? Luckily, you won't have to search for a wireless network often, especially if you have network discovery enabled as described in the preceding section. But when you're on the road, you'll want to find available networks in your area and log on to one, providing you have the proper credentials.

1. Pass your mouse pointer over the network connection icon in the System Tray. An alert message appears saying that wireless networks are available.
2. Single-click the icon and choose Connect to a network.
3. Click the network you want to connect to.
4. Click Connect.

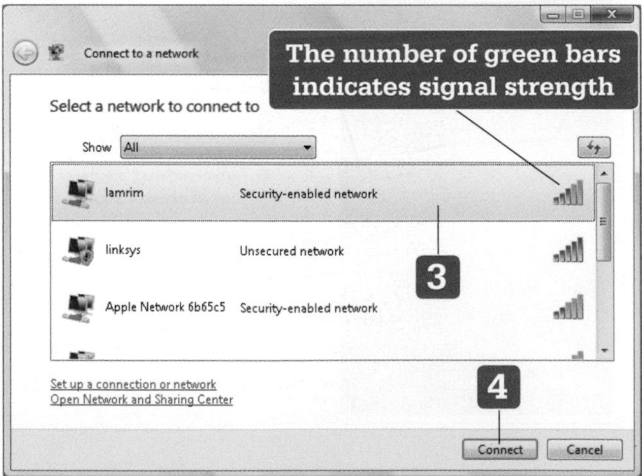

ALERT: Logging on to an unsecured wireless network is convenient, but not secure. Others in the area may be running software that can 'spy' on your computer while you work. Be aware of this danger and log on to such networks sparingly.

WHAT DOES THIS MEAN?

A red X over the connection icon: this means you are not connected to a wireless network.

A yellow alert icon: this means you are connected, but with limited access: you may not be able to access the Internet, for instance.

A blue circular icon appears: this means you are connected fully, so you can access both the local network and the Internet.

Troubleshoot connection problems

Sometimes, connections don't work for some reason. Perhaps the signal strength isn't strong enough, or Windows needs to refresh its network settings. Windows includes convenient diagnostic tools to help you troubleshoot the problem.

1. Open the Network and Sharing Center.
2. If your Internet connection is not functioning, click Diagnose and repair.
3. Click the first option to repair the problem.
4. Chances are the problem will be resolved. If not, follow additional steps shown in the Windows Network Diagnostics utility.
5. Click the X in the top right corner of the Network and Sharing Center window to close it.

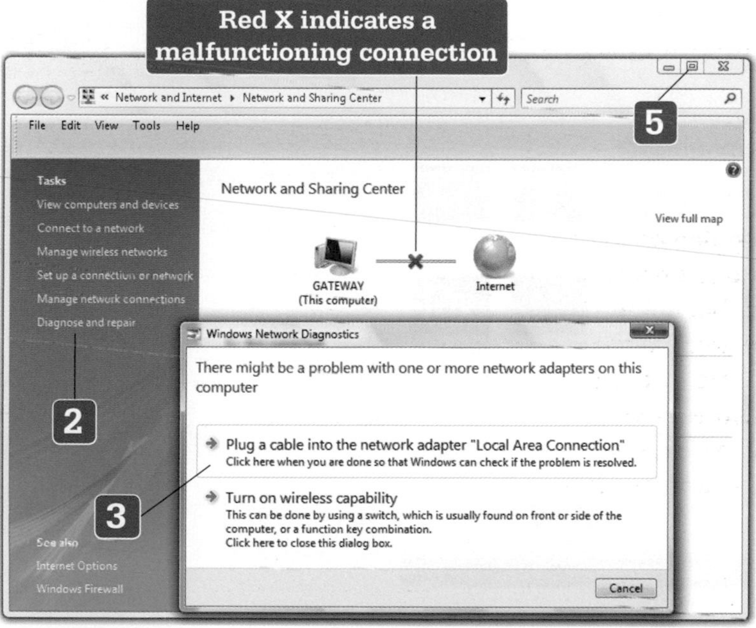

HOT TIP: You can also access the Diagnose and repair utility by right-clicking the network connection icon in the System Tray and then choosing Diagnose and repair from the context menu.

HOT TIP: You might see a message instructing you to enable the network adapter. You can do this manually by right-clicking the network connection icon and choosing Enable from the context menu.

Navigate to a website

Once you are connected to the Internet, either wirelessly or via a wired Ethernet connection, you can start browsing websites. Windows provides Microsoft's own web browser, Internet Explorer, so you can start using it right away.

1. Click the Internet Explorer icon just to the right of the Start button on the taskbar (it looks like a blue letter 'e').
2. Click once in the Address bar to highlight the current webpage's address (also called a URL or Uniform Resource Locator).
3. Type a new address and press Enter to go to a new webpage.

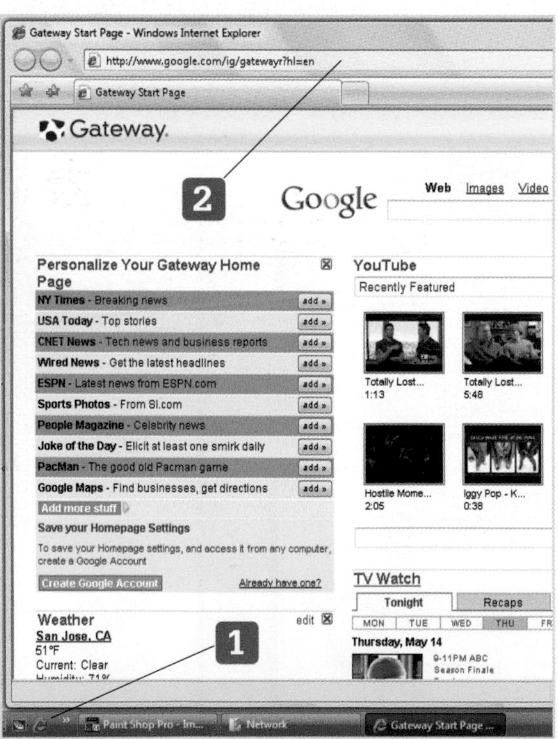

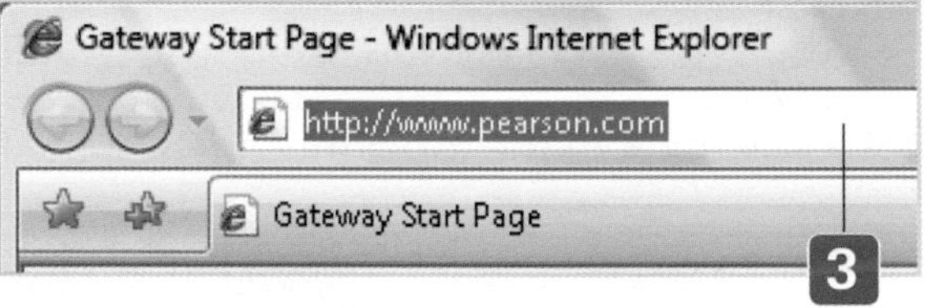

SEE ALSO: When Internet Explorer first opens, it displays the default start-up page – probably one configured by your computer manufacturer. You can change this to your own start-up page as described later in this chapter (Change your browser's home page).

DID YOU KNOW?

Internet Explorer is not the only web browser around. Many users (including me) prefer a free web browser called Firefox, which you can download and install from www.mozilla.org.

Change your browser settings

A web browser brings you text, images, sounds, video and many other wondrous bits of content from around the world. But if you find webpage text hard to read, you can change your browser's settings. You can choose a different type face or type size, for instance. It takes some fancy mouse/finger scrolling to do so, however.

1. Click Page.
2. When the menu appears, scroll down to Text Size (don't click it!).
3. When the submenu appears, slide your mouse pointer straight to the left and choose one of the text size options.

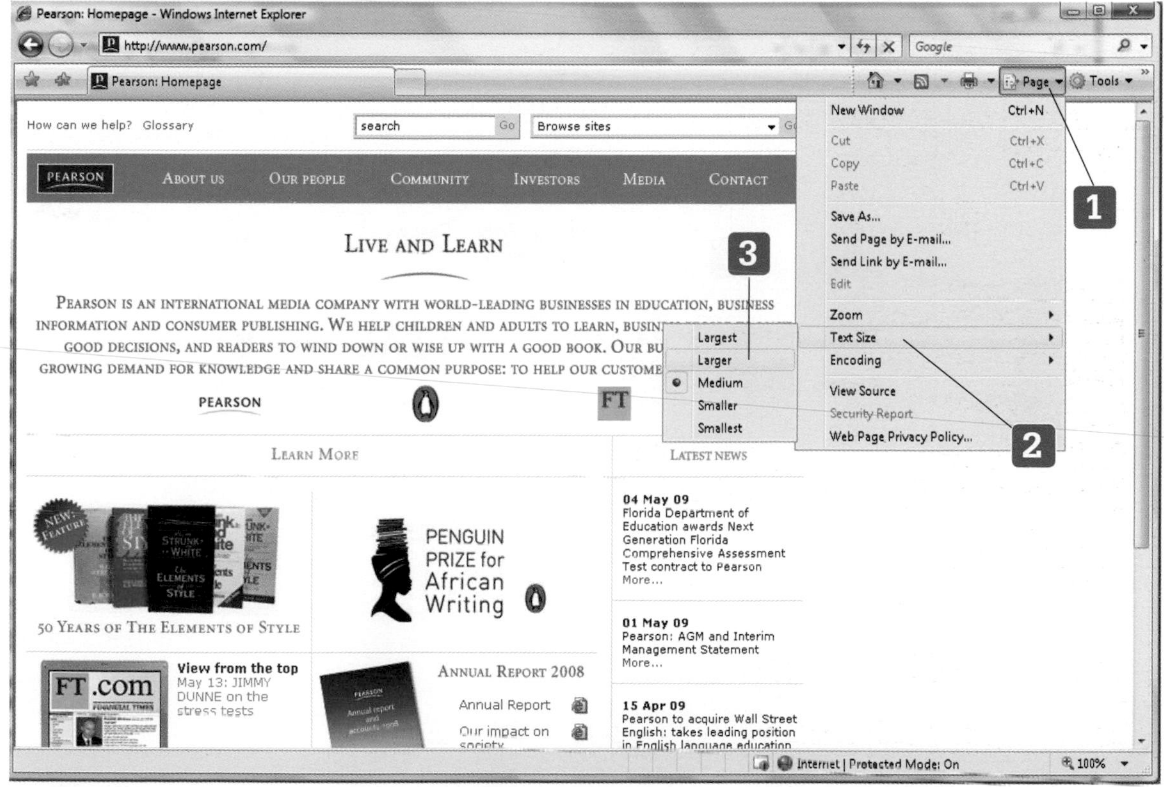

DID YOU KNOW?

Changing text settings in your browser won't enlarge all the type on the webpage; some text is formatted as a graphic image and won't be affected.

4 To enlarge all contents on the page (not just text) click Page and click Zoom.

5 Choose a Zoom option (the default is 100%).

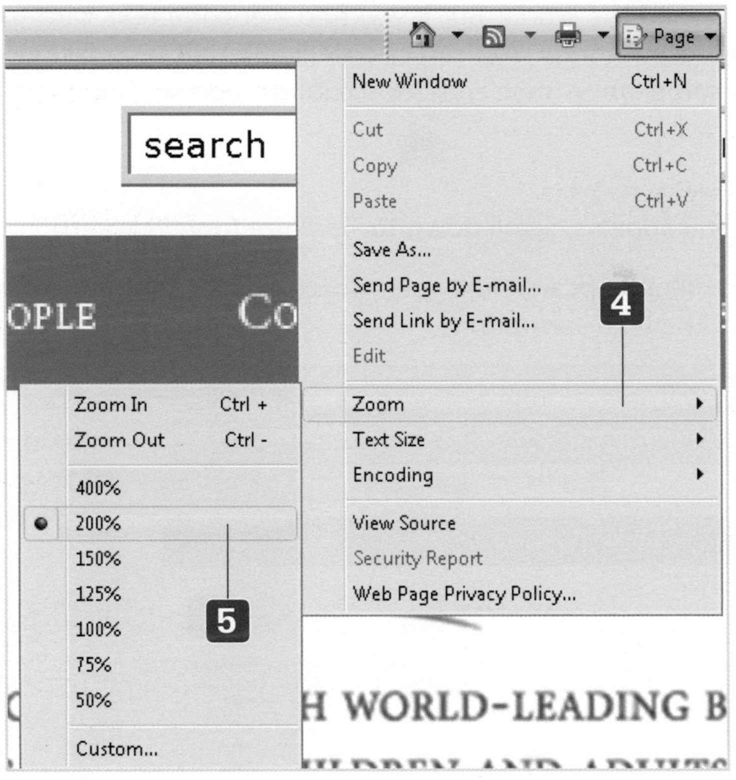

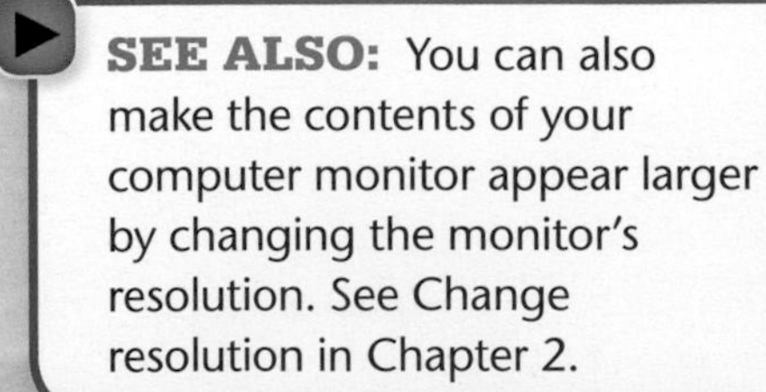

SEE ALSO: You can also make the contents of your computer monitor appear larger by changing the monitor's resolution. See Change resolution in Chapter 2.

Visit multiple websites with browser tabs

You don't have to visit one webpage at a time. You may want to keep one open while you visit another one (or two, or three, etc.). You can do so by opening a website in a new tab. When the new tab opens, simply type the address of the site you want to visit.

1. Open Windows Internet Explorer.
2. Click the New Tab icon, which appears just to the right of the tab for the current page.
3. When the new tab opens, the address is highlighted so you can quickly type or paste a new one.
4. Press Enter to go to the new page.

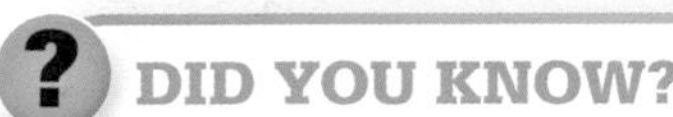

DID YOU KNOW?

Viewing pages in multiple tabs is useful because it consumes less computer memory than opening a separate browser window for each webpage.

HOT TIP: Type the following: http://www.microsoft.com/uk.

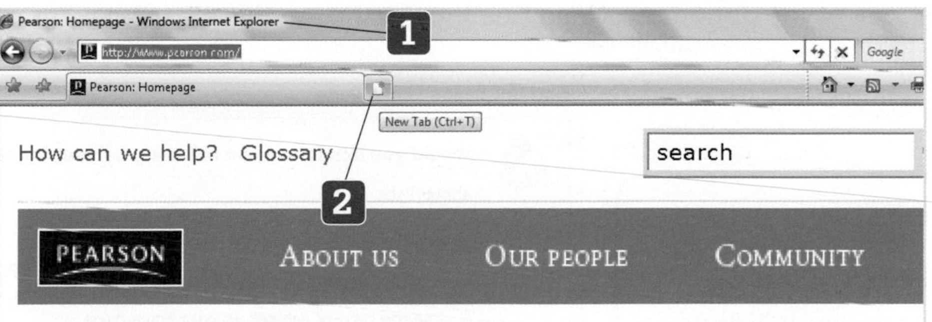

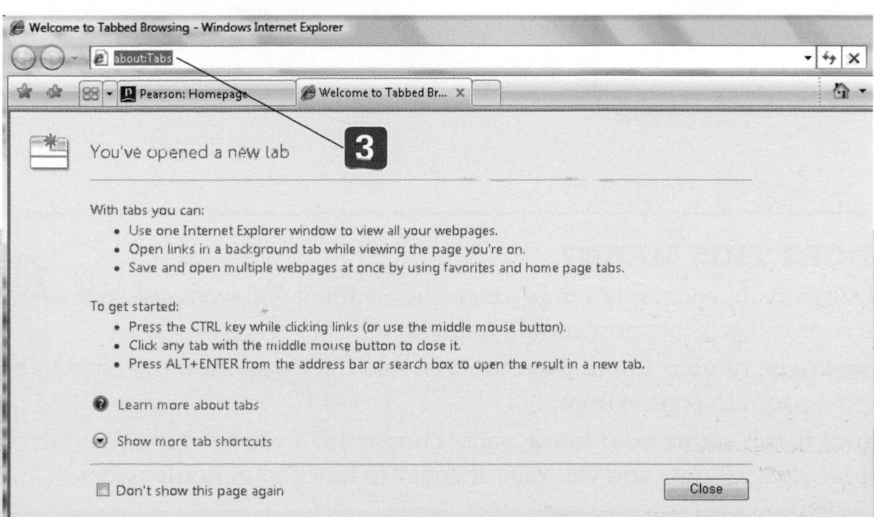

Change your browser's home page

Some people hate to move and stay in the same house their whole lives. The same applies to home pages. When you first start up your computer, you might want to have a page appear that contains photos of your family, or that lets you search the Web (like Google, http://www.google.co.uk). To change your browser's home page, follow these steps.

1. Visit the page that you want to use as your home page.
2. Click the down arrow next to the home icon (it looks like a house).
3. Click Add or Change Home Page.

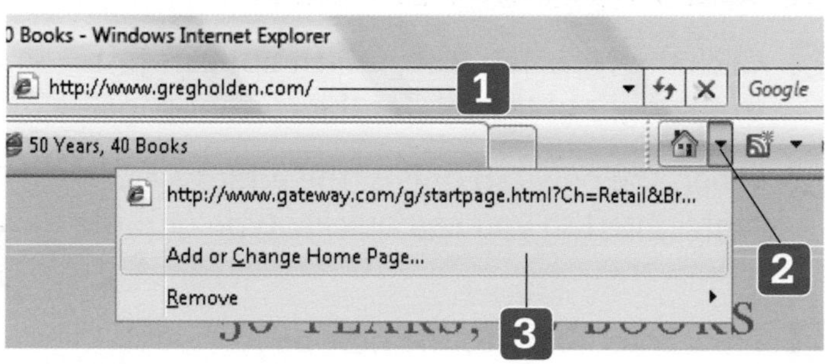

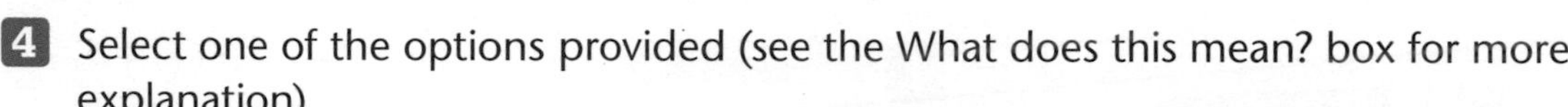

4. Select one of the options provided (see the What does this mean? box for more explanation).
5. Click Yes.

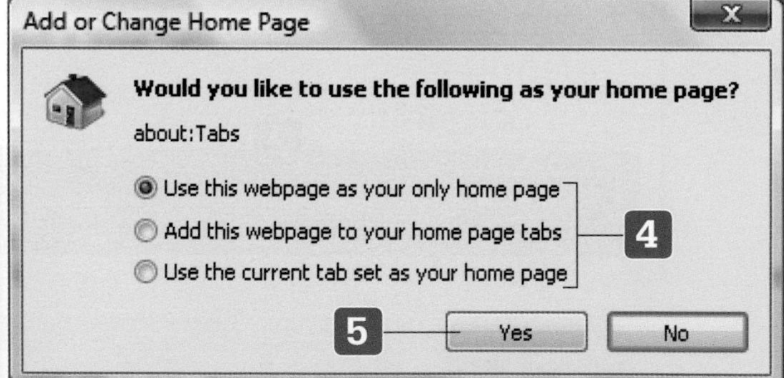

ALERT: Make sure you have located the webpage you want and that it is currently displayed in your browser window before you designate it as your home page.

WHAT DOES THIS MEAN?

Use this webpage as your only home page: choose this if you want only one page to be your home page. (This is the most common option.)

Add this webpage to your home page tabs: choose this if you want the page to be one of multiple home pages to choose from.

Use the current tab set as your home page: choose this if you have multiple tabs open in the current browser window and you want them all to function as home pages.

Save a page as a favourite

An old-fashioned bookmark with a tassel helps you return easily to a spot you want to revisit in a book. A 'favourite' serves much the same purpose: it helps Internet Explorer return quickly to a webpage you want to revisit.

1. Navigate to the webpage you want to designate as a favourite.
2. Click the Add to Favorites icon, which looks like two stars.
3. To add a single page as a favourite, click Add to Favorites.
4. Type a name for the website.
5. Click Add.

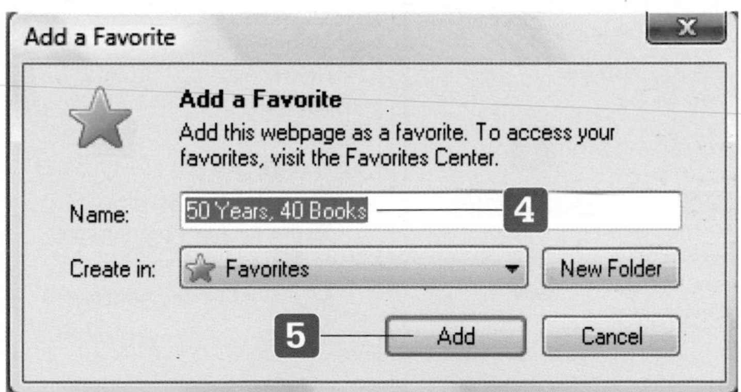

SEE ALSO: Once you have accumulated a lot of favourites, you can organise them to make them easier to find. Create subfolders within the favourites folder to organise them, as described in Organise your favourites, later in this chapter.

HOT TIP: The option under Add to Favorites, Add Tab Group to Favorites, lets you add all the webpages you currently have open in different tabs to your list of favourites. You add the entire group of tabs together. When you choose this option from the Favorites Center later on, you open all the pages at once.

Revisit webpages

The single star icon next to the Add to Favorites icon opens the Favorites Center, which is where you view and organise the pages you have saved. You'll also find a useful history of webpages you have visited recently, in case you want to revisit a page and can't find the address.

1. When you want to revisit a page, click the Favorites Center icon.
2. Open a folder to find a page you have saved as a favourite.
3. Click a page to jump to it instantly.
4. Click the down arrow next to History.
5. Click the date when you previously visited a page.
6. Click the page you want to revisit.

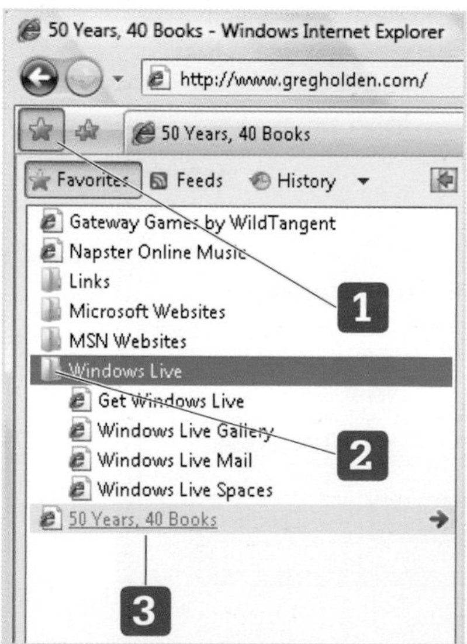

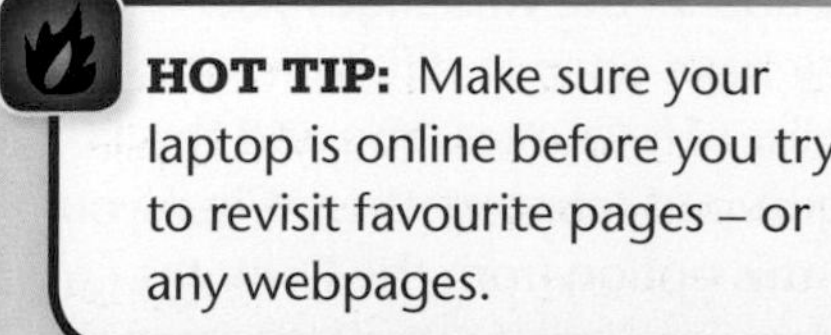

HOT TIP: Make sure your laptop is online before you try to revisit favourite pages – or any webpages.

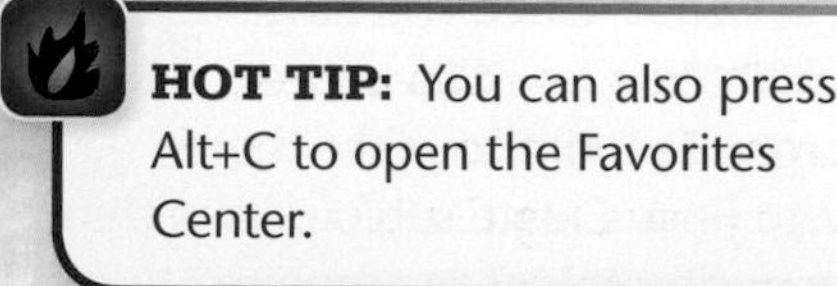

HOT TIP: You can also press Alt+C to open the Favorites Center.

Organise your favourites

A list of favourite pages can get quite long very quickly. By creating folders and storing favourite pages in them, you can find them conveniently.

1. Click Add to Favorites.
2. Choose Organize Favorites.
3. Click New Folder.
4. Type the name of your folder and press Enter.
5. Click a page you want to file, click Move, and choose a folder to move the page into it.

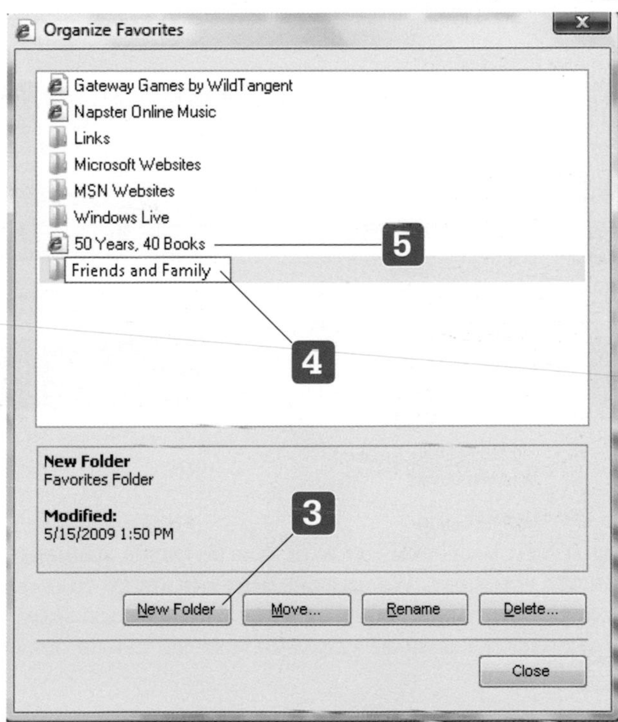

HOT TIP: You can also access the Add to Favorites menu options by pressing Ctrl+Z.

HOT TIP: It's a good idea to delete pages periodically so they don't pile up in your Favorites folders.

Erase your browsing history

In an earlier section you learned how to view your browsing history – a list of webpages you have revisited. This is a useful tool for those of us who are having 'senior moments'. But it can work against you – you may not want others to be able to see where you've been and what you've been viewing online. You can erase your history as well as other information about your online activities that's stored on your laptop.

1. Open Internet Explorer.
2. Press the Alt key on the keyboard.
3. Click Tools.
4. Click Delete Browsing History.

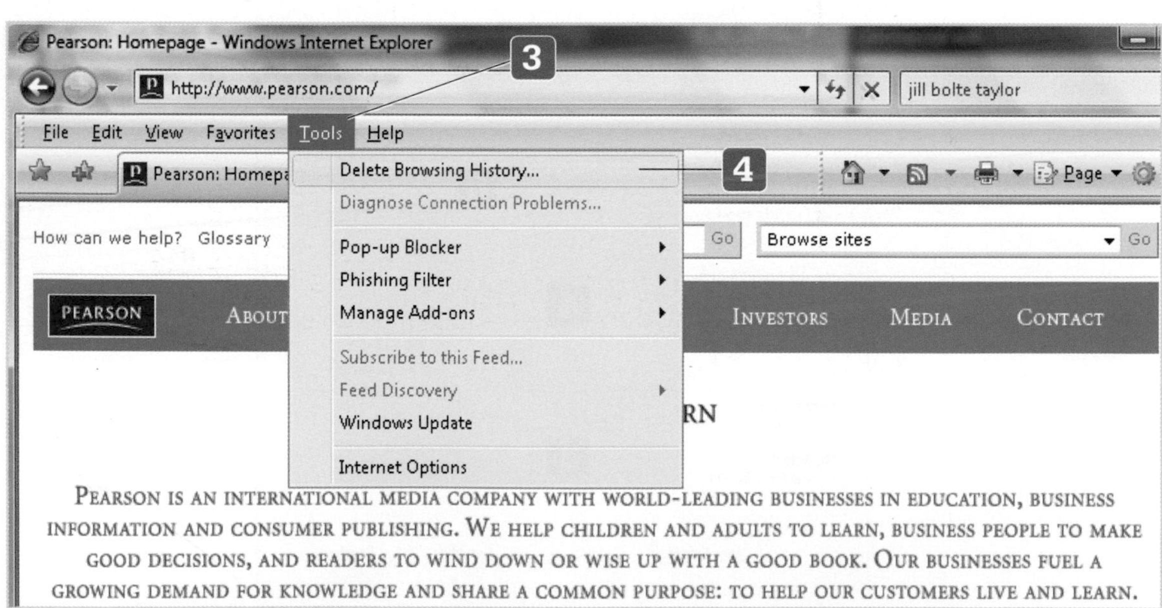

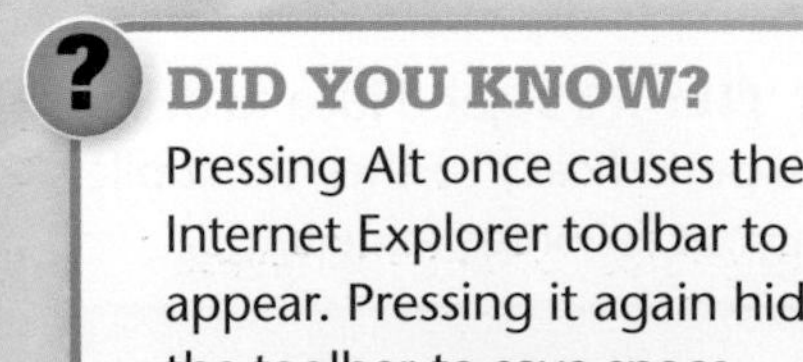

DID YOU KNOW?

Pressing Alt once causes the Internet Explorer toolbar to appear. Pressing it again hides the toolbar to save space.

5 Click the Delete button next to the item you want to erase.

6 Click Delete all to erase all stored information at once.

7 Click Close.

WHAT DOES THIS MEAN?

History: the list of webpages you have visited.

Cookies: bits of data that some websites store on your computer so that, when you revisit them, the site will 'know' who you are.

Maintain your security online

You have probably heard about computer security issues that are associated with being on the Internet: viruses, hackers, dangerous emails. These are real concerns. But if you follow a few commonsense practices and take some precautions you'll be able to browse sites, exchange email and shop online safely.

1. Install antivirus software and update it when prompted: this is the most important way you can protect yourself online.
2. Make sure before you submit credit card numbers or other sensitive information to a website that it is secure (it should begin with **https:** in the address).
3. Do not respond to emails from strangers, especially those that ask you to click on a link or open an attachment.
4. Don't store confidential information online.
5. Once you sign in to enter a website, always make sure you sign out when you are done.
6. Keep drinks, pets and other hazards away from your laptop.

You are logged in as **gholden** | Log Out |

5

HOT TIP: Secure webpages have addresses that begin with https:// instead of http://. The 's' indicates that the site uses security methods to encrypt the data you send.

ALERT: Don't publish your phone number, address or other personal information on sites such as Facebook.

ALERT: Windows comes with a firewall program, which you should activate. But it does not come with firewall software, which you have to purchase. Some laptops provide you with trial versions of antivirus programs, but be sure to subscribe and update them after the trial period is over.

HOT TIP: Free antivirus programs such as AVG (free. avg.com) aren't as full-featured as paid antivirus packages but they are better than no protection at all.

Control pop-ups

A pop-up is a webpage that appears (or pops up) while you are viewing another webpage. Sometimes, pop-ups appear in response to an action on your part: you click a link on a page, or you submit information to a remote site by filling out a form, for instance. Other times they appear without warning because simply viewing a webpage causes an advertisement to appear. The unwanted pop-ups can be annoying; the 'wanted' pop-ups need to be enabled so they appear if you want them.

1. Open Internet Explorer.
2. Click Tools.
3. Click Pop-up Blocker.
4. Choose Turn On (or Turn Off) Pop-up Blocker if needed.
5. Choose Pop-up Blocker Settings if you want to specify a website that you want to show pop-ups.

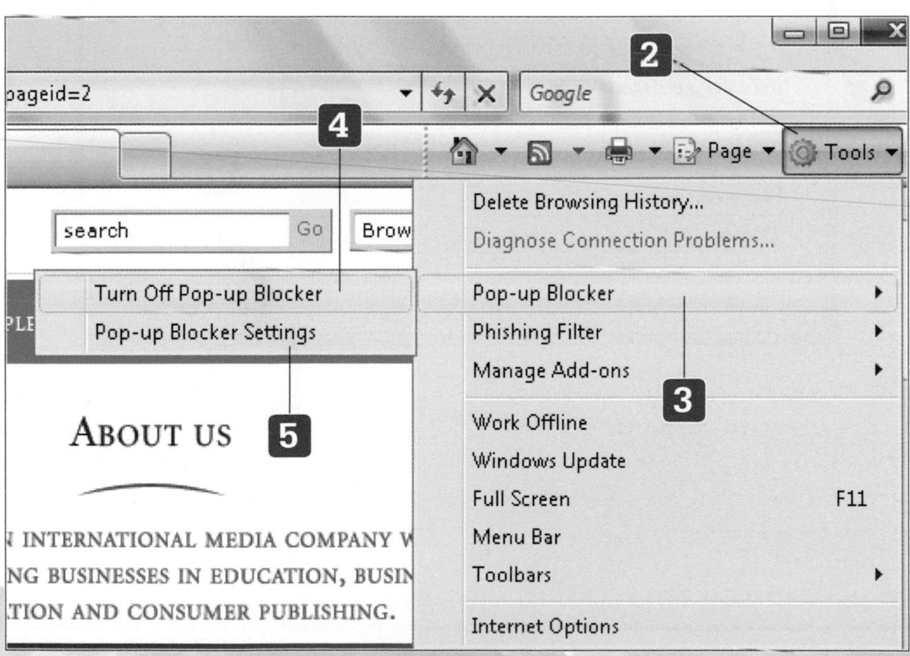

6. Type the name of the site.
7. Click Add.
8. Click Close.

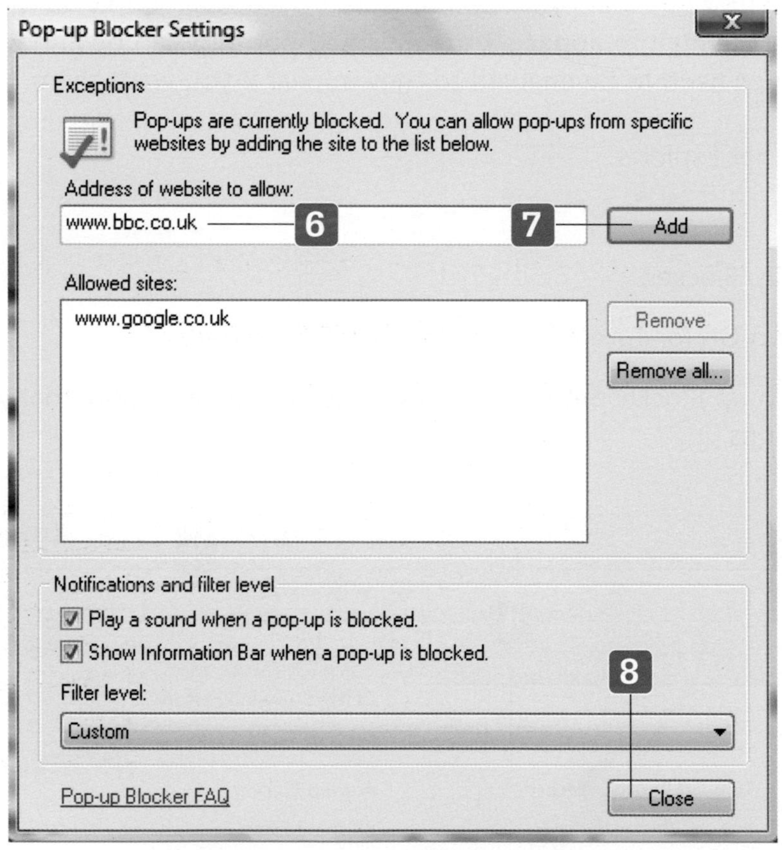

ALERT: Be selective about the pop-ups you block – not all pop-ups are bad. Some websites generate pop-up windows to play music or display username and password boxes so you can log in. If you need to log in and the screen doesn't appear because you have blocked pop-ups for that site, look just beneath Internet Explorer's menu bars for a yellow alert bar. Click the bar to allow the pop-up to appear.

Add or remove toolbars

Toolbars are areas near the top of an application window that contain tabs, buttons and other controls. With a web browser, the more toolbars you have open, the less room you have to view webpage content. You can add toolbars to gain functionality or remove them to save screen space.

1. Open Internet Explorer.
2. Click Tools.
3. Click Toolbars.
4. Slide your mouse pointer over to an unticked toolbar to add it to your browser.
5. Slide your mouse pointer over to a ticked toolbar to remove it.

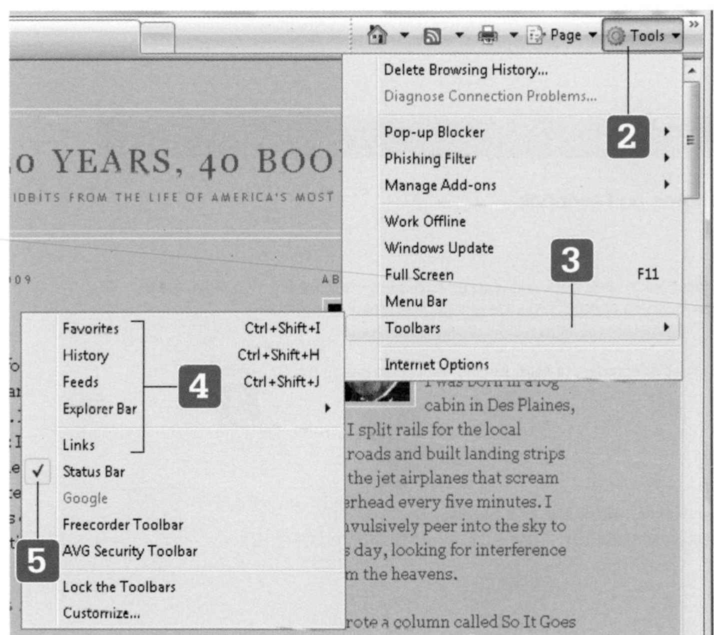

HOT TIP: The Lock the Toolbars option prevents you or others from adding or removing toolbars until you choose the Lock the Toolbars option again to deselect it.

HOT TIP: Click Customize to add or remove buttons from existing toolbars.

WHAT DOES THIS MEAN?

Favorites: this toolbar is one you configure yourself. You add buttons to it that function as shortcuts to websites you want to revisit frequently.

History: this isn't a toolbar like the others, but a pane that opens and shows websites you have visited recently. It has its own toolbar.

Feeds: a pane that lists websites with RSS feeds you have subscribed to.

Explorer bar: a pane that allows you to research terms in reference books that are included with Windows.

Create a Facebook page

One of the benefits of buying a laptop and connecting to the Internet is the ability to keep in touch with your children and grandchildren. Where do you find the young people and learn about what they are doing? You go to sites like Facebook. Ask your grandchildren: chances are they (or their parents) have a Facebook page where they post photos and gather 'friends'. You, too, can be counted among their fortunate friends.

1. Ask a grandchild or other relative who is already on Facebook to invite you to be their friend.
2. Use Windows Mail to open the email invitation and click the link supplied in the email.
3. Create your Facebook page.

HOT TIP: You don't need an invitation to create a Facebook page. Simply to go www.facebook.com and sign up for an account (it's free) by filling out the form on the home page. You may need to ask someone with a digital camera to photograph you so you can include a picture with your Facebook profile, however.

SEE ALSO: See Read an email message, in Chapter 5, for more about signing up for the Windows Mail email service and opening email messages.

4 Getting to know Windows

Introduction

Most new laptops come preinstalled with Windows Vista or Windows 7. These are operating systems and are what allow you to operate your computer's system. That means, in addition to learning how to navigate and use your laptop's physical controls, you need to navigate and use various aspects of your Windows operating system, too. You don't need to become a computer expert, however. In this chapter you'll learn a little about how the system folders are organised (like Documents, Pictures and Music), how to locate and open applications and files, and learn how to customise your laptop's look and feel. You'll also learn some new techniques for working in open windows, like Flip and Flip 3D, how to add icons to the desktop and even how to choose a new power setting.

Discover which version of Windows you have

Your laptop most likely runs one of three Microsoft operating systems. These are, in order of their release, Windows XP, Windows Vista and Windows 7. You could have any one of these installed on your laptop. It's important to find out exactly what operating system and version you have, so you can learn more about it. (You would not want to purchase a book on Windows XP if your computer runs Windows 7, for instance.)

1. Click Start.
2. Right-click Computer.
3. Click Properties.
4. Locate the Windows edition at the top of the system window.

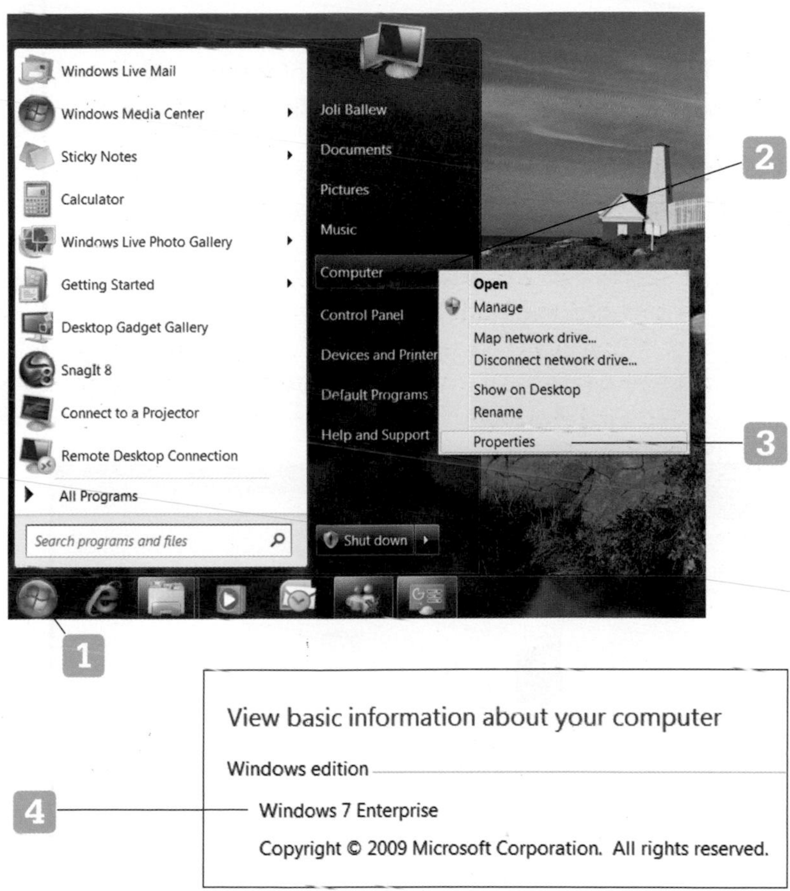

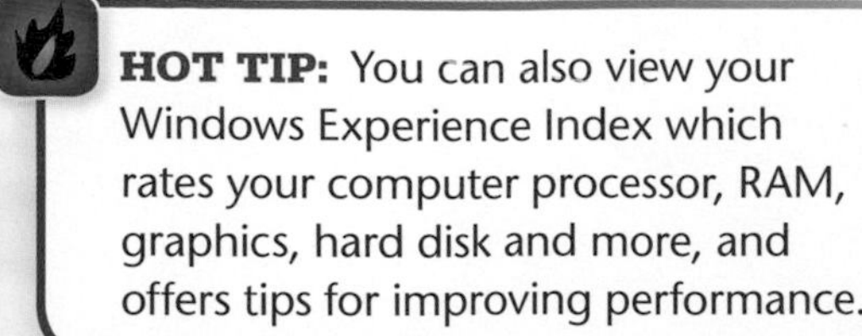

HOT TIP: You can also view your Windows Experience Index which rates your computer processor, RAM, graphics, hard disk and more, and offers tips for improving performance.

Explore system folders

All Microsoft operating systems offer system folders. These include folders called Documents, Pictures, Music, Games, Videos and more. You store your data in these folders. As you might expect, pictures go in the Pictures folder, documents and presentations in the Documents folder, and so on.

1. Click Start.
2. Click Documents.
3. Note the items already in the folder. You may see Microsoft Word documents, subfolders, or other items (like WordPad or Notepad files).
4. Repeat Steps 1 and 2 to open the Pictures folder. You may only see Sample Pictures, as shown here.

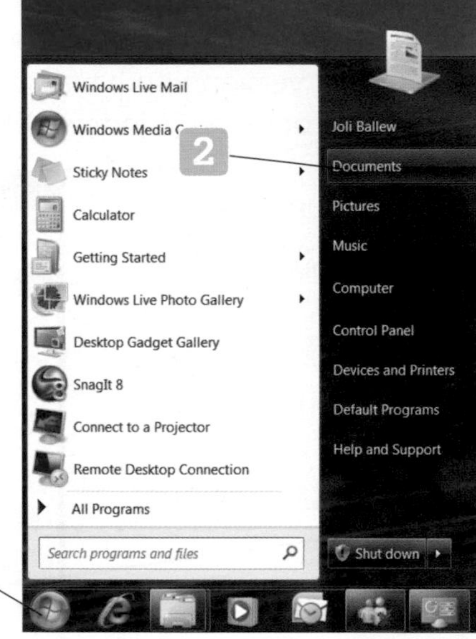

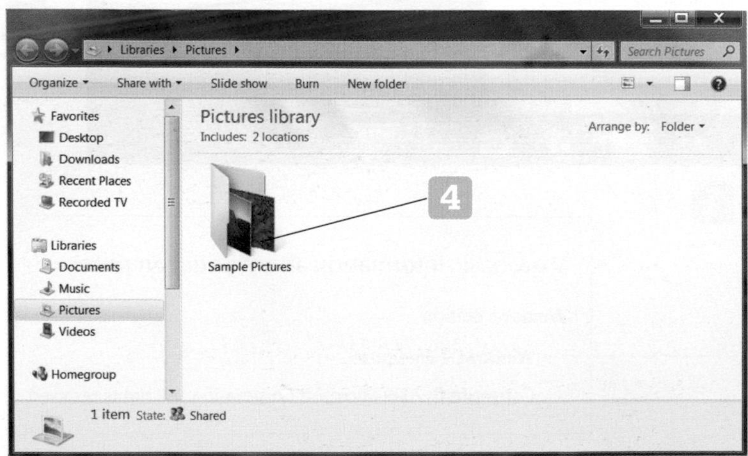

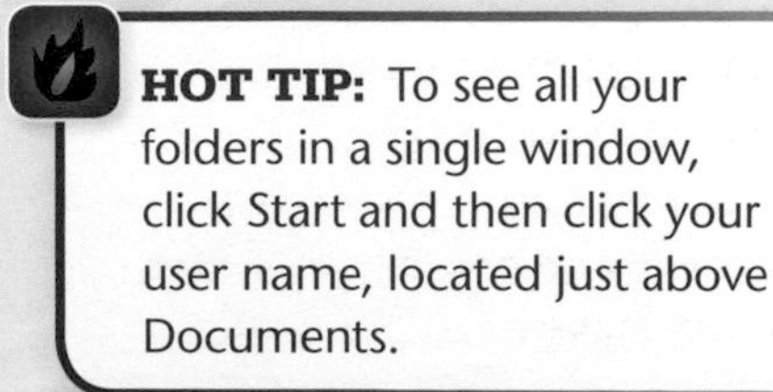

HOT TIP: To see all your folders in a single window, click Start and then click your user name, located just above Documents.

Open programs and files

If you're new to Windows Vista or Windows 7, you are probably unfamiliar with the new Start menu's Search option. Just click the Start button (the blue orb in the bottom left corner), type what you're looking for and click the program to open in the list.

1. Click the Start button, also called the Start Orb.
2. Type something in the Start Search window. For now, type Printers.
3. In the list that appears, note you can open the Devices and Printers window in Windows 7, shown here, or the Printers window in Vista (not shown). You will see additional results.

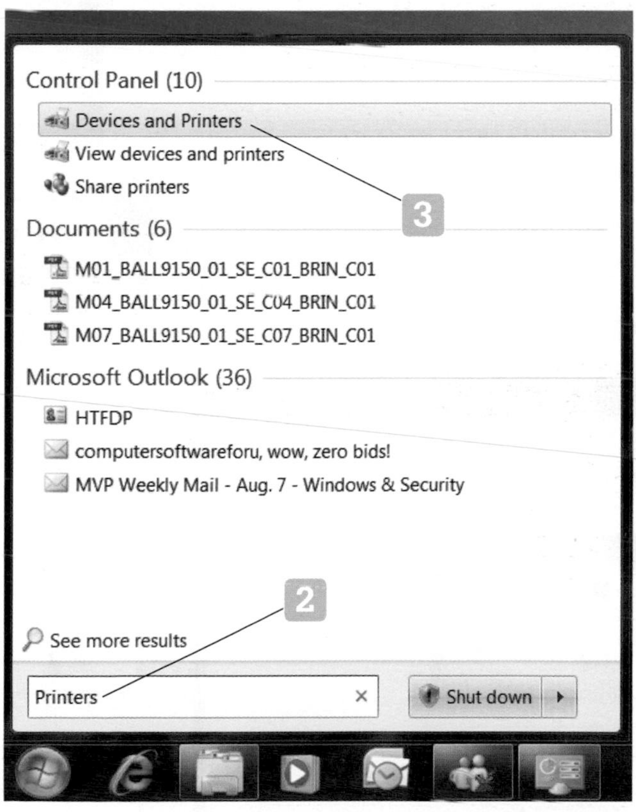

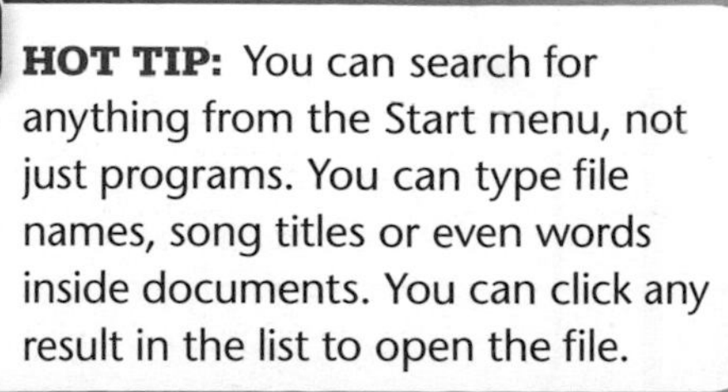

HOT TIP: You can search for anything from the Start menu, not just programs. You can type file names, song titles or even words inside documents. You can click any result in the list to open the file.

Change the screen saver

It used to be that screen savers saved your computer screen from image burn-in. Now they are either used as a visual enhancement or for security purposes. (You can require the user to type a password to get past the screen saver and back to the computer screen, preventing someone from accessing your laptop while you're away from it.) Here's how to customise your screen saver just how you like it:

1. Right-click an empty area of the desktop.
2. Click Personalize.
3. Click Screen Saver.
4. Click the arrow to see the available screen savers and pick your favourite.
5. Use the arrows to change how long to wait before the screen saver is enabled.
6. If desired, click On resume, display logon screen, to require a password to log back into the computer.
7. Click OK.

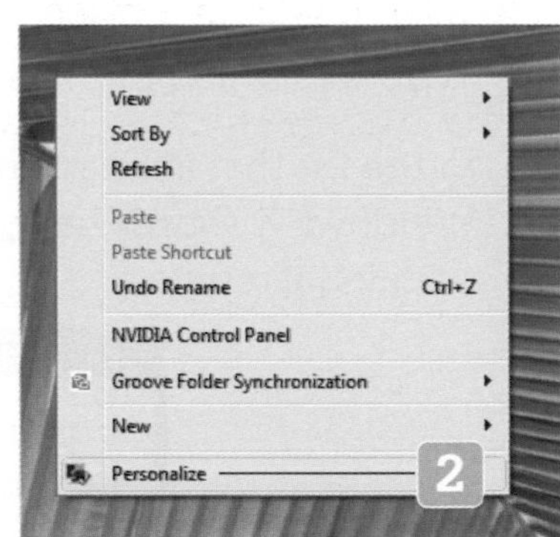

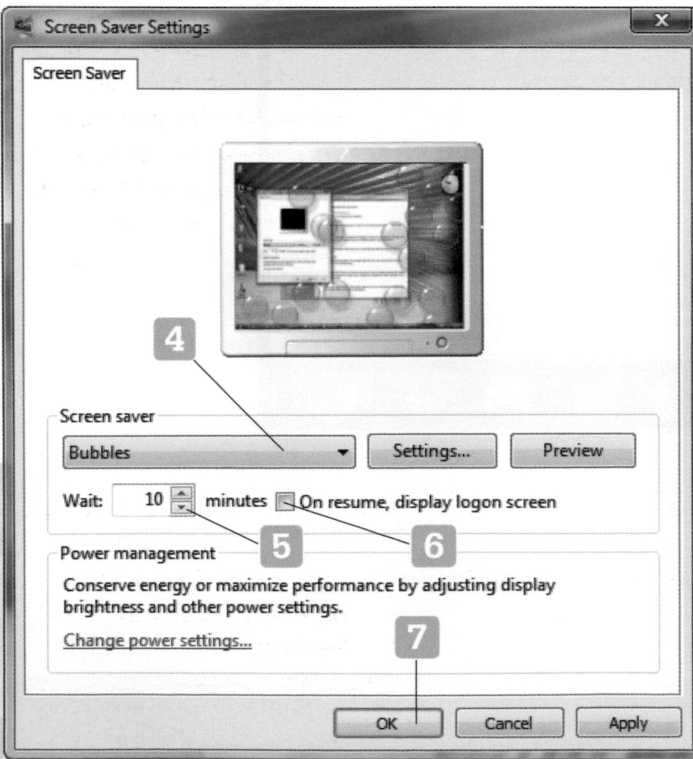

HOT TIP: Click Preview once and wait several seconds. A preview of the selected background will appear in the small screen in the Screen Saver Settings window. Click Preview again, and you'll see the actual screen saver in the background, but only momentarily. Click OK to make the change permanent.

HOT TIP: Click Apply to change the screen saver and put it on the background of your desktop but keep the Screen Saver Settings dialogue box open. That way you can choose a different screen saver without having to reopen Screen Saver Settings.

Use a personal photo as a screen saver

If you have taken some photos and saved them on your computer, you can use one of them as a screen saver. That way, when your computer is idle and you come back to it, a familiar image of a place or an acquaintance will be there to greet you.

1. Open Screen Saver Settings.
2. Choose Photos from the Screen saver drop-down list.
3. Click Preview once to view a 'slide show' of images.
4. Click Preview a second time to view the photo in your screen saver window.
5. Click OK or Apply to adopt the screen saver.

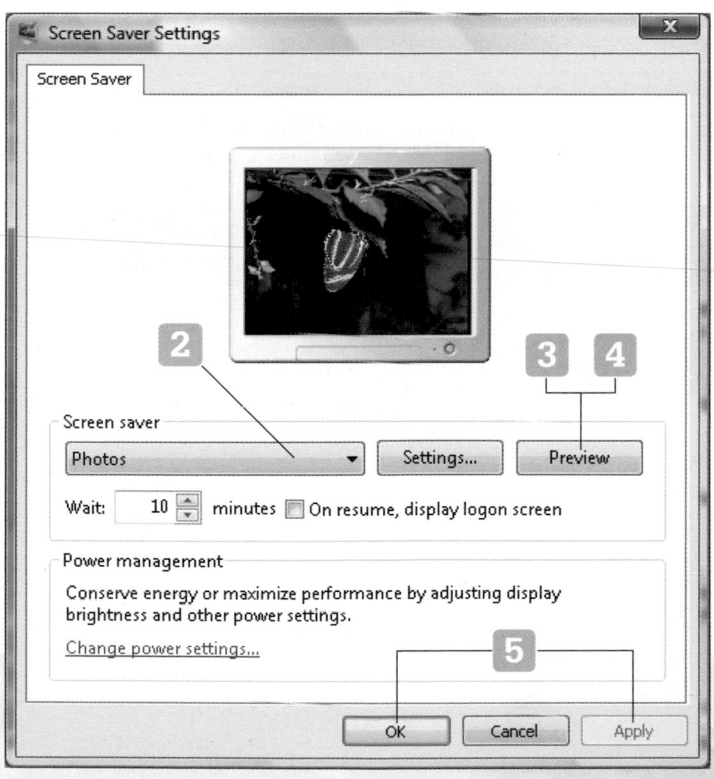

DID YOU KNOW? The photos shown as screen saver settings are taken from the My Pictures folder, which is located within My Documents. If you have an image you want to use, make sure you put it in My Pictures.

SEE ALSO: See the previous section to learn how to open Screen Saver Settings.

Change the background

The picture on the desktop, which is called the background, can tell the world who you are … similar to the ring tone on your mobile. Unlike a screen saver, which only appears after your laptop has been idle for a period of time, the background is always there, while you're working.

1. Right-click an empty area of the desktop.
2. Click Personalize.
3. Click Desktop Background.
4. For Location, select Windows Wallpapers. If it is not chosen already, click the down arrow to locate it.
5. Use the scroll bars to locate the wallpaper to use as your desktop background.
6. Select a background to use. In Windows 7 you can select as many backgrounds as you like, and change them every so often.
7. Select a positioning option (the default is the most common).
8. Click OK.

Personalize 2

Desktop Background 3

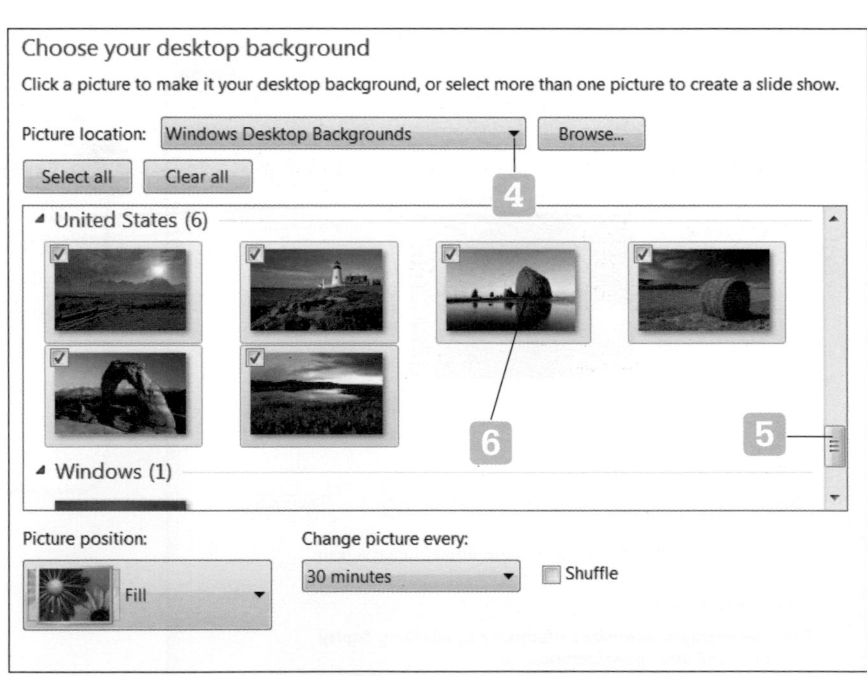

HOT TIP: Click Browse and navigate to another location if the image you want is not in your My Pictures folder.

DID YOU KNOW?

Screen savers and backgrounds used to be needed to save your screen from burn-in, but that is no longer the case.

Use Flip

Flip is a fun name that refers to a fun-to-use Windows utility. Flip gives you a quick way to choose a specific window when multiple windows are open. You are able to scroll through open windows until you land on the one you want to use, and then select it. Here's how.

1. With multiple windows open, on the keyboard hold down the Alt key with one finger or thumb.
2. Press and hold the Tab key. A set of open windows appears in one screen.
3. Press the Tab key again, making sure that the Alt key is still depressed.
4. When the item you want to bring to the front is selected, let go of the Tab key and then let go of the Alt key.

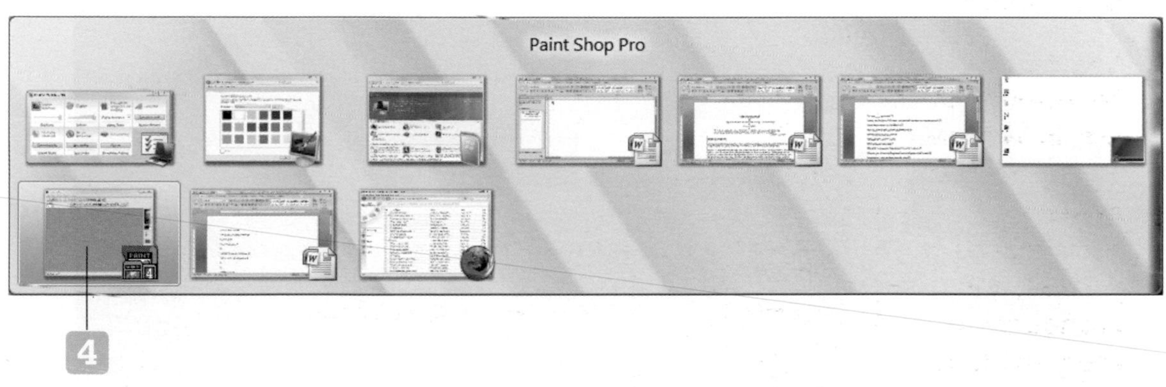

HOT TIP: The windows you have open can either be from a single application (multiple Internet Explorer windows) or from multiple applications (Internet Explorer, WordPad, Paint, Windows Media Center, and so on).

HOT TIP: The Alt key is usually found in a standard position on either side of the spacebar (or on some computers, only on the left side of the spacebar). The tab key is just to the left of the Q key.

Use Flip 3D

Flip 3D offers a quick way to choose a specific window when multiple windows are open. With Flip 3D, you can scroll through open windows until you land on the one you want to use, and then select it.

1. With multiple windows open, on the keyboard hold down the Windows key with one finger or thumb.
2. Click the Tab key once, making sure that the Windows key is still depressed.
3. Press the Tab key again, making sure that the Windows key is still depressed, to scroll through open windows.
4. When the item you want to bring to the front is selected, let go of the Tab key and then let go of the Windows key.

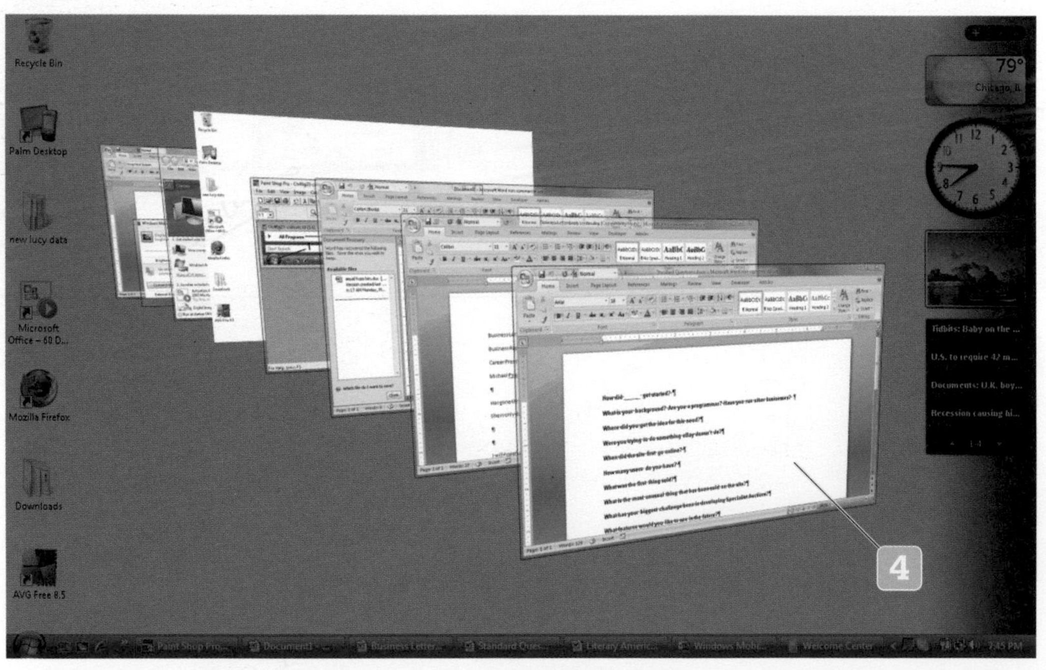

HOT TIP: The Windows key is to the left of the Alt key on the left side of the spacebar. It has the Windows logo printed on it.

HOT TIP: For Flip 3D to work in Windows Vista, the windows you want to view must be actually open, not reduced to taskbar buttons. In Windows 7, that limitation is gone.

Add a desktop icon

Icons on your desktop are shortcuts: instead of having to fish around your Program Files folder or the Start menu, you double-click an icon and the program starts immediately. Adding an icon to your desktop is similar to that for adding one to the Start menu.

1. Click Start.
2. Type the name – or part of the name – of the application you want in the Start menu box.
3. Right-click the application you want to add to the desktop.
4. Click Open file location.

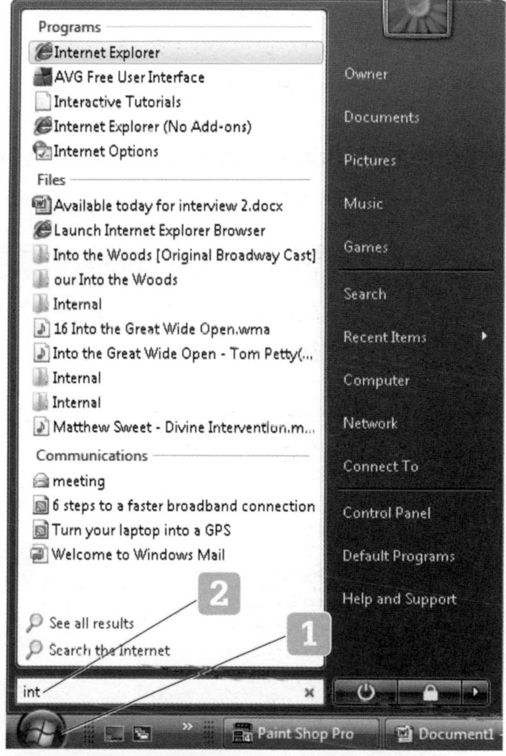

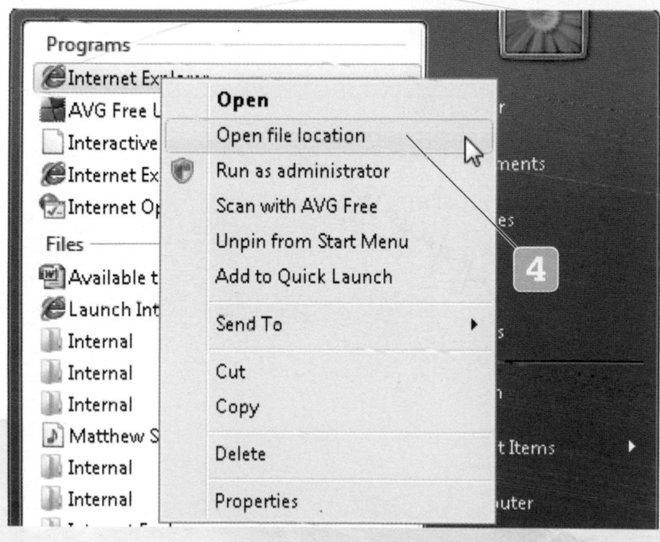

5 When the application appears in Windows Explorer, right-click its icon and choose Create Shortcut.

6 Click Yes to create the shortcut on your desktop.

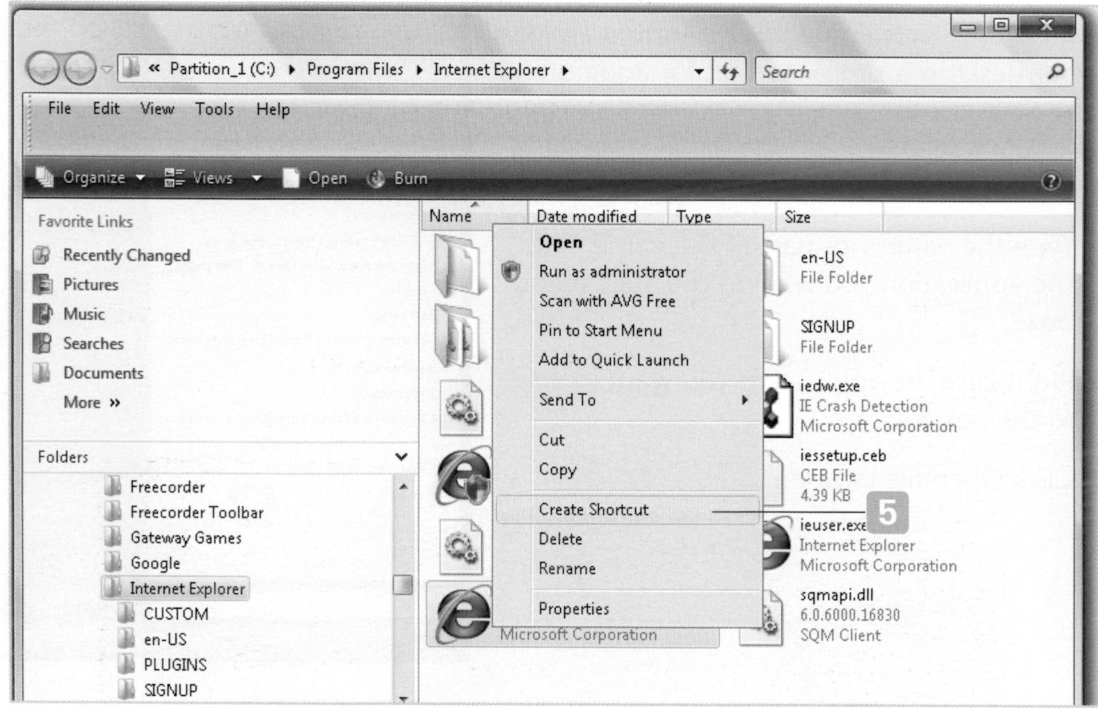

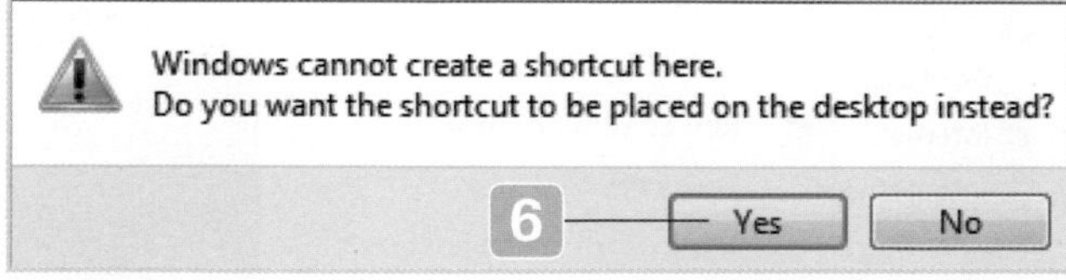

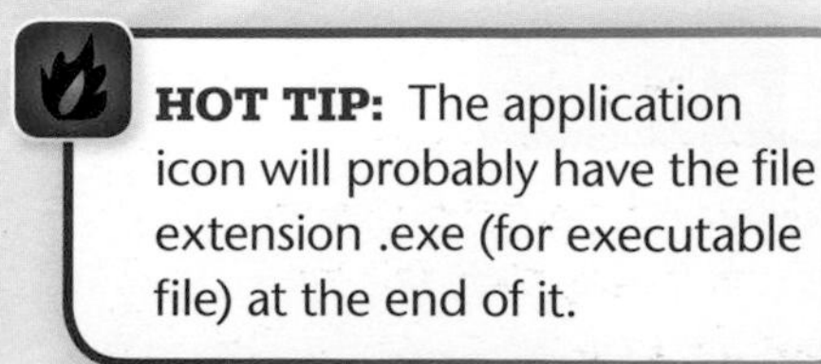

HOT TIP: The application icon will probably have the file extension .exe (for executable file) at the end of it.

Adjust when your laptop goes to sleep

Windows automatically causes your computer to sleep after a period of inactivity. You can adjust the time when your computer 'falls asleep' in order to save battery power.

1. Open Mobility Center by clicking start and typing Mobility in the Start Search window.
2. Click the battery icon in the Battery Status part of the centre.
3. Click Change when the computer sleeps.
4. Edit the plan settings to the desired configuration and click Save Settings.

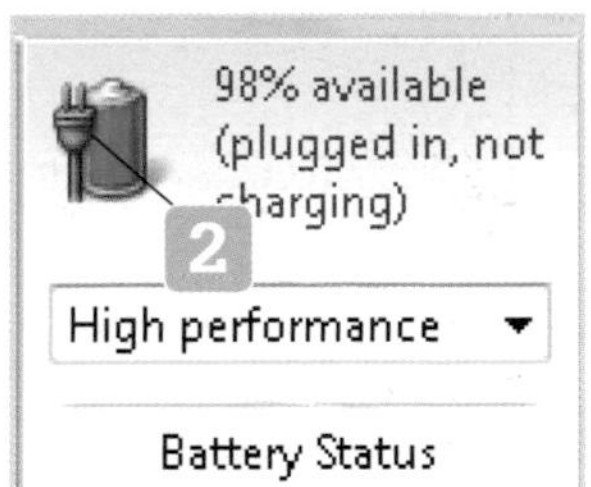

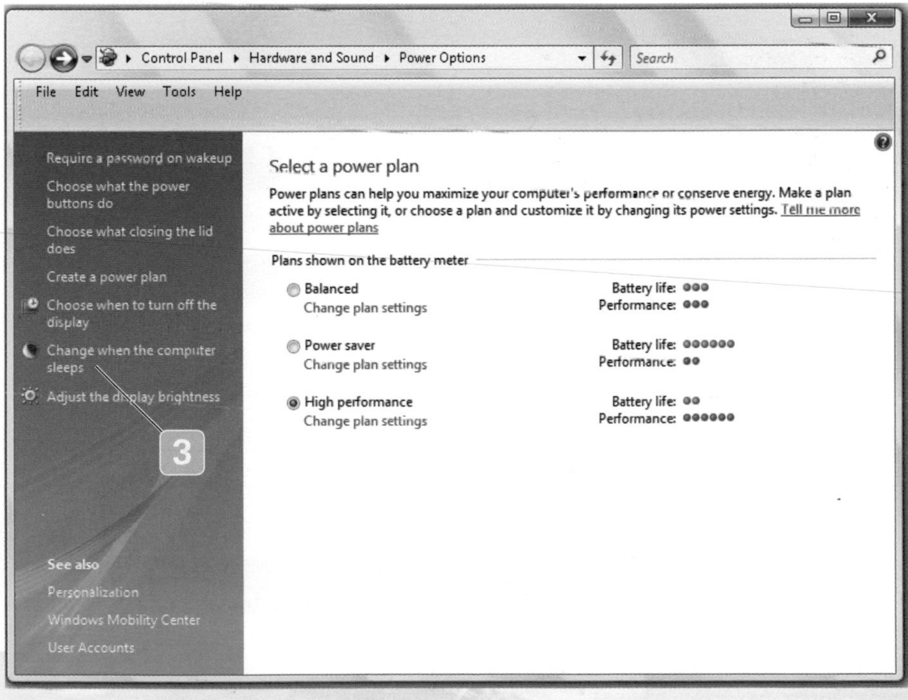

DID YOU KNOW? You can also adjust your power plan in the Power Options window.

HOT TIP: If you don't understand what the power settings mean, click Tell me more about power plans in the Power Options window.

Find Help

If you can't find an answer to a question in this chapter or other parts of this book, turn to Windows' built-in Help system for answers.

1. Click Start.
2. Click Help and Support.
3. When the Help window opens, type your question or subject in the search box and press Enter.
4. Click on a topic to browse through answers by subject.
5. Ask for assistance.

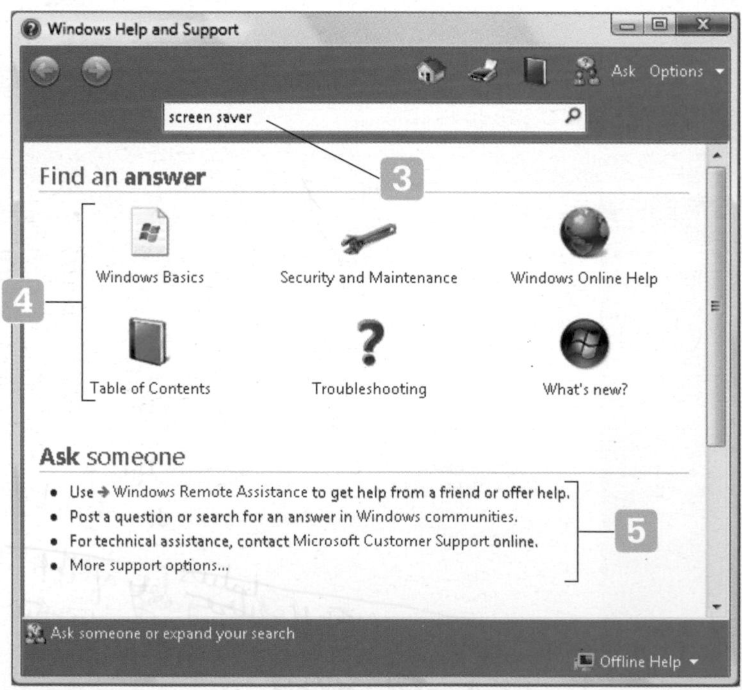

HOT TIP: Press the F1 key to open the Help window. You can do so from within any open application.

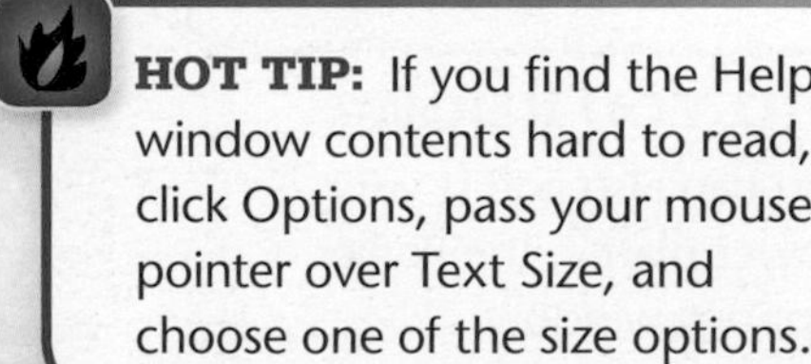

HOT TIP: If you find the Help window contents hard to read, click Options, pass your mouse pointer over Text Size, and choose one of the size options.

5 Keeping in touch with friends

Introduction

Mums and grandmothers of the world rejoice: you now have even more ways to keep in touch with your adult children thanks to your laptop, Internet connection and email. In truth, though, everyone over 50 may so enjoy connecting with their own friends that they might forget about connecting with family. In this chapter, you'll become proficient at the email service that's either already installed on, or can be downloaded onto, your laptop, Windows Mail, and other Internet technologies to communicate instantly with both new and old acquaintances.

Windows Mail makes it easy for you to view email, send messages, manage your contacts and print and store your electronic correspondence as well. To use Windows Mail, you need an email address and two email server addresses, which you obtain from your ISP. In fact, you have probably already gathered that information from Chapter 3. With this information to hand, you can set up email using the new connection wizard. In no time, you'll be online, sending and receiving your own email.

Sign up for Windows Live Mail

I still listen for the postman or woman to come down my drive. But more and more, it's all about email. The first time you open Windows Mail, you're prompted to gather the information about your email address and mail servers. You can't send and receive email without the proper information, after all.

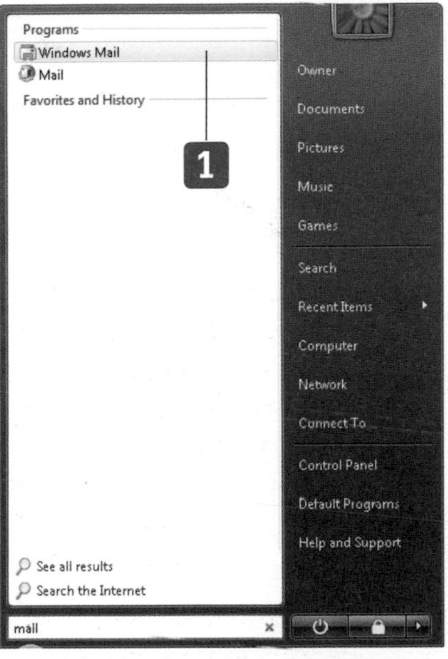

1. Click Start, and click Windows Mail.
2. Click E-mail Account. Click Next.

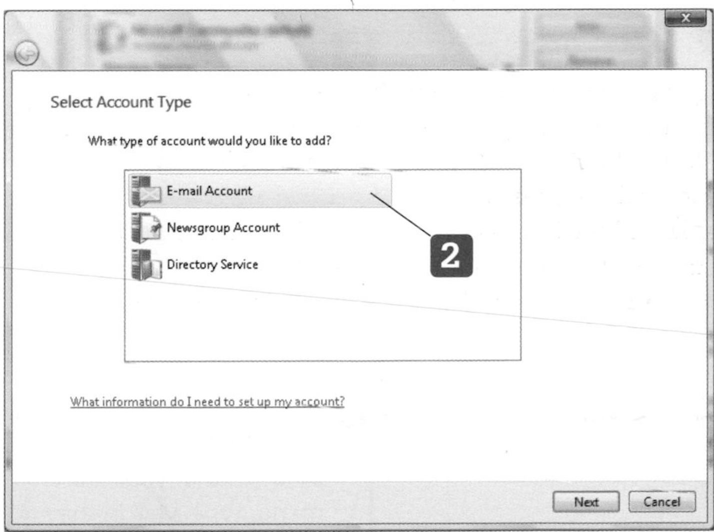

HOT TIP: In case you don't want to use Windows Mail, or if you just want an alternative email service, you can obtain free email from Google (with its Gmail service) or Yahoo! (with Yahoo! Mail).

WHAT DOES THIS MEAN?

Display name: when you send an email message, this is the name that appears in the From line. Put your real name and address here rather than your email address.

User name: when you connect to your ISP's website to pay bills or change other account information, you use a user name. The password is essential; it keeps your email and account information private. Usually passwords are case-sensitive.

Email address: when you obtained Internet access from an Internet Service Provider you received a default email address. If your user name is rkipling and your provider's URL ends with provider.co.uk, chances are your email address is rkipling@provider.co.uk. But check with your ISP to make sure.

3. Type your display name. Click Next.
4. Type your email address. Click Next.
5. Fill in the information for your incoming and outgoing mail servers. Click Next.
6. Type your email user name and password. Click Next.
7. Click Finish.

Display name: Greg Holden
For example: John Smith
3

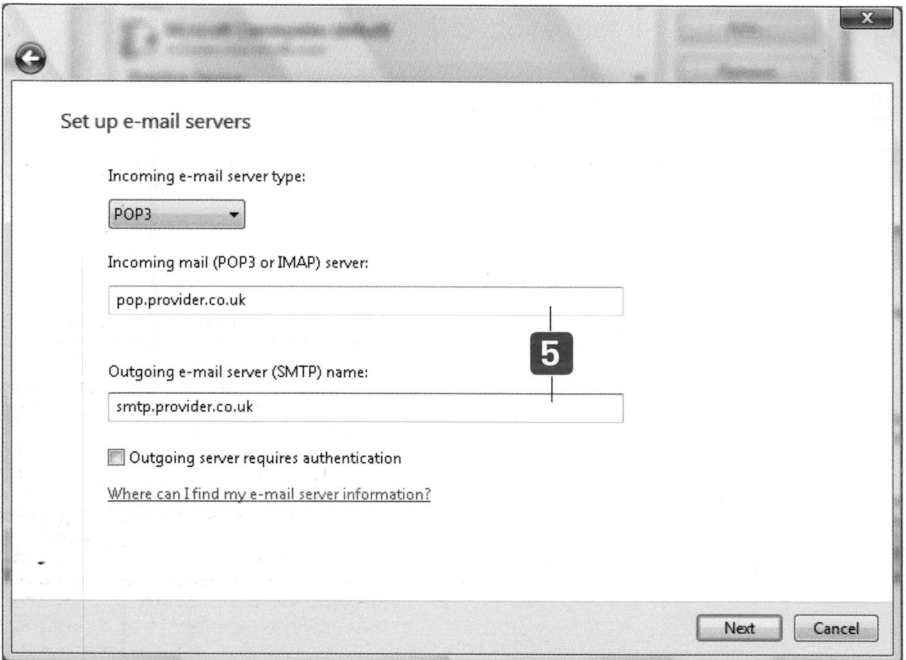

HOT TIP: If Windows Mail is not in your Start menu, type Mail in the Start box.

HOT TIP: Make sure, when you enter your password, that you tick the box telling Windows Mail to remember it, so you don't have to enter it each time you check for new mail.

DID YOU KNOW?

What you need to obtain from your Internet Service Provider, if you haven't already, is an email address and the names of the servers that will route your outgoing and incoming mail.

Read an email message

If you are wondering when your first email message will arrive, you don't have to wait long. Windows Mail provides you with your first welcome message. You can have a friend or relative send you another just to test the system out.

1. Click the Send/Receive button.
2. Click the email once.
3. View the contents of the email.
4. Click the yellow bar if the email contains images that are not being displayed.

ALERT: Email is received in the Inbox. If Inbox is not selected, do that first.

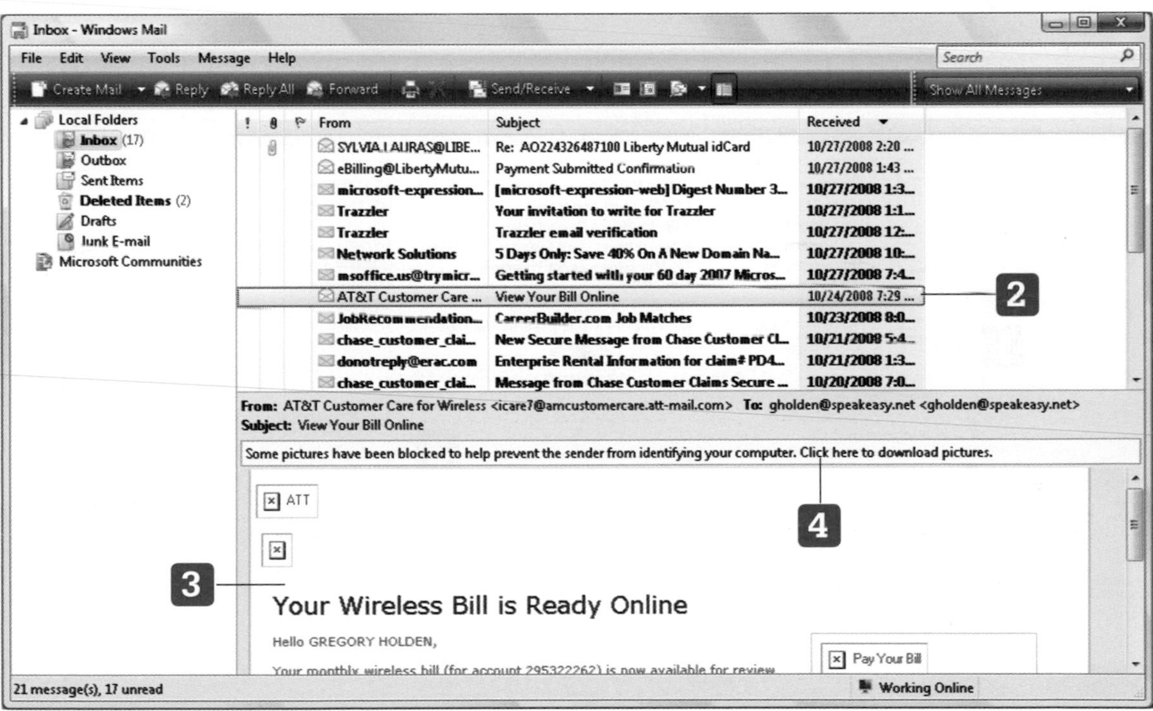

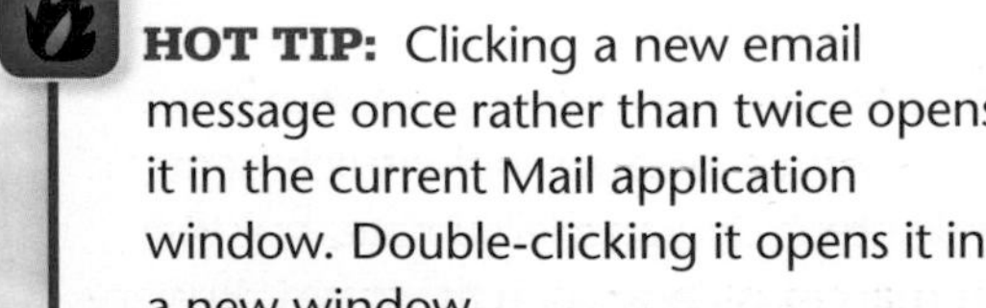

HOT TIP: Clicking a new email message once rather than twice opens it in the current Mail application window. Double-clicking it opens it in a new window.

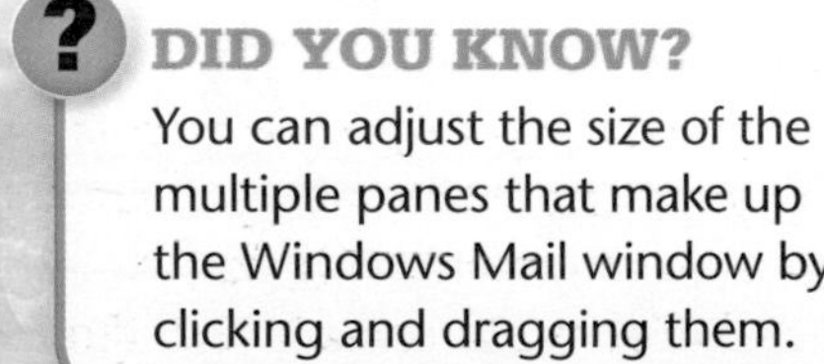

DID YOU KNOW?
You can adjust the size of the multiple panes that make up the Windows Mail window by clicking and dragging them.

Open an attachment

Just like a package attached to a card, an attachment can be an extra treat such as a picture, document or video clip. When you see a paperclip, here's how to unwrap the gift inside.

1. Click the email once in the Message pane.
2. Click the paperclip in the Preview pane.
3. Click the name of the attachment.
4. Click Open.

DID YOU KNOW?
Not all surprises are pleasant. Hackers often use attachments, and they can contain viruses. Never open an attachment, especially if it ends in .zip, unless you know that the email is from a legitimate source.

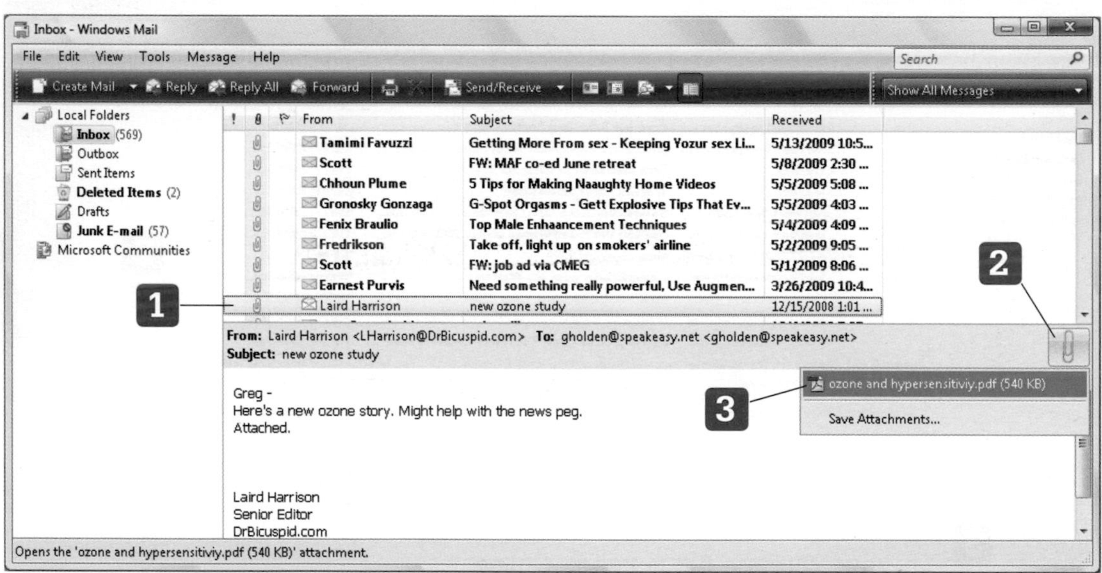

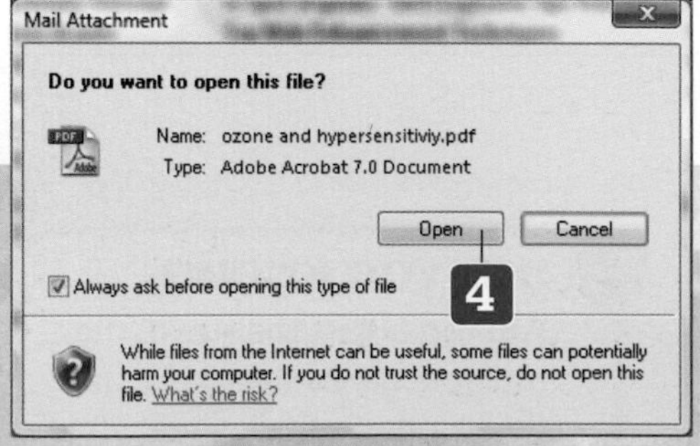

ALERT: Attachments can be dangerous when you don't know who they're from. Hackers frequently send messages with attachments that look interesting and legitimate, but that contain malicious code such as viruses. Be very careful when opening such attachments.

Reply to an email message

Like playing ping-pong, an email message can keep bouncing back and forth between sender and receiver. Follow the steps below to reply to someone who has sent an email to you.

1. Select the email you want to reply to in the Message pane.
2. Click Reply.
3. Make sure the email address is accurate.
4. Change the subject line in the Subject field if you wish.
5. Type the message in the body pane.
6. Click Send.

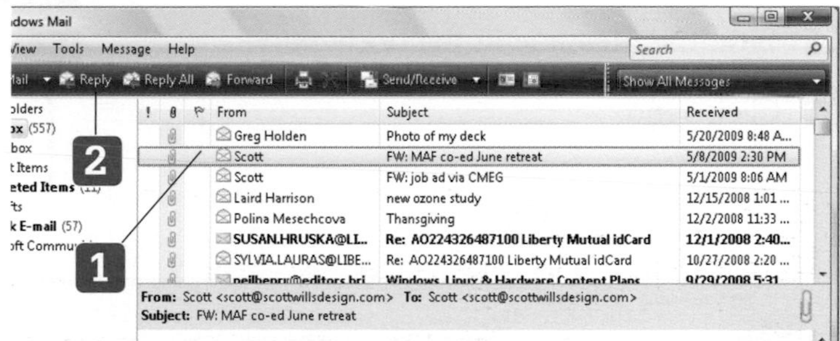

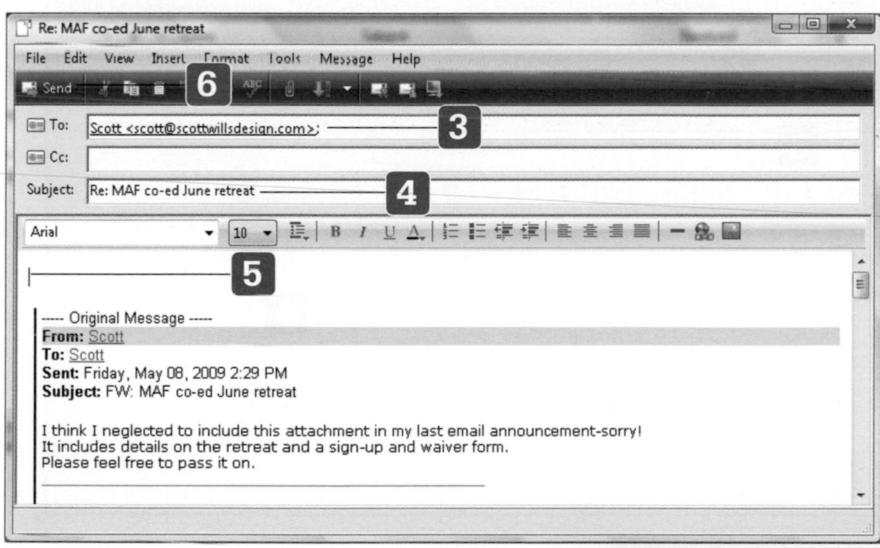

ALERT: If you're not the only one who received the email, you'll send your response to all of the original recipients if you click Reply All. If you only want the sender to read your response, click Reply.

DID YOU KNOW?

Type an email address in the Cc field if you want to copy someone in on your message. To send your email to multiple recipients, separate each address by a semicolon. When you are responding to a message, the To address has a semicolon pre-entered at the end.

Send an email message

Responding to a message you have received is particularly easy because the subject, sender's email address and original text are already entered for you. But often, you'll want to send a message from scratch. The steps are nearly the same.

1. Click Create Mail.
2. In the To field, type the email address of the recipient.
3. Type a subject in the Subject field.
4. Type the message in the body pane.
5. Click Send.

HOT TIP: Make sure your subject is clear and specific so recipients know what the email is about if they want to open it later.

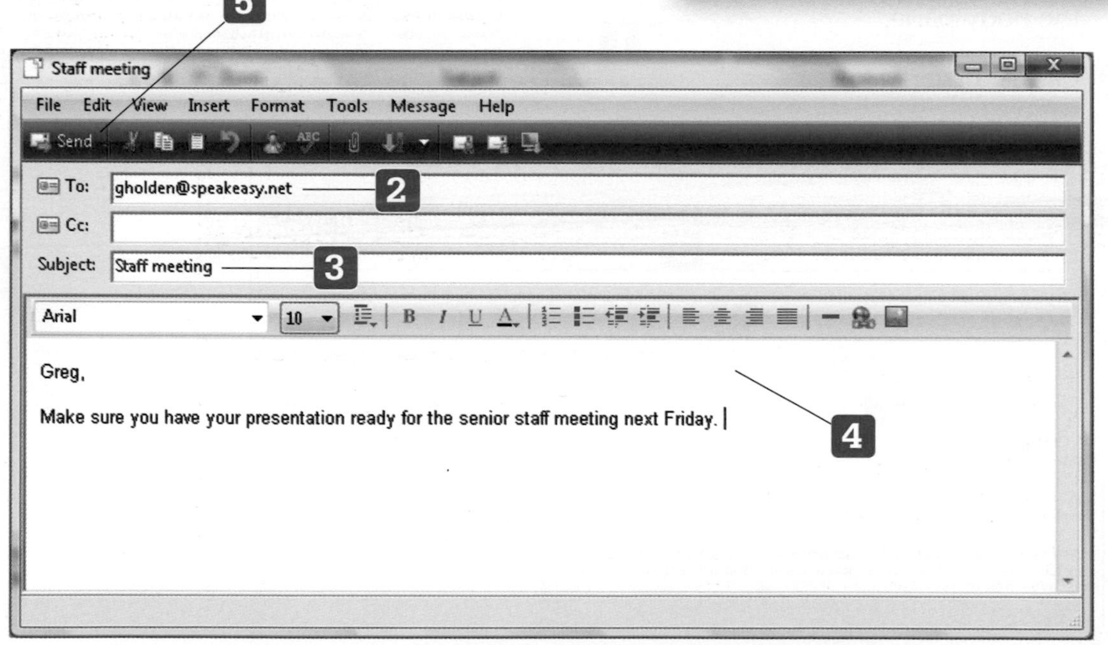

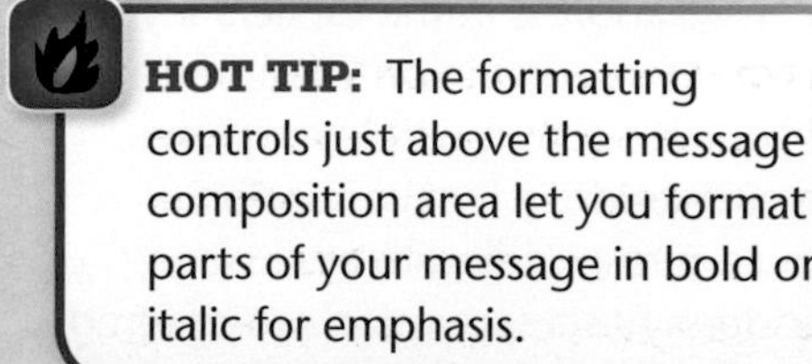

HOT TIP: The formatting controls just above the message composition area let you format parts of your message in bold or italic for emphasis.

DID YOU KNOW?
The menu bar at the top of the message composition window lets you cut, paste and spell check a message's contents. The tools let you copy text from a word processing file, for instance.

Forward an email message

Some news is just too good to keep to yourself. You can forward an email message to others with just a few mouse clicks.

1. Select the email you want to forward in the Windows Mail Message pane.
2. Click Forward.
3. In the To field, type the email address for the recipient.
4. Type a subject in the Subject field if you wish, or leave the previous one in place.
5. Type the message in the body pane, above the text of the message you are forwarding.
6. Click Send.

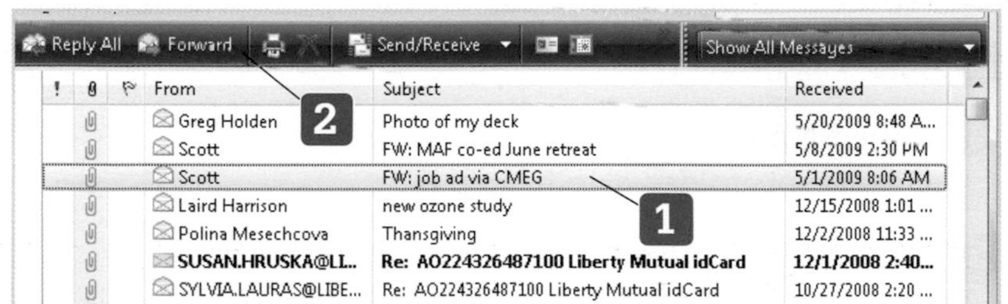

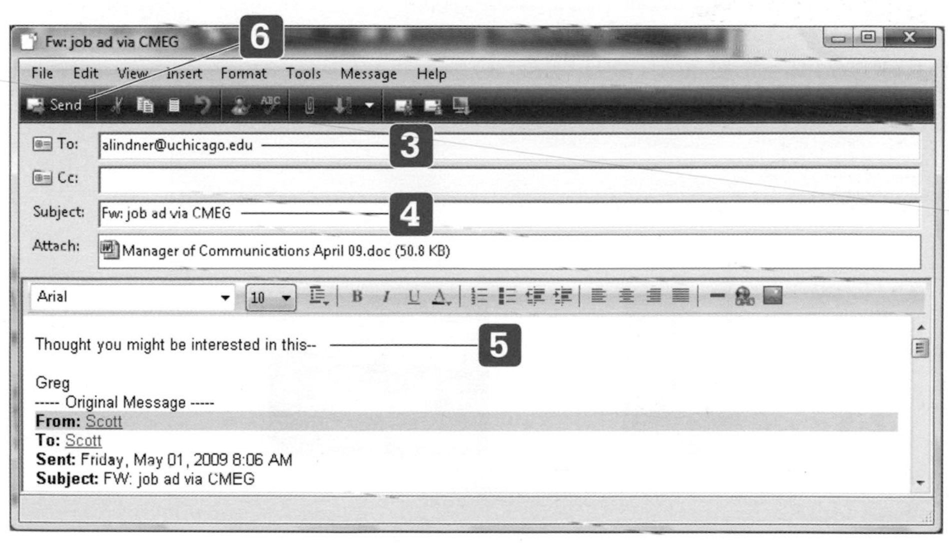

DID YOU KNOW? Your recipient will know the message has been forwarded because 'FW:' will be contained in the subject line by default.

ALERT: Make sure your recipient will want to receive the message you forward. Sometimes people can be offended by 'chain' emails or jokes that they regard as time-wasters.

Attach an image to a message

Sometimes you want to send someone more text than you want to put in the body pane. Or maybe you have a totally adorable photograph, a short video or a sound recording that you want to include. The important thing to remember is that a photo attachment works the same as a text attachment: you use Mail's Insert function to send the image along with your message, rather than cutting and pasting the image into the body of the message.

1. Click Create Mail.
2. Click Insert.
3. Click File Attachment.
4. If the item you want to attach is saved in your Documents folder, skip to step 6.
5. If the item you want to attach is not in the Documents folder, browse to the location of the folder.
6. Click the item that you want to add, and select Open.

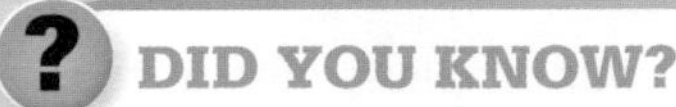

DID YOU KNOW?
A copy is created for the attachment so don't worry, your document will not be removed from your computer.

ALERT: Email services differ on the limit for the size of a file attachment. Some digital photos, when taken at the highest quality setting, can be 2 MB or more in file size. They may take a long time to 'attach' and they may not send properly. Try to keep file attachments to 1 MB maximum.

Include an image within your message

When you attach a file, it is sent along with the text of your message but it is separate. It is up to the recipient to open the image. Windows Mail also lets you insert an image directly into the body of the message. That way it appears instantly the moment the recipient starts to read your text.

HOT TIP: If the image you have added is too big or you want to delete it, click it once and then press the Delete or Backspace key.

ALERT: The same size rules that apply to attaching image files apply to inserting them into message text. But in this case, the bigger the image, the harder it will be for someone to see in its entirety. Only insert images that are small in size – perhaps 200 K to 300 K. Otherwise, attach them.

1. Click Create Mail.
2. Type the email address of the recipient.
3. Type a subject line.
4. Type your message and press Enter twice to provide some space.
5. Click Insert.
6. Choose Picture.
7. Navigate to the image file and double-click it to insert it.

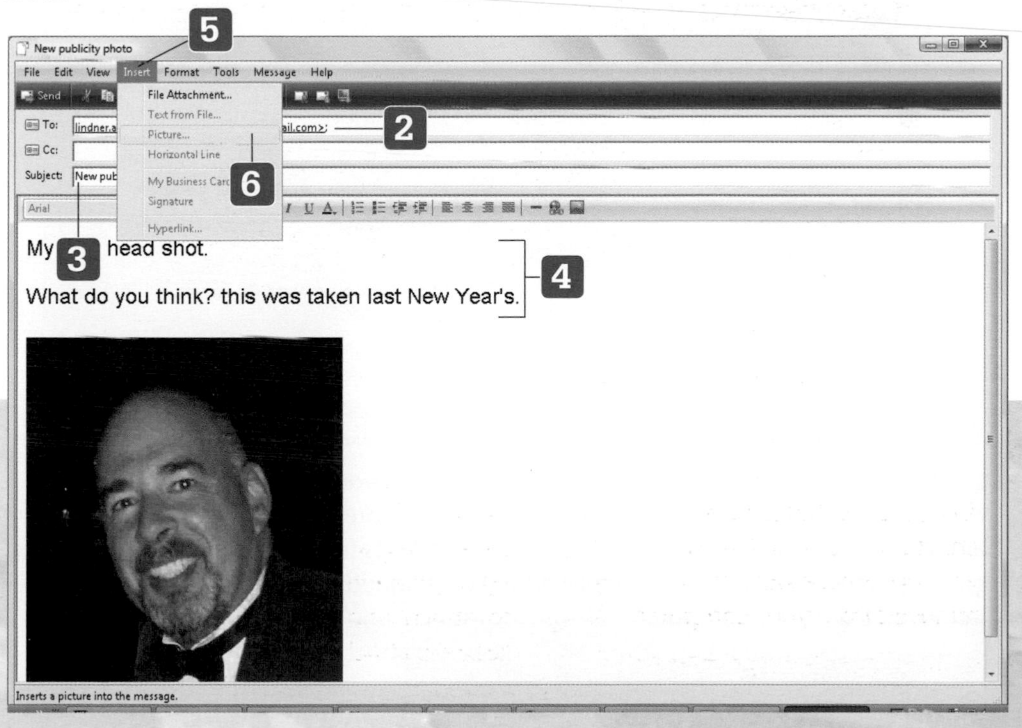

Add someone as a contact

Inside your personal folder, you can store your contacts in a Contacts folder. That way, you don't have to remember and then retype their email address each time you want to send them a message. Follow the steps here to add someone to this new version of your 'little black book'.

1. From Windows Mail, click the Contacts icon on the toolbar.
2. Click File.
3. Pass your mouse over new and click Contact.

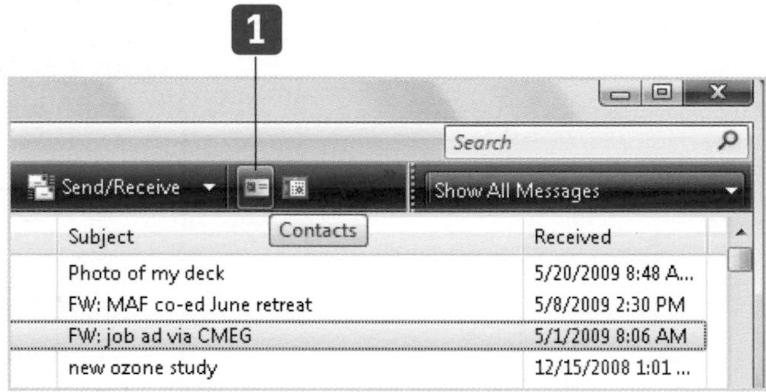

HOT TIP: There's a quicker way to add someone to your contacts. Right-click their name in your Inbox, after you receive a message from them. Choose Add sender to contacts from the context menu. Their name and email address are added instantly.

4 Type all of the information you want to add. Be sure to add information to each tab.

5 Click Add.

6 Click OK.

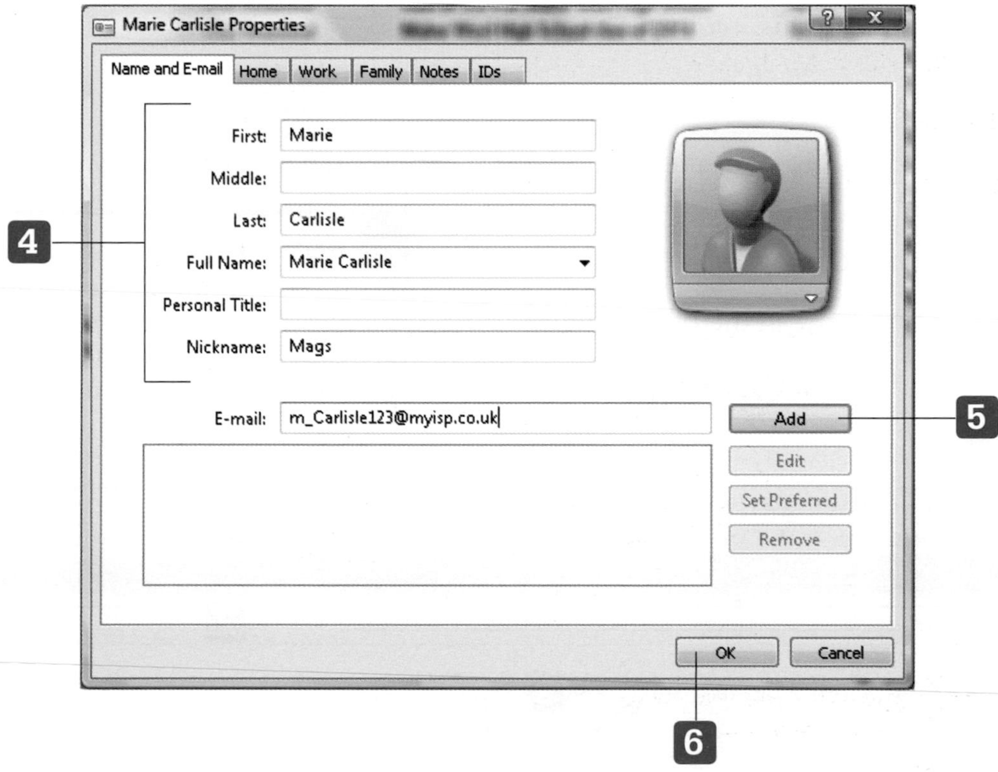

DID YOU KNOW?

Once you add someone to your Contacts list, you click the Contacts icon and then double-click their name in your list of contacts.

Send a message to more than one person

An email 'blast' is a general statement or announcement that you send to a group of people. It's a great way to communicate with many acquaintances at once if you don't need to individualise the information to each person.

1. Click Create Mail.
2. In the To field, type the email addresses for each recipient, separated by a semicolon.
3. Type a subject in the Subject field.
4. Type the message in the body pane.
5. Click Send.

HOT TIP: The easy way to send an email to multiple recipients is to click the Tools menu and then click Select Recipients to quickly add recipients from your Contacts list.

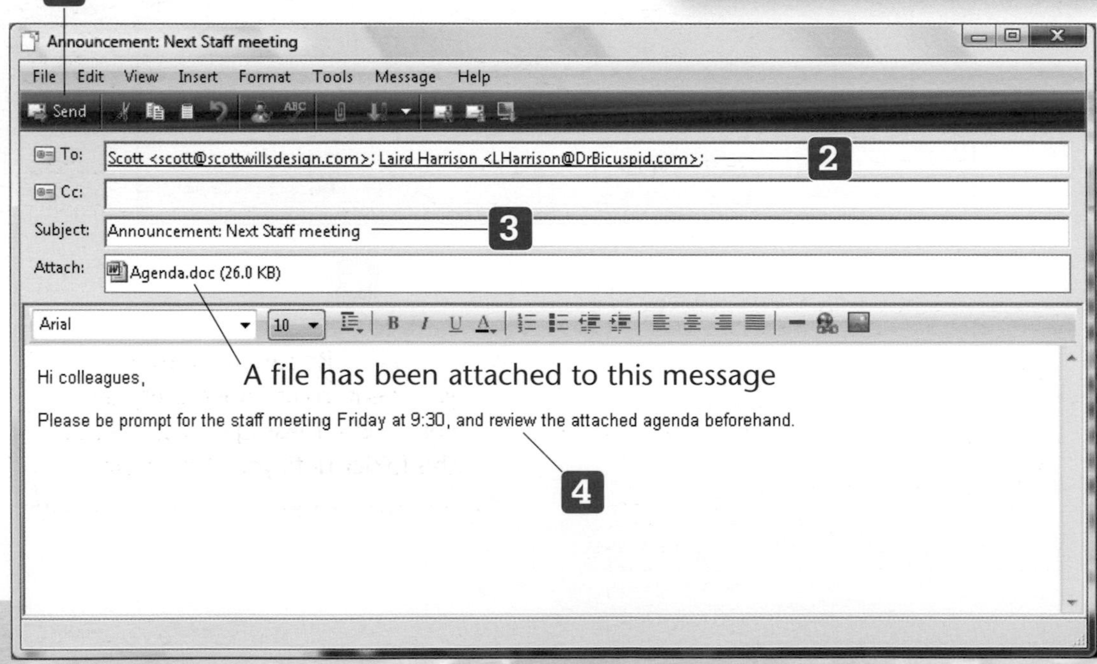

DID YOU KNOW?

If you receive an email message that was sent to you and others at the same time, you can reply to the entire group at once. Click Message and choose Reply to All, or press Ctrl+Shift+R.

Delete your email

Rubbish bin collection day at my house signals a flurry of cleaning activities, and the same can be said about cleaning up your email inbox. Here's how to send an individual message to the trash and then empty the trash.

1. Right-click the email message.
2. Click Delete to send the message to Deleted Items.
3. Right-click Deleted Items.
4. Click Empty 'Deleted Items' Folder.

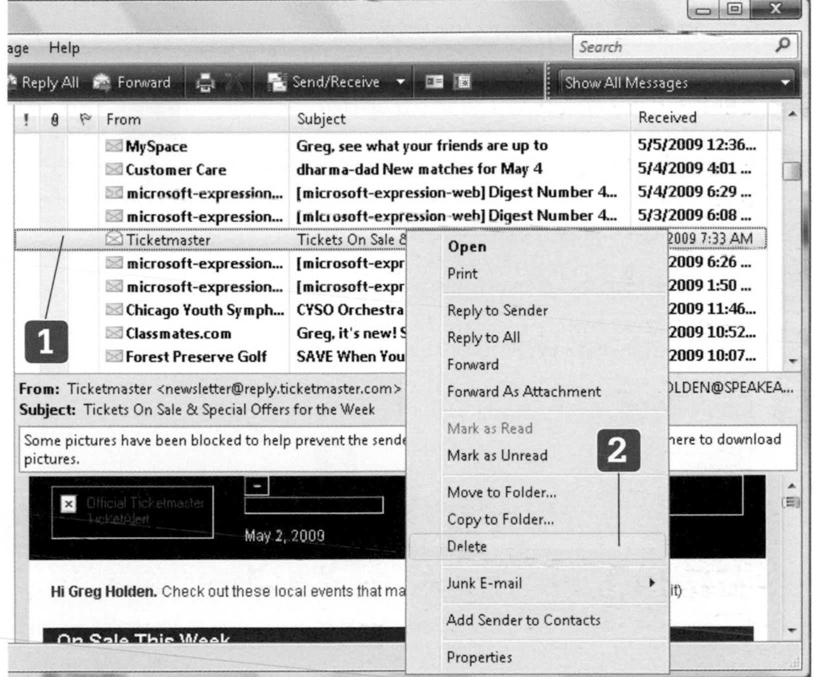

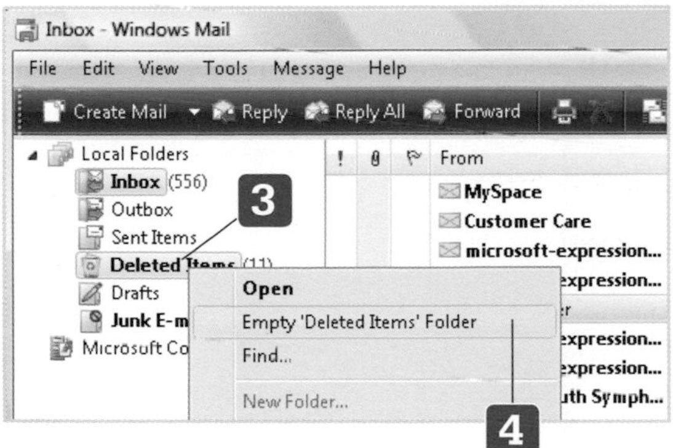

ALERT: Be sure to clean out your Sent Items folder. Every time you send a message, a copy sits in this folder until you clean it out.

ALERT: Cleaning out your trash is especially important if your ISP sets a limit on the amount of storage space you can use for email. The more email sitting in your Inbox and other folders, the more memory you consume. If you go over your limit, you won't be able to send or receive email until you clean out old messages and free up more memory.

HOT TIP: Select any email in any folder, and click the red X to delete it.

Print an email message

Some messages are worth saving offline, and Windows Mail gives you the chance to do this by printing either the mail message itself or an attachment. The Print icon in the Mail toolbar is the place to start. After clicking the Print icon, the print dialogue box appears so you can select a printer, the range of pages you want, the number of copies, and other options.

1. Select the email you want to print.
2. Click the Print icon.
3. Choose the printer you want to use.
4. Click the up or down arrows to adjust the number of copies.
5. Click here and type the number of pages, if necessary.
6. Click Print.

HOT TIP: You can also press Ctrl+P to open the print dialogue box.

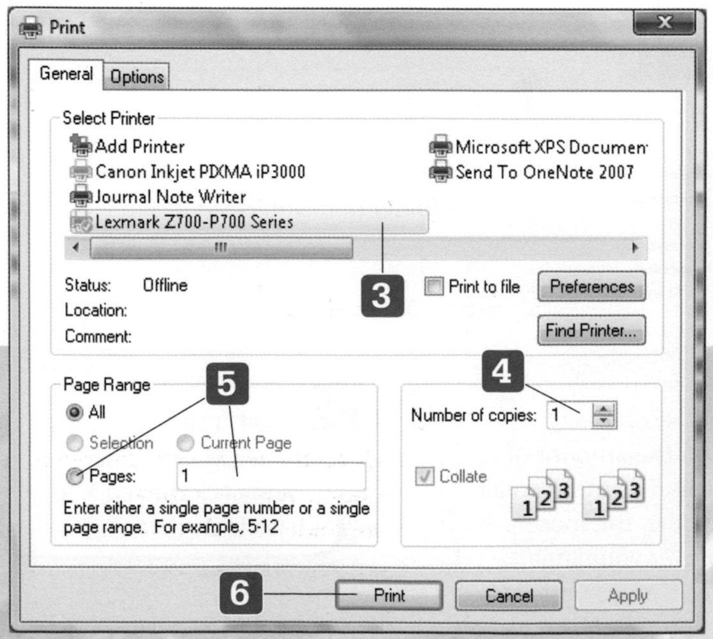

DID YOU KNOW?

You can configure print preferences by clicking Preferences in the Print dialogue box. Preferences depend on the printer, but typically include print quality and black-and-white versus colour.

Create an email folder

You have a wardrobe for your clothes and a cupboard for your dishes. You should also have a folder for email that you want to save. That will make you feel so organised, plus it will prevent Windows Mail from getting bogged down and performing more slowly than it should.

1. Right-click Local Folders.
2. Select New Folder.
3. Type a name for the new folder.
4. Select Local Folders.
5. Click OK.
6. Note the new folder in the Local Folders list.

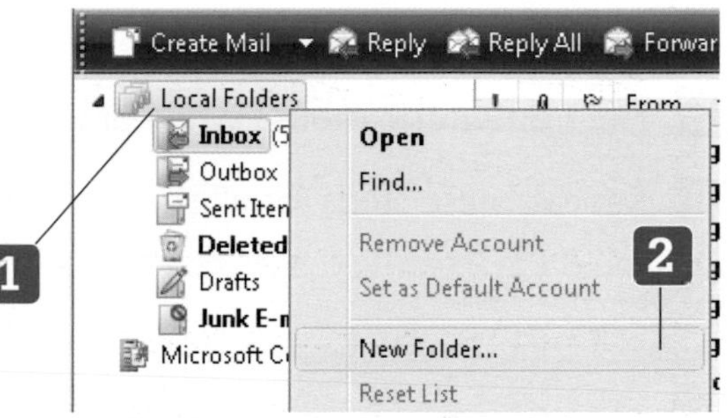

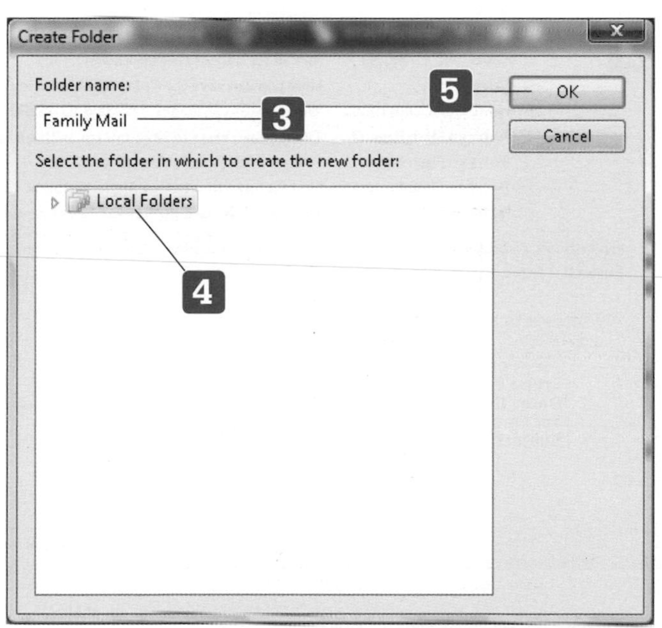

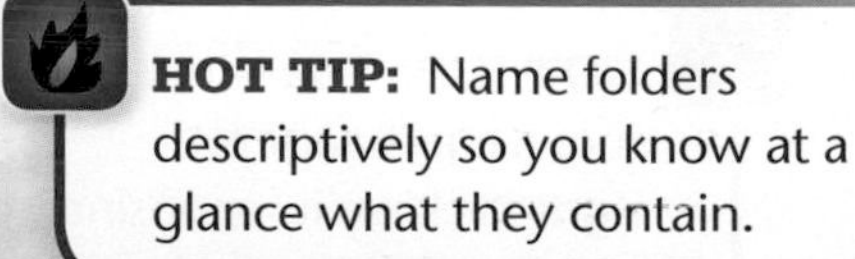

HOT TIP: Name folders descriptively so you know at a glance what they contain.

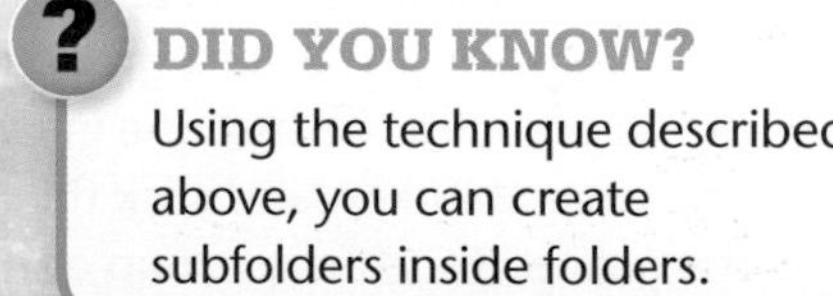

DID YOU KNOW?
Using the technique described above, you can create subfolders inside folders.

File your email in a folder

If you've ever had a sloppy teenager living in your house, you know that providing the storage space doesn't guarantee that items will be put away. You can avoid having your inbox turn into a disorganised mass of messages by moving email from one folder to another. The steps below are really easy.

1. Click the email message that you want to move in the Message pane.
2. Hold down the mouse while dragging the message to the new folder.
3. Repeat these steps for all the messages you want to move.

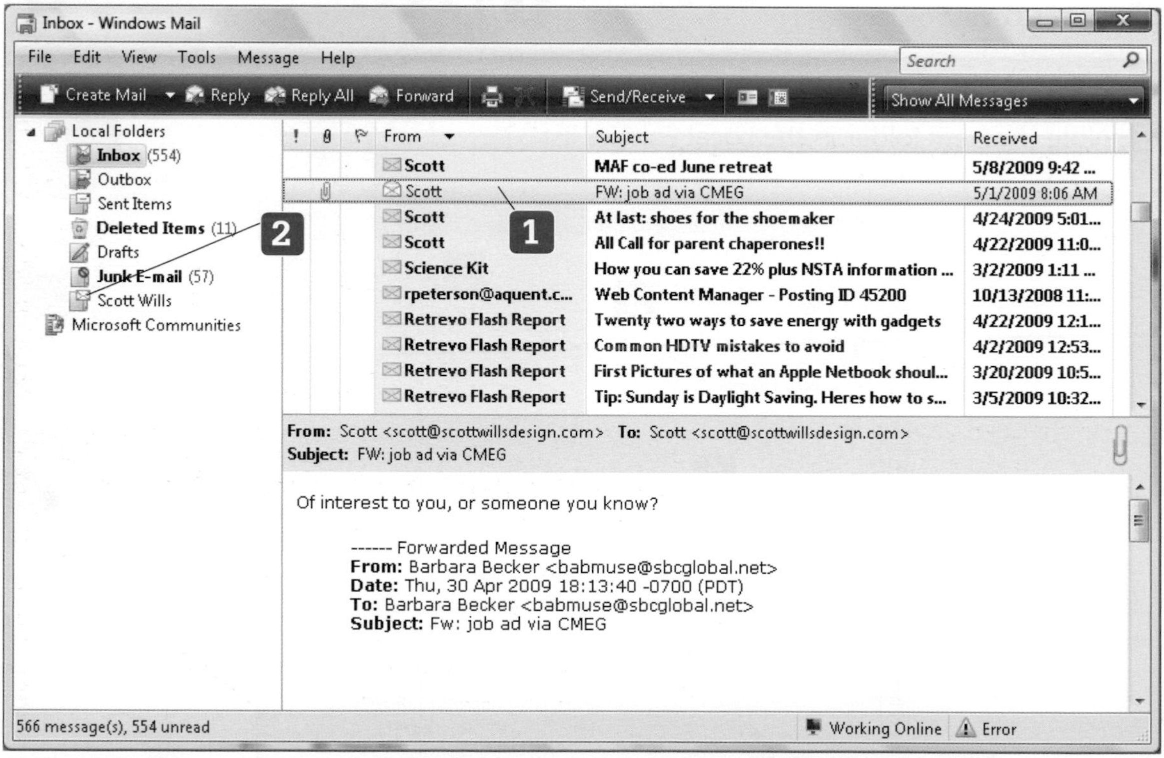

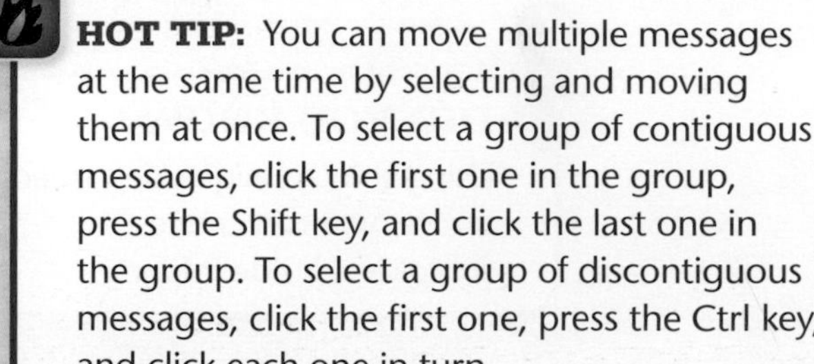

HOT TIP: You can move multiple messages at the same time by selecting and moving them at once. To select a group of contiguous messages, click the first one in the group, press the Shift key, and click the last one in the group. To select a group of discontiguous messages, click the first one, press the Ctrl key, and click each one in turn.

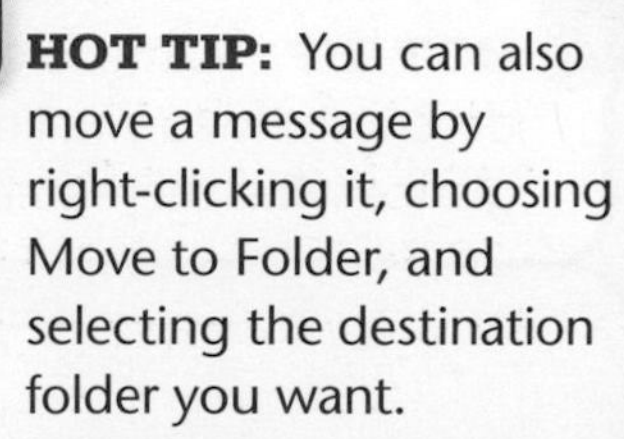

HOT TIP: You can also move a message by right-clicking it, choosing Move to Folder, and selecting the destination folder you want.

Check for your email

Windows Mail, like other mail programs, will automatically connect to your ISP's email server periodically and retrieve any new messages you have. But you don't have to wait for the program to work. You can manually check for mail at any time. You can also change how often Mail looks for email.

1. To check for email manually, click the Send/Receive button.
2. To control how often Mail checks for email, click Tools.
3. Click Options.
4. Click the General tab.
5. Change the number of minutes from 30 to a different period.
6. Click OK.

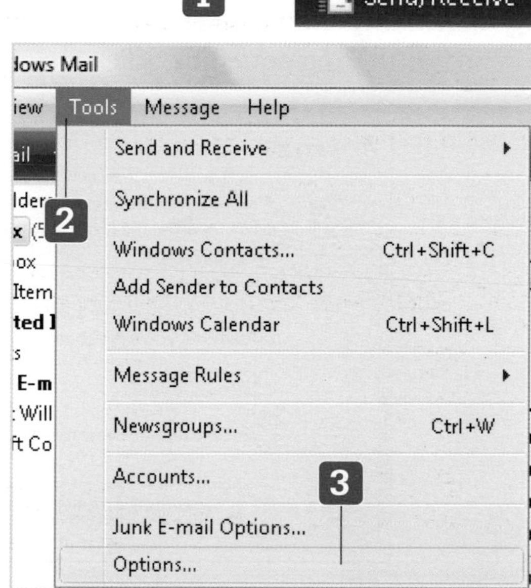

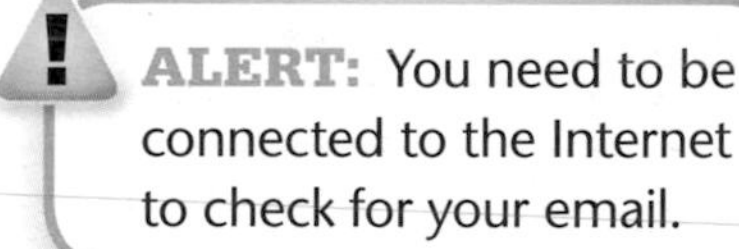

ALERT: You need to be connected to the Internet to check for your email.

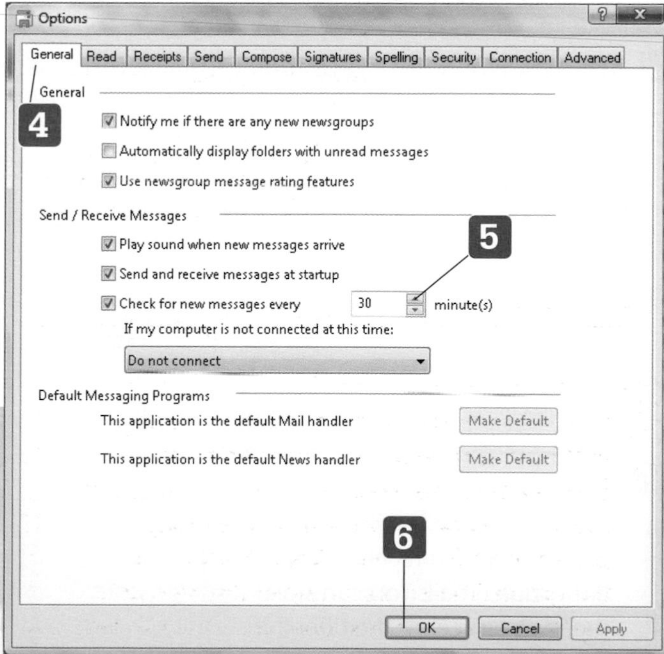

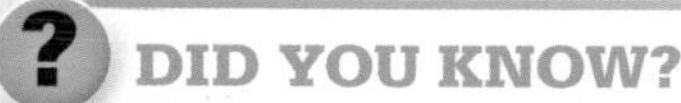

DID YOU KNOW?

You can change other settings in Mail from the other tabs in the Options dialogue box.

Create a junk mail filter

I can go weeks without getting a real letter or card from an actual person, but my mail carrier is loaded down with all the junk mail that comes to me. Luckily in the case of Windows Mail, you can do something about unwanted advertisements. Follow the steps below to block messages from scam artists:

1 If Windows Mail detects an incoming message that it determines is 'junk' mail it shows this dialogue box. Click Junk E-mail Options.

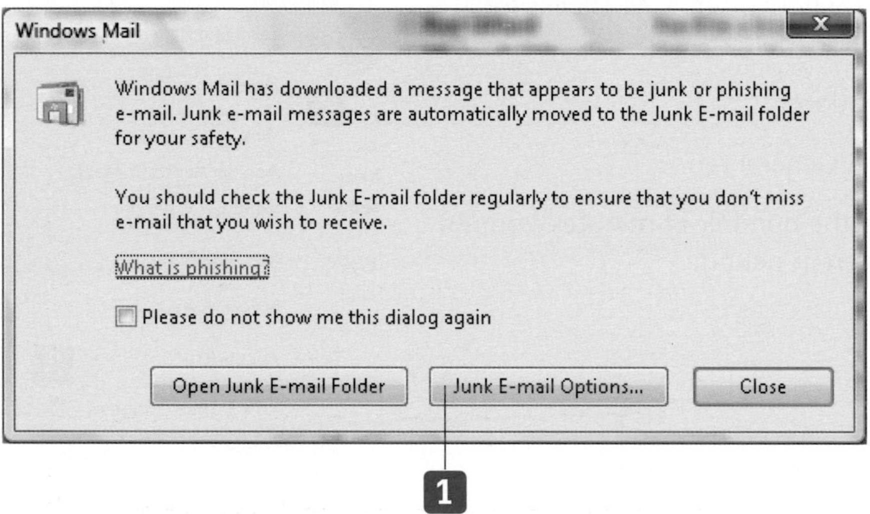

2 To manually adjust your junk e-mail settings at any time, click Tools.

3 Click Junk E-mail Options.

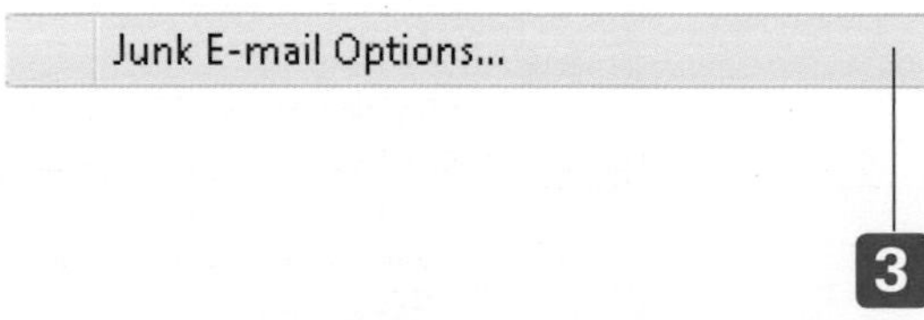

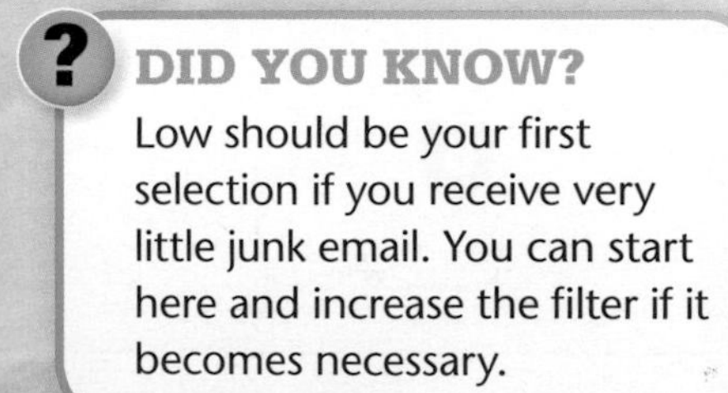

DID YOU KNOW?

Low should be your first selection if you receive very little junk email. You can start here and increase the filter if it becomes necessary.

4 Choose one of the following: No Automatic Filtering, Low, High, or Safe List Only.

5 Click the Phishing tab.

6 Select Protect my Inbox from messages with potential Phishing links. Move phishing email to the Junk E-mail folder.

7 Click OK.

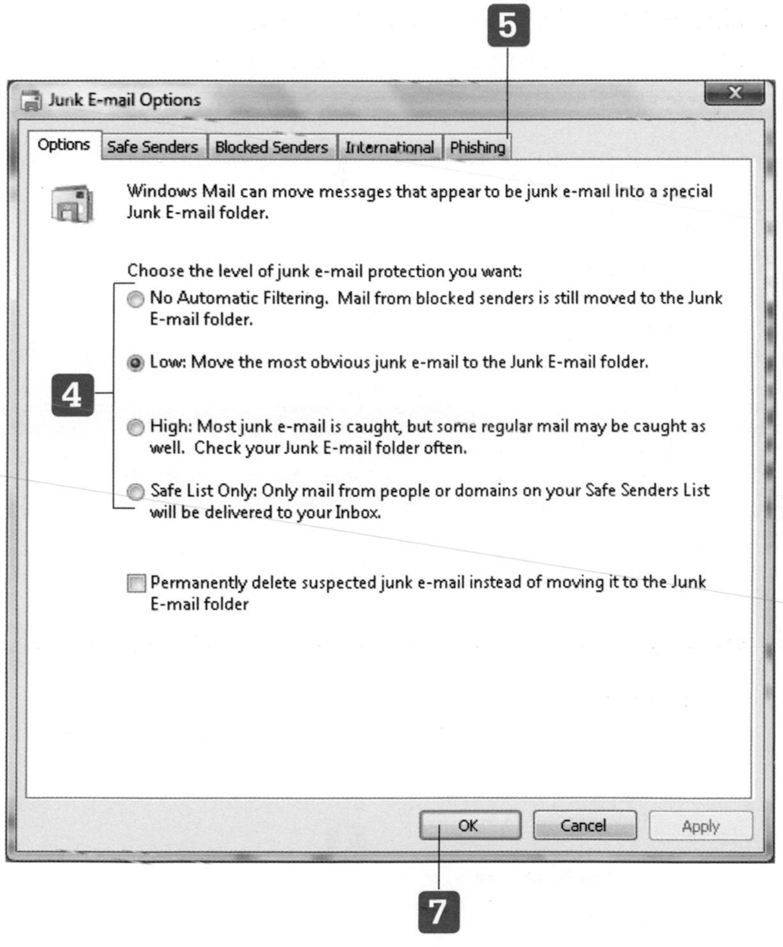

DID YOU KNOW?

If you choose High or Safe List Only, you should review the junk email folder occasionally to make sure you aren't missing any important email.

Avoid spam

The Monty Python characters may have liked spam, spam, spam, but you don't want it in your inbox. 'Spam', in the slang of the Internet, is mail that is unwanted and that usually advertises products or services you aren't interested in. Some forms do bad things if you open them up, and some are just plain annoying. Here's how to make your email a spam-free zone.

1. Never give your email address to websites or companies or include your email in any registration you perform unless you are willing to accept junk email from the companies or their constituents.
2. If you are given the opportunity to opt out of receiving mailings from businesses from which you make purchases, do so.
3. Never buy anything advertised in a junk mail message or give money to anyone you don't know just on the basis of an email message.

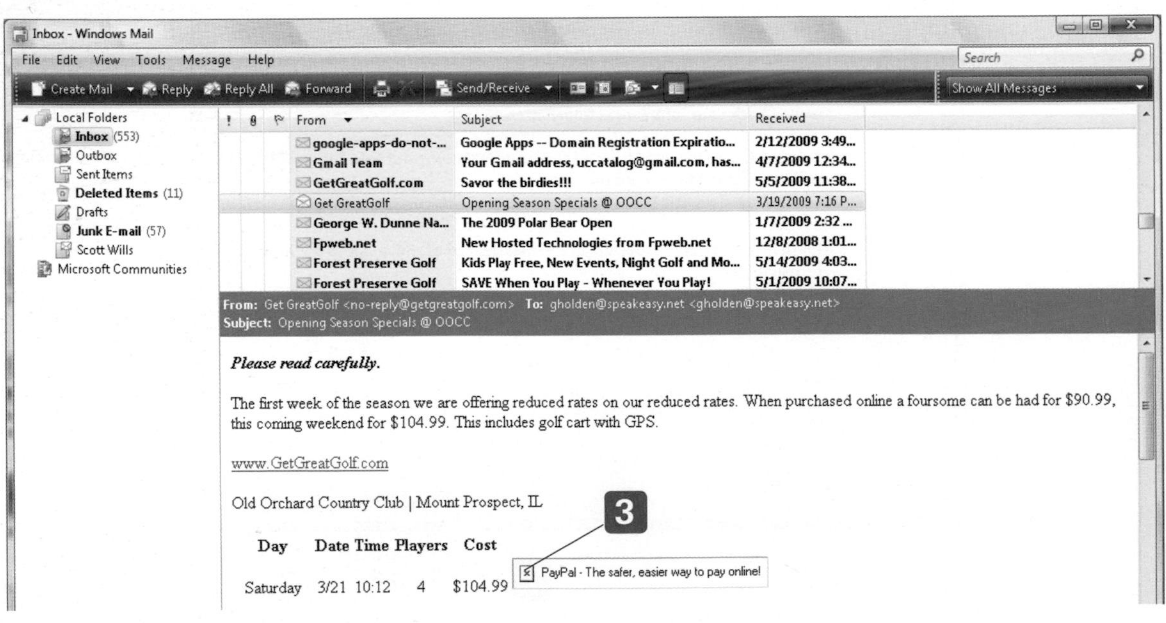

? DID YOU KNOW? Don't fall for common spam hoaxes by buying anything from a junk email or sending money for your portion of a winning lottery ticket or to a 'sick' person.

! ALERT: It's a good idea periodically to check your junk email folder in case legitimate email was moved there by mistake.

? DID YOU KNOW? Giving your email address to a company on its website or on a registration card is an invitation to be spammed by it and all its partners.

6 Working with text, music, videos and more

Introduction

By now, you know that your laptop can perform many different functions. It can get you online, where you can exchange messages with friends and family and keep up with current events. But your laptop can do much more, and enable you to do much more. You can write letters, entertain yourself and indulge your creative side too.

In this chapter, I have collected tasks that describe some common ways you can use your new laptop. You'll learn how to write and format a letter and juggle numbers. You'll also learn how to use your laptop as a source of entertainment; it can bring you music, television and lots of photographic images as well.

Write a letter

You can always write personal letters by hand, but when it comes to business communications or group messages, typing a letter on your computer is by far your most convenient option. Here's how to get started with Windows' built-in application, WordPad:

1. Click Start.
2. Select All Programs.
3. Click Accessories.
4. Click WordPad.

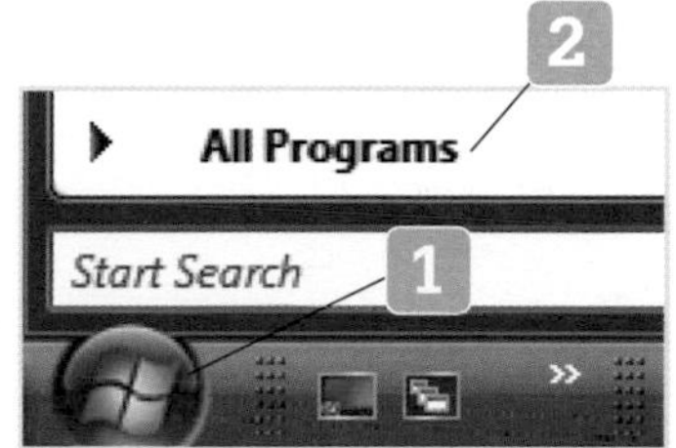

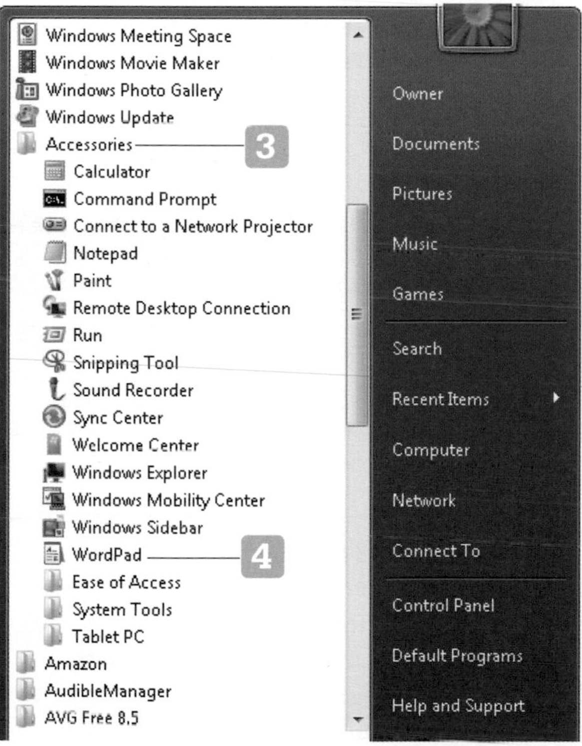

DID YOU KNOW?
You'll see another word processing application under Accessories: Notepad. This application is for creating plain-text documents with virtually no formatting. It's best suited for creating webpages and computer programs, not formatted text documents.

HOT TIP: As you might suspect by now, you can also open WordPad by clicking Start, typing WordPad in the start box, and choosing the application when it appears in the Start menu.

DID YOU KNOW?
WordPad, which is a built-in word processor that comes with Windows, is perfect for straightforward word processing.

5 Notice the text cursor, which is positioned so you can start typing. Type your message; press Enter to break a line when needed.

6 Click Center to centre a paragraph.

7 When you are done, click Save.

8 Give your file a name and press Save to save it on your laptop.

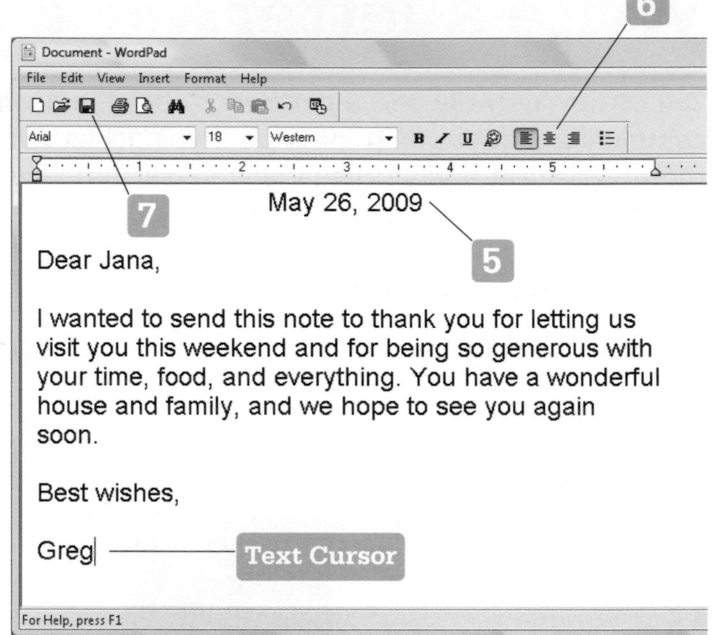

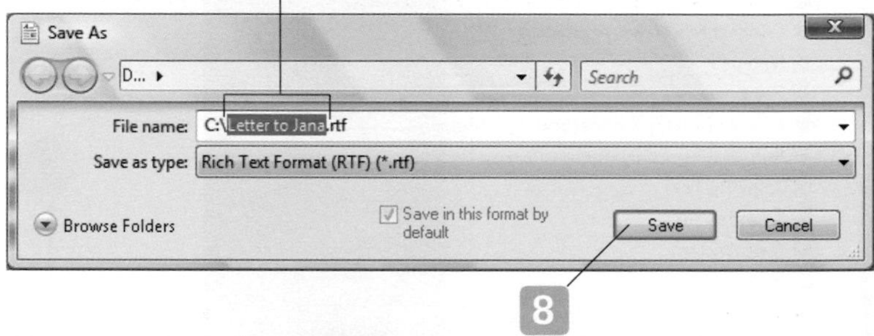

HOT TIP: To print your letter, click the Print icon (next to the Save icon in the toolbar).

HOT TIP: The bar right above the ruler provides options so you can select font type and size (to the left) and buttons to add bold, italics, underlining, text colour, alignment and bullet points (to the right).

WHAT DOES THIS MEAN?

.RTF: stands for Rich Text Format, a file format commonly used by word processing applications.

.TXT: stands for Plain Text Format.

.DOC: is used to signify a Microsoft Word document.

Format and print a letter

One of the advantages of using a word processing application to create a letter, as opposed to writing it by hand, is the ability to add formatting after you do the composition. Once you have typed the text and saved the file, you can edit words and add emphasis before you print it out.

1. To format text, first select it.
2. Click one of the options in the Format bar to change text size or add emphasis.

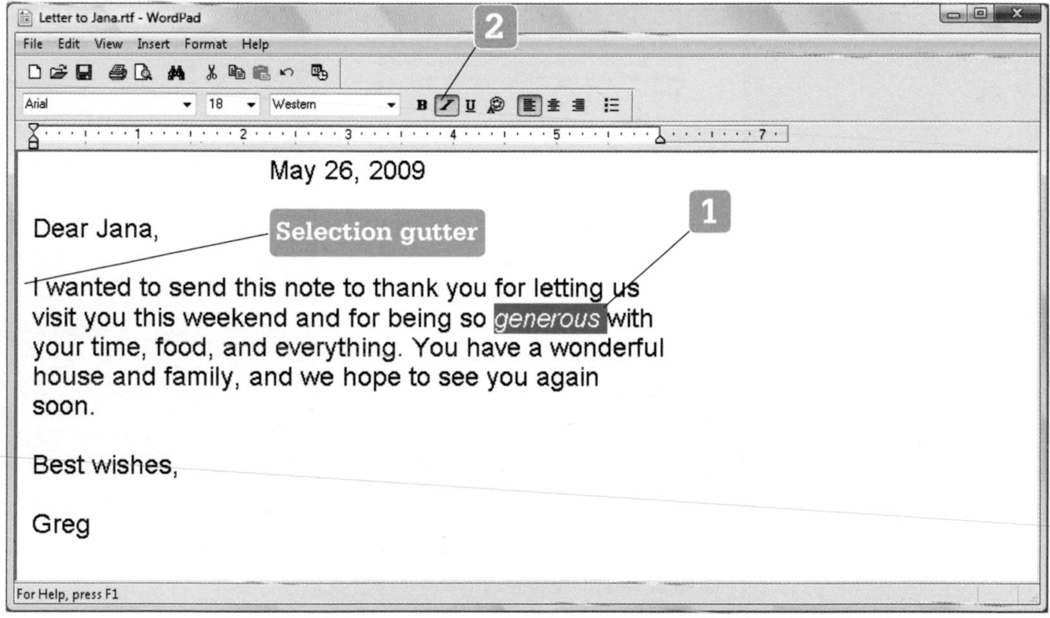

3. If you want to preview your document before printing, click File and select Print Preview.

HOT TIP: To select a single word, double-click it. To select an entire paragraph, triple-click anywhere in the paragraph. To select a line, position your mouse pointer in the selection gutter near the left margin. Click once to select the adjacent line. You can also select multiple words by clicking at the beginning of a selection and Shift+Clicking at the end of the selection.

4. Click Zoom In to zoom in.
5. Click Print if you are ready to print.
6. Click Close if you need to do more editing.
7. Click File and choose Print.

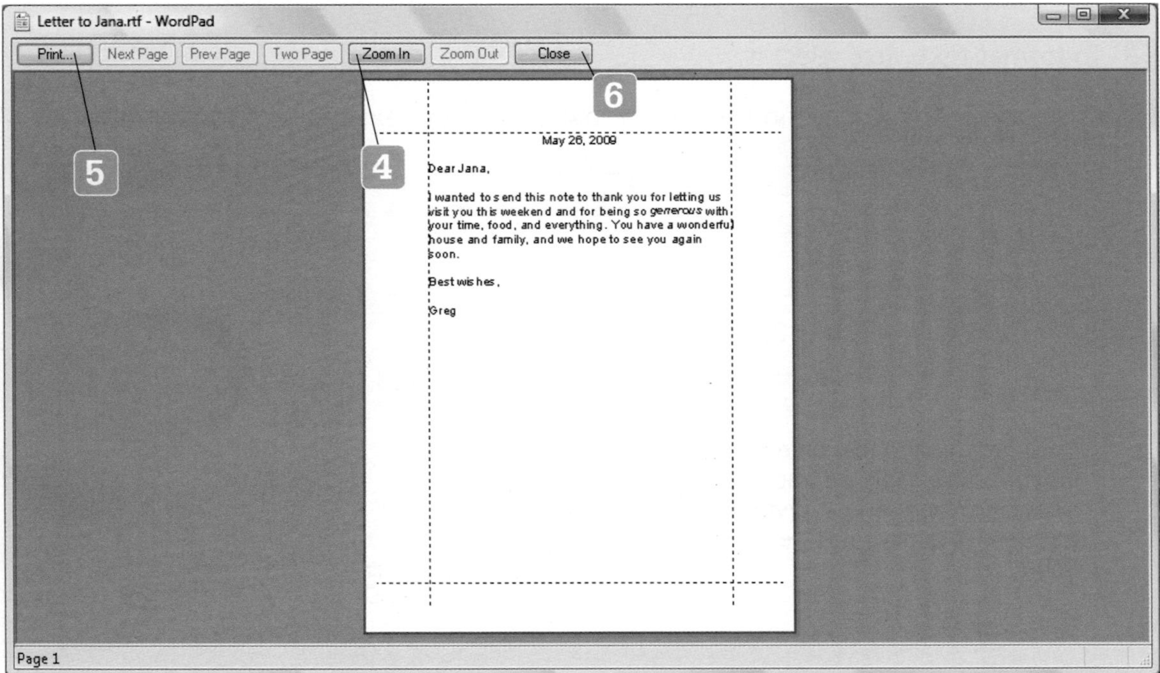

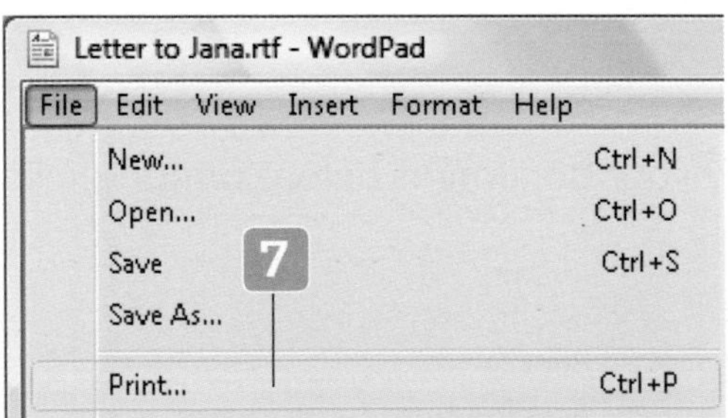

DID YOU KNOW?

Microsoft Word, which is part of the Microsoft Office suite, comes installed with many new laptops in a trial version. After the trial period (perhaps 60 days) is over, you either have to uninstall the program or purchase Microsoft Office, the suite of applications that includes Word.

8 Select the number of copies you want.

9 Click Print to print your file.

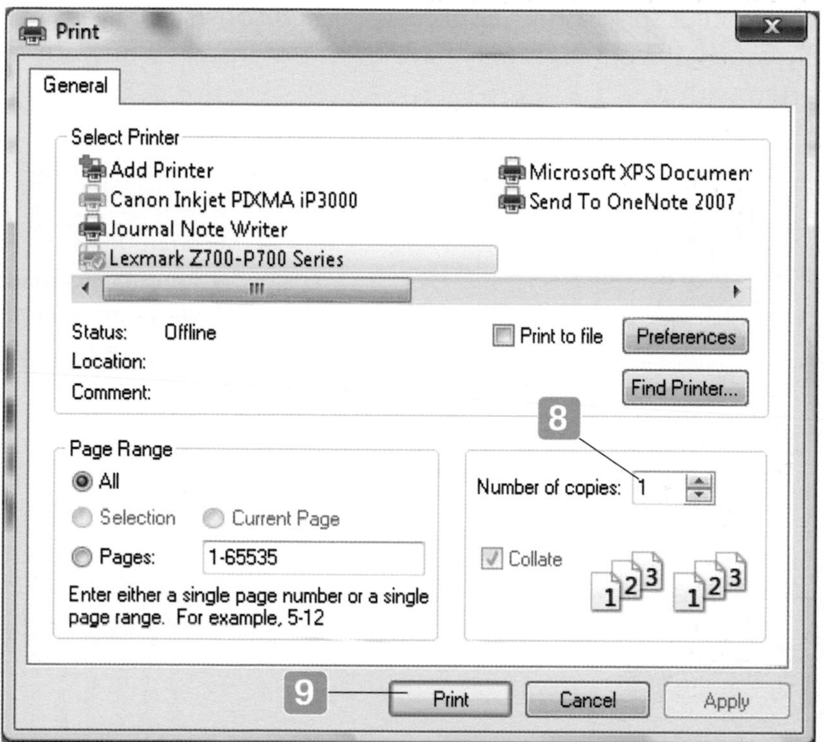

ALERT: Make sure your printer is connected and switched on before you try to print. If the printer is not connected or not turned on, you'll see an alert message telling you that your laptop cannot communicate with the external device.

HOT TIP: If you click the Print icon in the WordPad toolbar, the document will be sent to your printer immediately, and one copy will print. If you want to print more than one copy or choose other print options, click File and choose Print to display the Print dialogue box.

Create a spreadsheet

People who think spreadsheets are more trouble than they are worth haven't used them. The most popular spreadsheet application, Microsoft Excel, is easy to use. It comes with Microsoft Office, which may have been pre-installed on your laptop. Here's how to get started with it.

1. Click Start, click All Programs, click Microsoft Office, and click the Microsoft Excel icon.
2. Click in a cell and type text or numbers.
3. Press Enter or click the tick mark to confirm your entry.

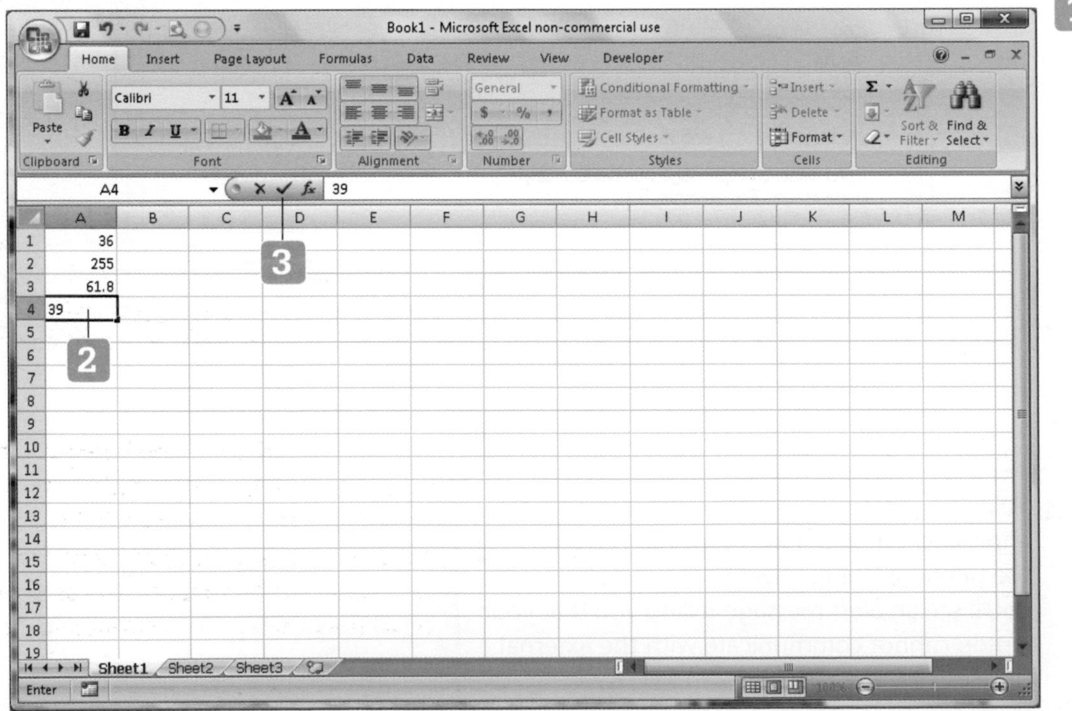

Spreadsheets are formatted into rows (identified by numbers) and columns (identified by letters). Each box is known as a cell.

HOT TIP: Use the toolbar and menu bar, which are situated at the top of the spreadsheet, to add and format data in the spreadsheet.

4 To add data you have entered in a spreadsheet, highlight the cells you want to add.

5 Click AutoSum to add the selected cells.

6 Note the result, which appears in the cell next to the selected cells.

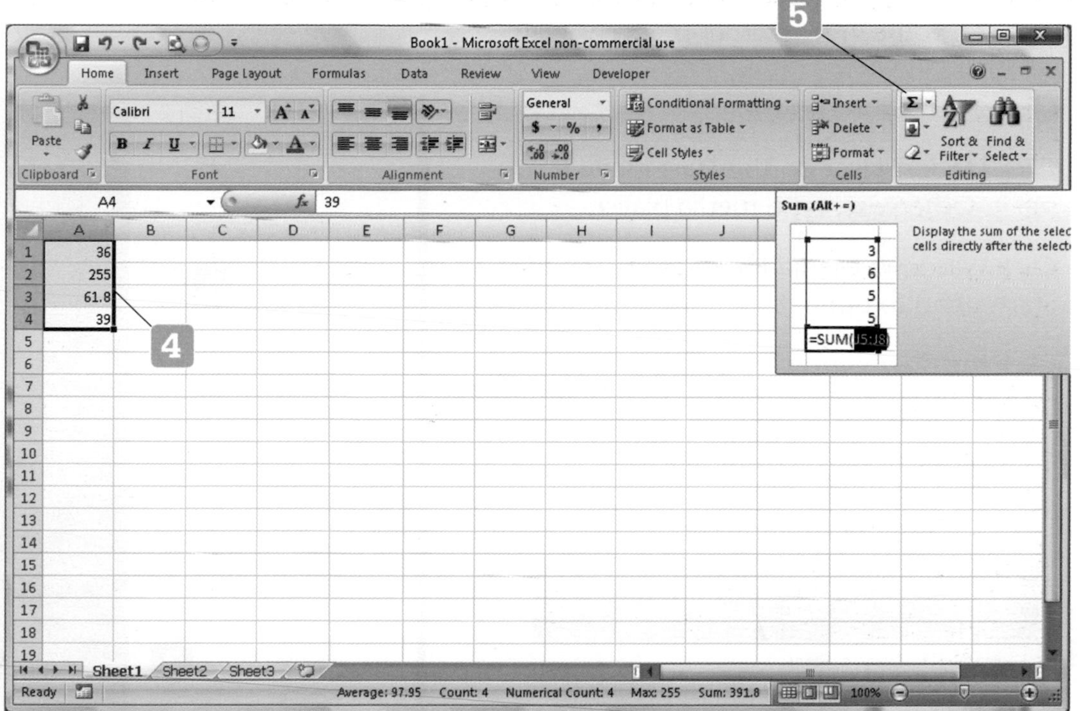

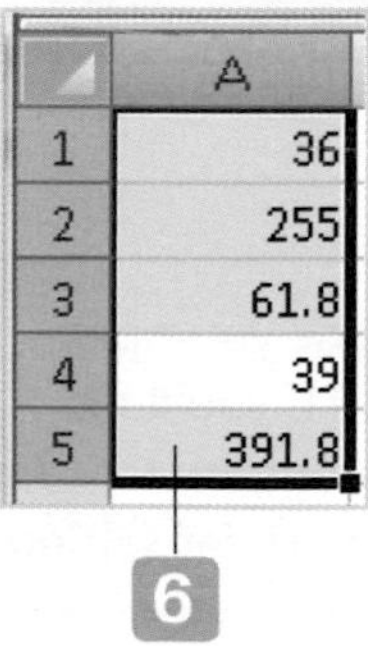

HOT TIP: Different workbooks can be used within the same spreadsheet for related topics such as household and holiday expenses. To move between workbooks, click on tabs that can have customised names if you double-click on the existing name and over-type it.

HOT TIP: It takes time to learn about all of Excel's features. To find out more about this complex program, turn to *Microsoft Excel in Simple Steps*, written by me and also published by Pearson.

HOT TIP: The sum, average and other results of selecting cells appear immediately in the Excel status bar without you having to choose AutoSum or another command.

Use Windows Media Player

When we use the word 'media' here, we're talking about digital content such as music or videos. Media Player is one of the applications that can play music and movies. By default, Media Player is configured to play music. But once you know where the right controls are, you can play other media as well.

1. Click on the Start button.
2. Click Media Player on the Start menu if you see it. Otherwise, type media player.
3. Click Windows Media Player at the top of the Start menu to open it.
4. Click the down arrow next to the music icon (Select a Category).
5. Click Music to play a music file.

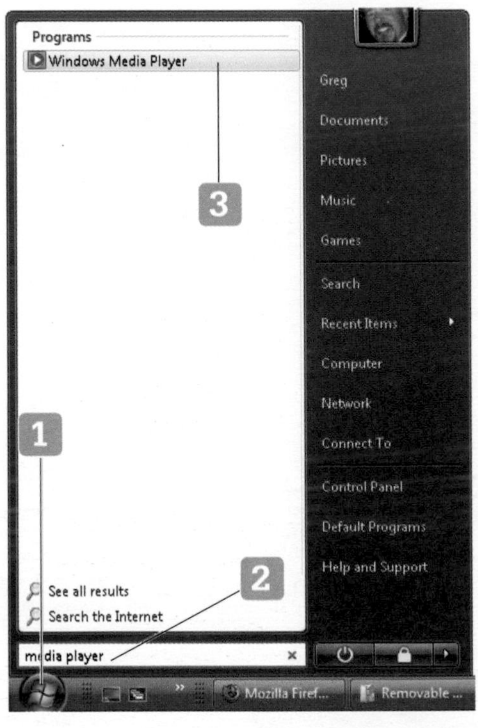

ALERT: The first time you open Media Player version 11, you'll be asked to set up the program. Choose Express to accept the default settings.

DID YOU KNOW?

The Windows Media Player can also be used to organise your music and videos by creating your own playlists.

DID YOU KNOW?

Windows Media Player can be used to copy music onto blank CDs. Insert a blank CD into your laptop's CD/DVD writer. Select songs, albums or playlists you want to burn. Select Burn>Audio CD from the Media Player menu bar.

Manage your music

Once you have Windows Media Player open, you'll find it easy to open any music track. You'll discover, in fact, that several music selections are provided for you along with Windows. Songs are listed in the navigation pane.

1. Open Media Player.
2. Click on the down arrow next to the Music icon to view the categories within Media Player.
3. To play a song or album, double-click it.
4. To add to the preloaded content of Media Player's Library, click on the Library button and select Add to Library.
5. Select My personal folders to add content from your laptop.

6. Click OK. The appropriate content (digital music, images, video) is accessed and placed in the relevant section of Media Player.

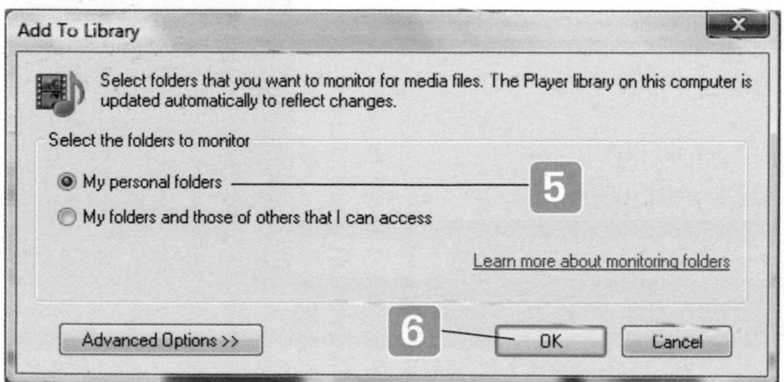

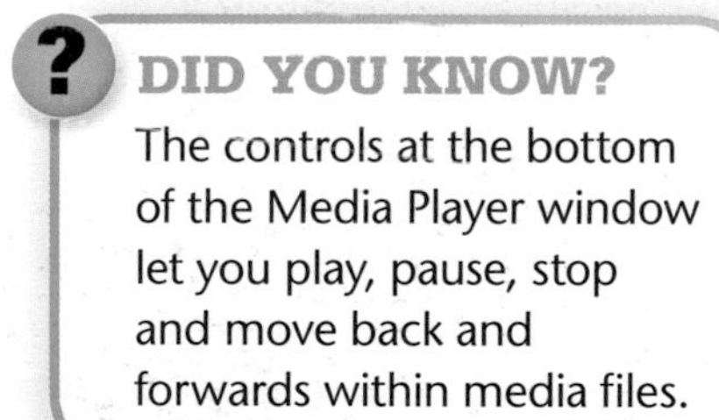

DID YOU KNOW?

The controls at the bottom of the Media Player window let you play, pause, stop and move back and forwards within media files.

DID YOU KNOW?

You can copy music onto Windows Media Player from CDs. Insert a CD and select Rip from the Media Player menu bar. This will give you the various options for copying the music from the CD.

Open Windows Media Center

Media Center is a Windows application that lets you play and organise a wider range of media than Media Player, including live television. By now you're probably getting the hang of how to find and open this and other Windows applications: just go to the Start menu.

1. Click Start.
2. Type media center.
3. Click Windows Media Center.

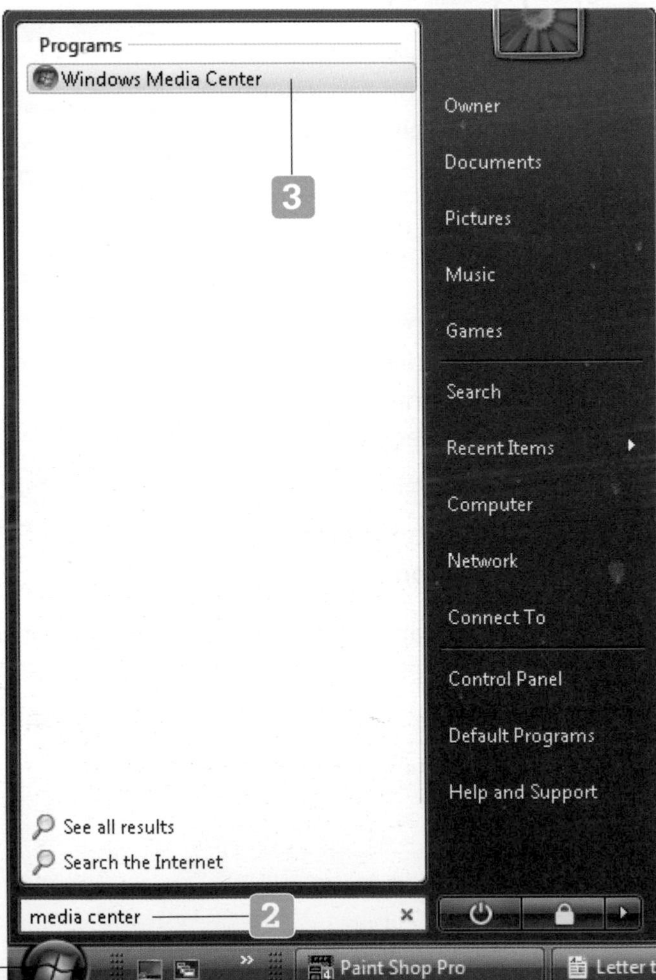

DID YOU KNOW?
Media Center's interface includes several menus: TV + Movies, Sports, Online Media, Tasks, Pictures + Videos, and Music.

ALERT: You have to type the US spelling of 'center' when you open this program.

ALERT: The first time you open Media Center, you'll be prompted to set up the program. Set-up can take a few minutes, but the set-up program walks you through the process, giving you clear choices with images and diagrams to help you along. Although some options are not required, it's best to go through the entire process.

Watch live TV

I just hate it when I miss my favourite TV shows. Now I catch them all, even when I'm out that night. Here's how to be a couch potato even if you're away from your couch. Media Center helps you watch TV, either on the Internet or on live television.

1. Open Windows Media Center
2. If necessary, under TV + Movies, click set up tv.
3. Once you have set up your TV, move to the right of recorded TV once and click live tv.
4. Position the mouse at the bottom of the live tv screen to show the controls you need.

HOT TIP: If you don't have TV tuner hardware at hand, keep in mind that many TV networks archive recent episodes of their most popular programmes on their websites so you can view them any time, using programs such as Media Player.

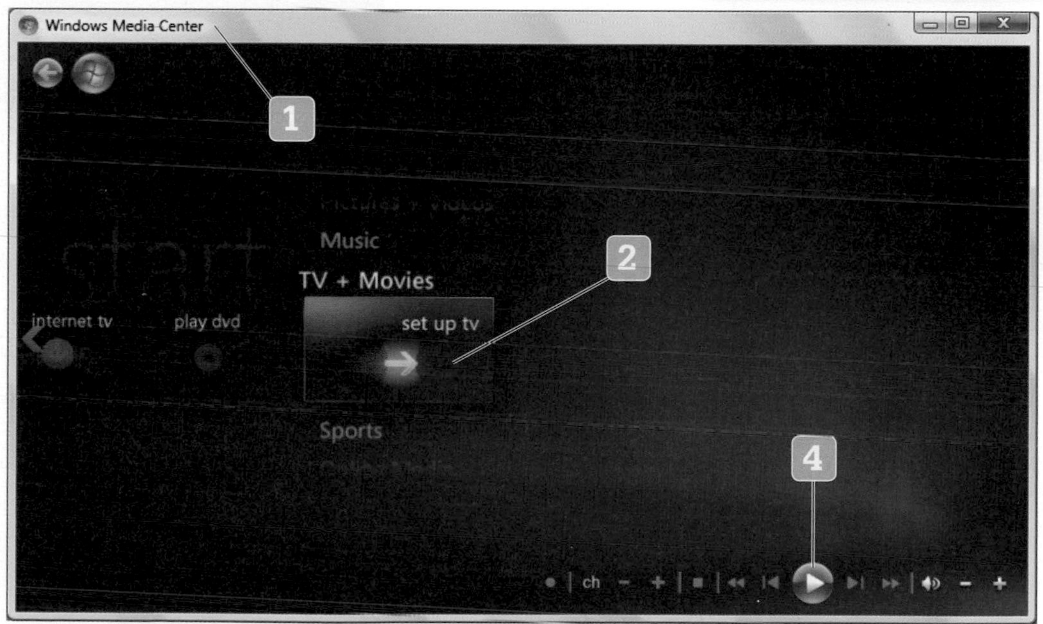

HOT TIP: If you receive an error when you click live TV, either you don't have the TV signal properly set up or you don't have a TV tuner. Many come with antennas, and you can find them for as little as £14.99 at Amazon.co.uk.

DID YOU KNOW?

There are lots of ways to navigate the Media Center. To name only three, you can use the mouse, the arrow keys on the keyboard, or a remote control.

Watch Internet TV

If you're curious about the sort of televised entertainment you can watch with your laptop and you haven't yet purchased a TV tuner add-on, you can watch a growing selection of Internet TV using Media Center as your guide.

1. Under TV + Movies, click internet tv.
2. By default, Top Picks appears first. Click tv series to view available shows you can watch online.
3. Pass your mouse over the episode on the far right or left; when an arrow appears, click to scroll through different options.
4. Double-click a TV show to watch it.

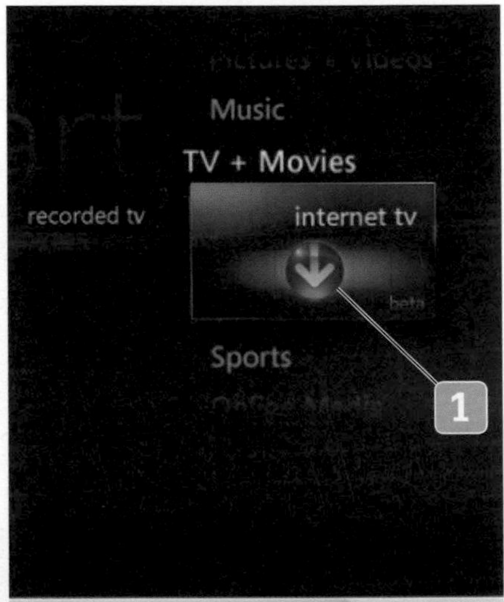

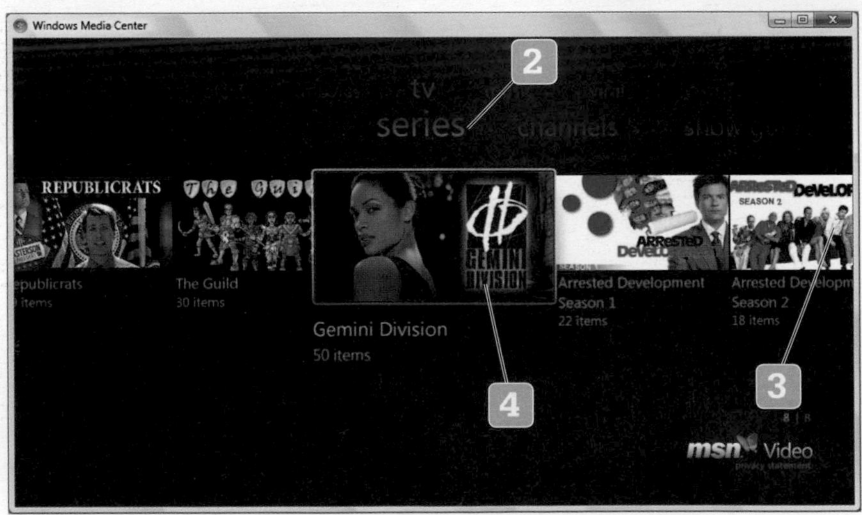

ALERT: You need to be connected to the Internet before you try to watch Internet TV. You also need a high-speed connection such as a cable or DSL line to view TV without delays.

DID YOU KNOW?
If you have a TV tuner connected to your laptop, you can use a hand-held controller to play TV and move from one programme to another.

Pause and rewind live TV

The hand that controls the clicker at home belongs to the person who rules the world. With Media Center on your laptop, it's all at your fingertips as well.

1. Open Windows Media Center.
2. Browse through TV shows and double-click one to play it.
3. Pass the mouse pointer over the bottom of the TV screen to display the controls.
4. Click the double vertical lines to pause the programme.
5. Click fast forward or rewind to move back or forwards through the programme.

DID YOU KNOW?

To fast forward through the commercials, press pause at the beginning of the show. For a 30-minute show, pause for 10 minutes; for a 60-minute show, pause for 20 minutes.

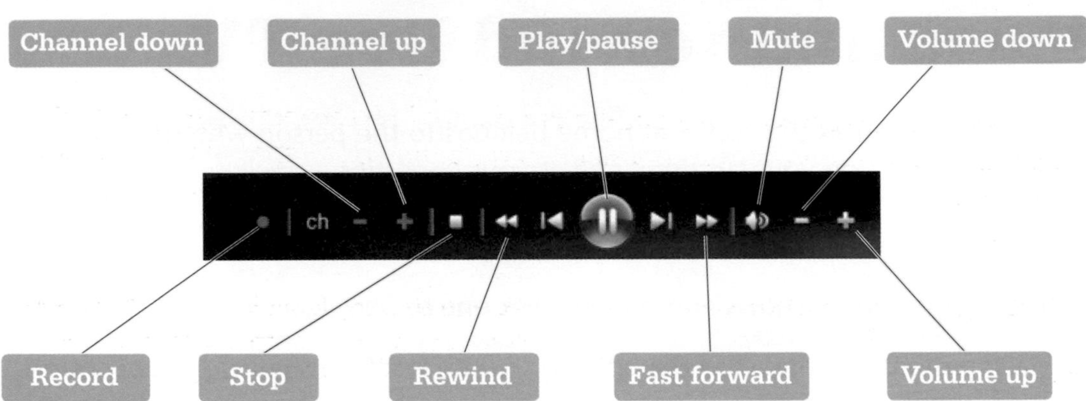

HOT TIP: Recorded TV is also an option with Media Center. If you record a TV show digitally and save it on a disk connected to your laptop, you can use Media Center to play it.

HOT TIP: Pass your mouse over the contents of the Media Center window in order to see controls. When you pass your mouse pointer close to the right or left edge of the window, navigation arrows appear. When you pass your mouse over the bottom right corner of the window, the stop, play, back, forward and other controls appear.

Obtain programme schedules

As you can probably guess, you'll get the Program Info screen when you click on Program Info. Then you can record a single programme or a series, plus you'll have access to more information about the show. Here's how to obtain programme schedules:

1. Open Windows Media Center.
2. Under TV + Movies, click live tv.
3. Right-click a show and choose Program Info or More Info from the context menu.
4. Click anywhere outside the context menu to remove it from the screen.

DID YOU KNOW?

You can click any items in the list to open a new dialogue box that contains additional choices.

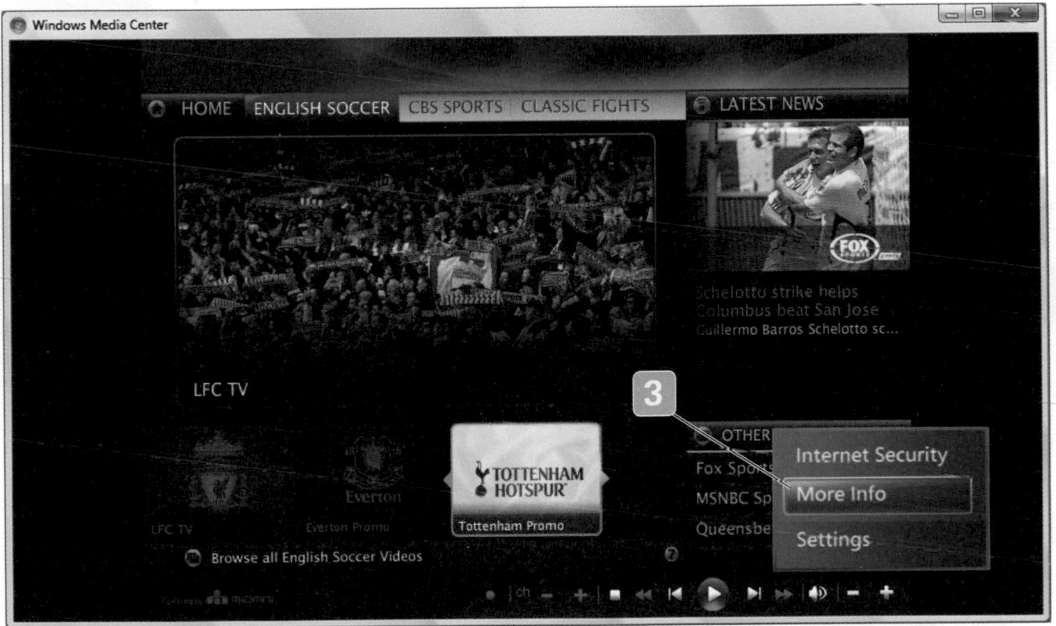

WHAT DOES THIS MEAN?

More Info/Program Info: presents you with information about the show, and lets you record a single programme.

Record: immediately starts recording the current show.

Record Series: starts recording the current show and schedules the rest of the programmes in the series so they can be recorded.

Zoom: lets you zoom in on the display.

Mini Guide: displays a miniature screen with information about the show.

Settings: opens Media Center Settings.

View a photo

Laptops come in handy for photo opportunities. Not only can you download photos while you are away from home, but you can also show them to other people when you're travelling or at a special event. Here's how to view digital photos.

1. Click Start.
2. Click on the Pictures button on the Start menu.
3. Select a folder containing photos. Double-click to view the photos inside.

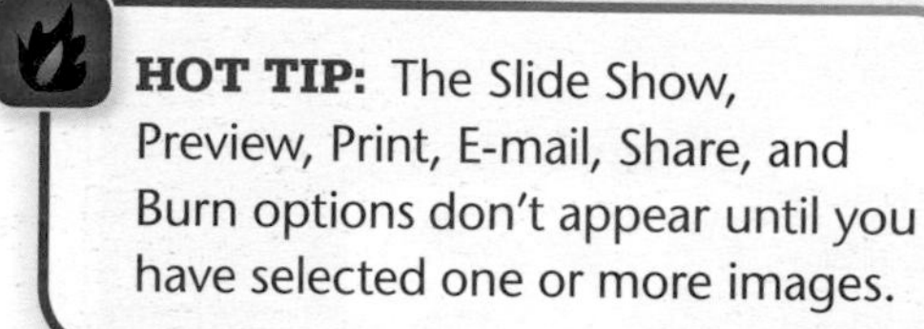

HOT TIP: The Slide Show, Preview, Print, E-mail, Share, and Burn options don't appear until you have selected one or more images.

HOT TIP: By default, your pictures are stored in the My Pictures folder, which is contained in the My Documents folder.

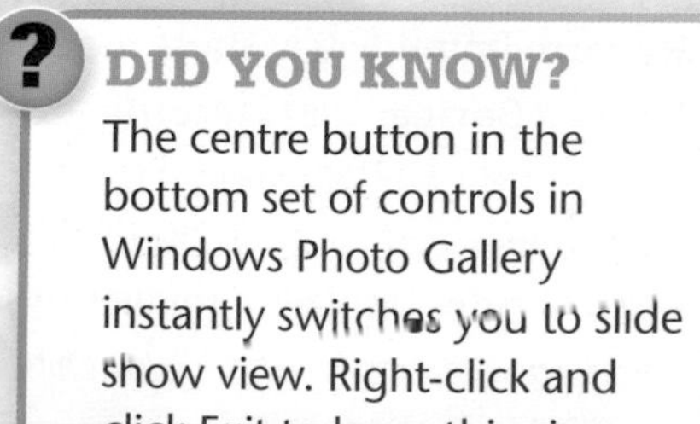

DID YOU KNOW?

The centre button in the bottom set of controls in Windows Photo Gallery instantly switches you to slide show view. Right-click and click Exit to leave this view.

4 Click on the Slide Show button to view the photos as a slide show.

5 Select a photo and click on the Preview button to open the photos in the selected folder in Windows Photo Gallery.

6 When the slide show plays, right-click an image and choose an option from the context menu to pause or control the show.

7 Click Exit to leave the slide show.

8 If you clicked Preview, use the controls at the bottom of the screen to move from one image to another.

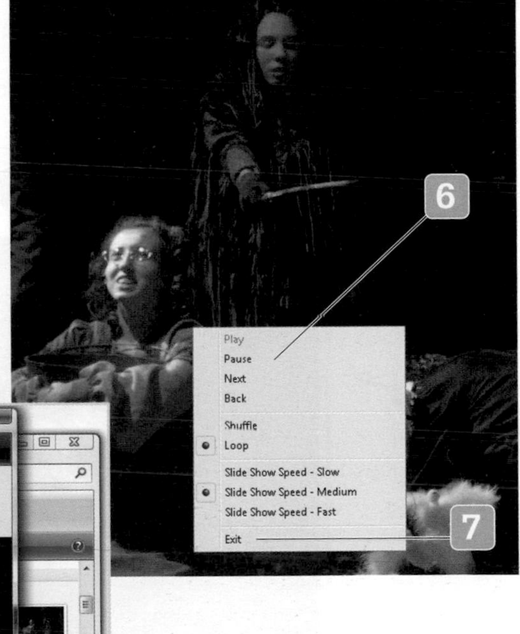

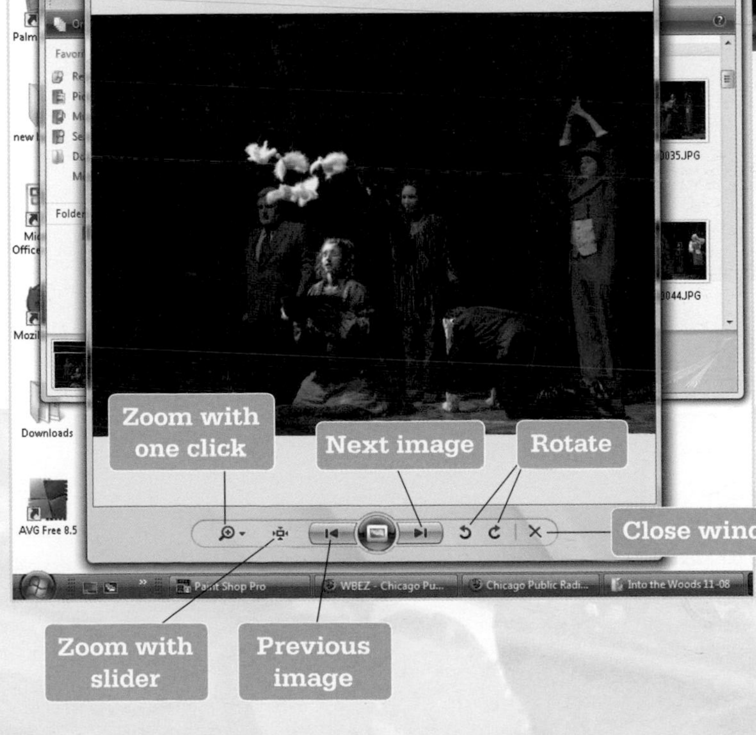

Edit a photo

When you heard the word 'edit', you used to think 'words'. Now you can give your photos a facelift without having to take classes to learn a complex program like Photoshop. Just turn to the Photo Gallery application that comes with Windows or can be downloaded and installed if you are using Windows 7.

1 Open a selection from Windows Photo Gallery.

2 Click the controls at the bottom of the Photo Gallery window which let you manipulate digital images so you can edit them more easily.

3 Click on the Fix button to access the editing tools you need.

ALERT: If you want to keep the original photo, make a copy before you start to edit. Don't forget to save your changes.

4 Adjust the individual controls that appear.

5 The edited image is displayed in Windows Photo Gallery.

6 Click the close box to accept the changes.

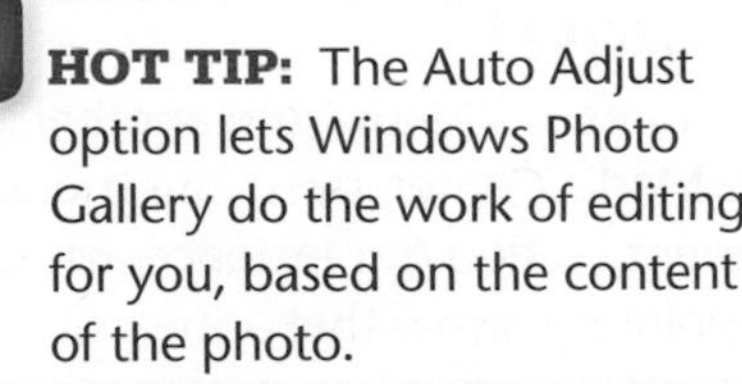

HOT TIP: The Auto Adjust option lets Windows Photo Gallery do the work of editing for you, based on the content of the photo.

Create a slide show with Media Center

Some people are bored with the holiday photos of others, not to mention babies with dirty faces that only a mother could adore. I'm always eager to take a look, especially if it's in the form of a slide show. If you already have Windows Media Center open, use it to create a slide show.

1. Open Windows Media Center.
2. Click Pictures + Videos.
3. Click picture library.
4. Browse through the available pictures and picture folders.
5. Click play slide show to display the images as a slide show.

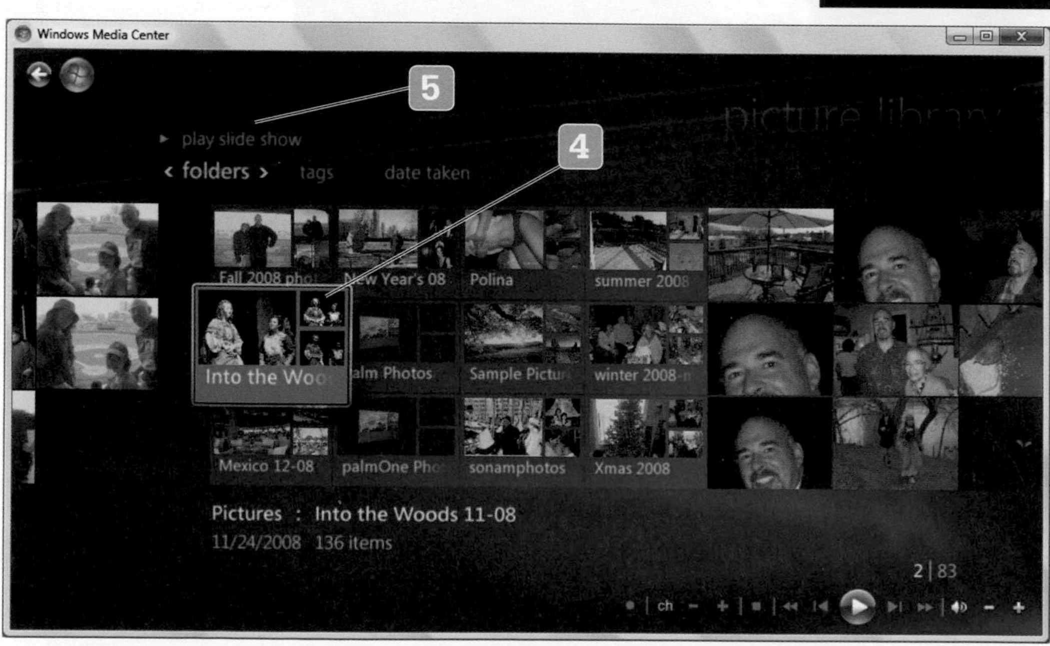

SEE ALSO: See Open Windows Media Center, earlier in this chapter, for instructions on how to open this application.

DID YOU KNOW?

To move to Pictures + Videos from another section of the Media Center, pass your mouse above the current section (for instance, Music). Click the up-pointing arrow that appears.

Import an image from your digital camera

Never again do you need to be caught without a camera when you view that perfect sunset. Follow the steps below to transfer what's in your camera to your laptop.

1. Turn on your digital camera.
2. Connect the camera to one of your laptop's USB ports.
3. Click Import pictures and videos to my computer.
4. Select your camera.
5. Click OK.
6. Follow the steps shown in the rest of the wizard to complete the transfer.

HOT TIP: The AutoPlay dialogue box automatically appears when you connect your digital camera and Windows detects it. Choose the first option, Windows, if you don't want to use the wizard and prefer browsing and copying photos with Windows Explorer.

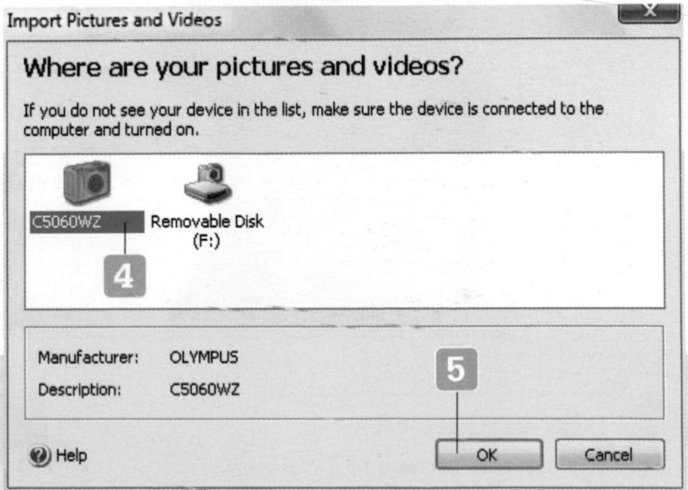

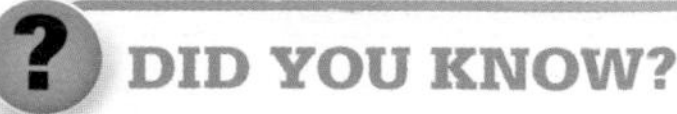

DID YOU KNOW?

You don't need to use AutoPlay. You can close the window and use Windows Explorer to find the camera under My Computer. You can then drag and drop photos to your laptop.

Play a DVD

One of the most common uses you'll have for your laptop is playing movies on DVD. You can play your disk using Windows Media Center or Windows Media Player. One or the other will probably start automatically – it depends on which application is configured to play DVDs by default.

1. Put a DVD in your laptop's DVD drive.
2. If prompted, choose play dvd using Windows Media Center.
3. Use the controls at the bottom of the screen to pause, stop, rewind and fast-forward.
4. Click PLAY ALL or one of the other options to play the DVD.

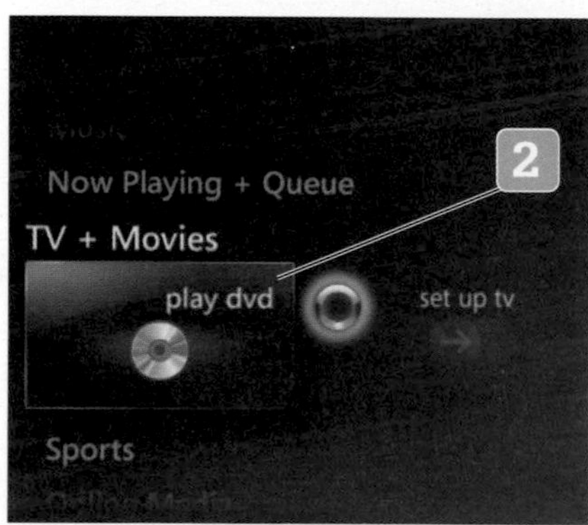

DID YOU KNOW?

You can also browse to TV + Movies in Media Center, and from the submenus choose play dvd.

HOT TIP: If you use Media Center, you can press fast-forward to skip the previews before the main feature. I find this doesn't always work with Media Player.

7 Taking your laptop on the road

Introduction

The whole point of having a laptop is that you can go mobile. There are actually two components, however, to what you need to do when you're using your laptop outside of your home or office. The first has to do with protecting the machine itself. The second involves the data that it contains. This chapter will help you make sure both the device itself and your information will be safe and secure.

Consider alternatives to taking your laptop

Unlike the credit card commercial that urges you to not leave home without it, I'm officially giving you permission to amputate your laptop from your wrist from time to time. I love to travel, but there are always unexpected adventures that can sometimes cause stress. If an alternative will work just as well, it's okay to let your laptop hold down the fort while you wander the globe. Consider the following before you pack your bags.

1. If you are staying with friends and relatives, you may be able to use their computer to go online and check your email.
2. If you will be near an Internet café or public library, you can use computers free of charge.
3. If you're not working on large documents, a mobile phone or small hand-held mobile device such as a PDA will work just as well as your laptop.

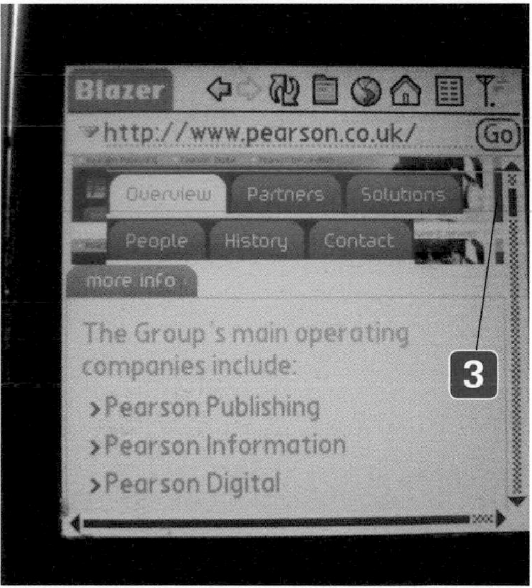

HOT TIP: A flashdrive, USB stick or CD can be used to move files and photos from computer to computer. You can also email documents to yourself.

DID YOU KNOW?

Allow extra time if you're going through airport security with your laptop and bring along a proof of purchase if you're going through customs. Even the smallest laptop involves some weight, so make sure you're prepared to carry all your luggage if necessary.

Connect to a Wi-Fi hotspot

'Free' is one of my favourite words, so my eyes are always scanning billboards and travel brochures for places to stay, eat and just hang out that provide free Wi-Fi hotspots. If your laptop has wireless capabilities, you can access the Internet without physically connecting to a router or phone line. What's not to love about one less monthly bill? Here's how to take advantage.

1. Turn on your wireless laptop within range of a wireless network.
2. Look for your prompt from the Notification area that wireless networks are available.
3. Right-click the network icon (which looks like two computers next to each other) and click Connect to a network.

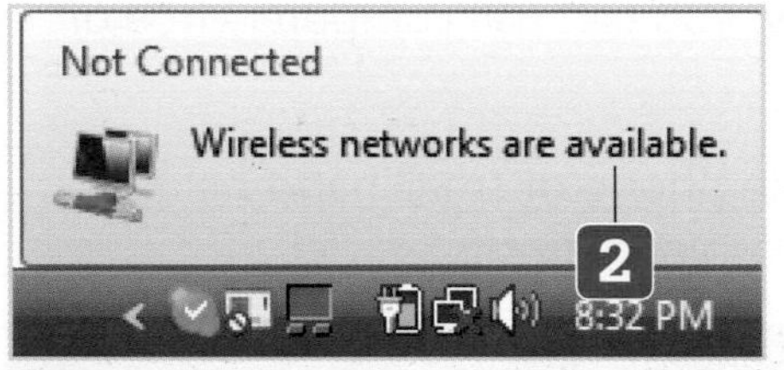

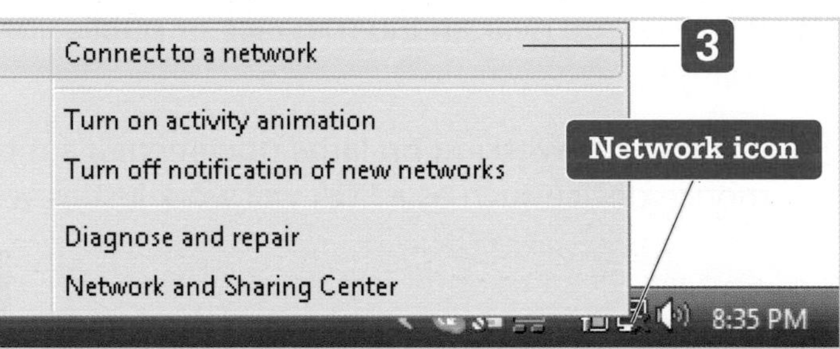

4. Click a network.
5. Click Connect.

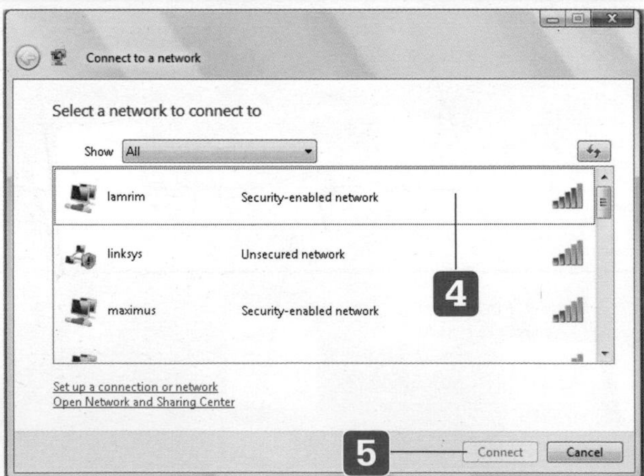

HOT TIP: If you don't see a pop-up, click Start and click Connect To. If prompted, choose Public network. Of the wireless options available, choose the one with the most green bars. The more green bars you have, the stronger the signal.

DID YOU KNOW?
If the Wi-Fi hotspot has a patio, you may be able to sit close to the door and still get access. Otherwise, you may have to actually be in the building itself.

Back up your files before you travel

Before you travel, you probably already go through a routine of making sure the iron is turned off and your rubbish has been taken out. So add backing up your computer to your list. That way you won't have to worry about precious photos and sensitive tax information.

1. Make a copy of all your important files.
2. Move the copy to an external drive, such as a removable disk or 'flash drive'.
3. Put the external drive in a safe place in your home or office.

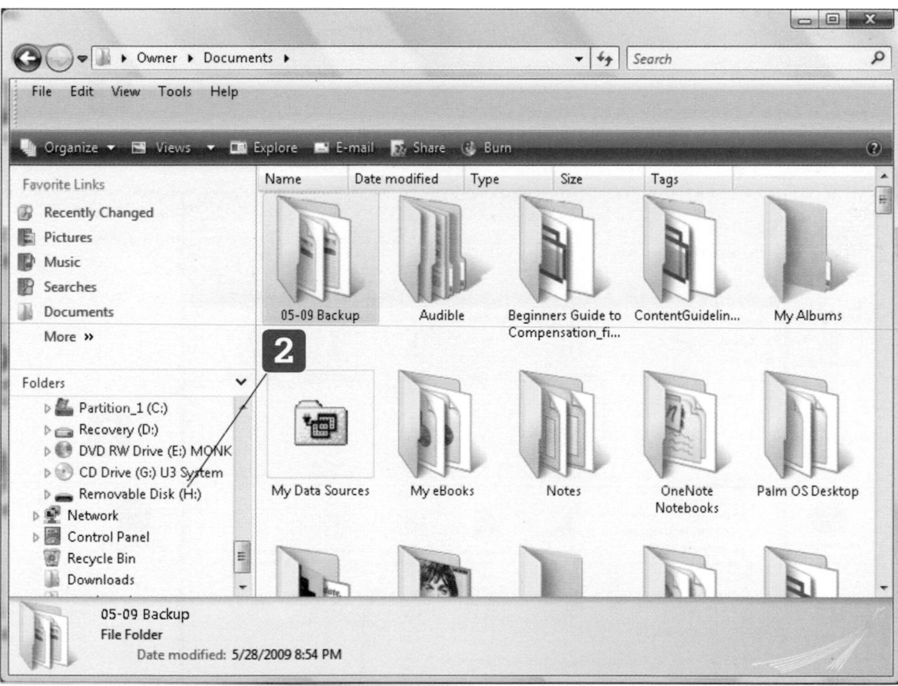

DID YOU KNOW?

There are secure online data storage services that you could use if it's necessary for you to have access to sensitive information while you're travelling. Check out Goggle Docs & Spreadsheets, Ibackup or Evault.com.

HOT TIP: It's not just personal and business documents that should be backed up. You'd be really sad to lose your photos, videos and music, so don't forget about them.

Create a virtual briefcase

Using a virtual briefcase will ensure that you always have backups of your important files. You can also use this feature to keep files in sync over multiple computers, such as between your desktop and your laptop.

1. You can right-click anywhere, but on Documents or on your desktop would be best. Right-click, choose New, then choose Briefcase.
2. Drag and drop into the New Briefcase the files you want to move.

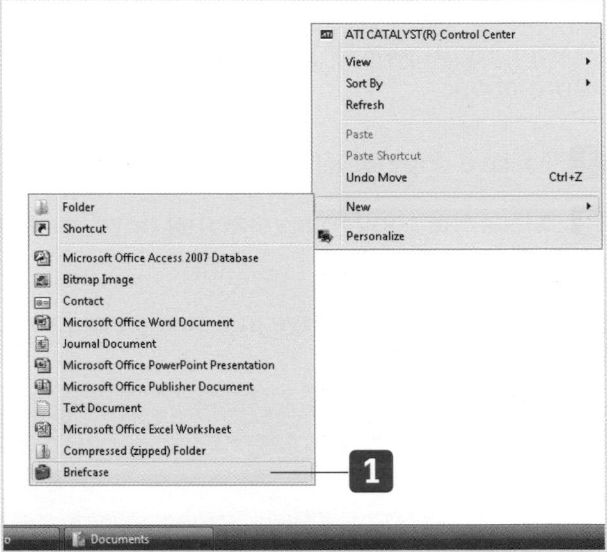

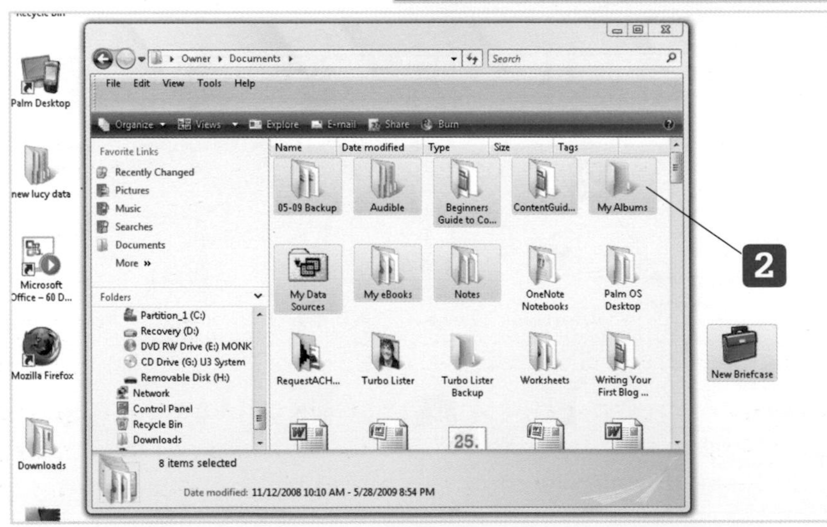

ALERT: The Briefcase is especially good if you want to synchronise files and you expect to be working at two different computers. Otherwise you might want to use a Windows application called the Sync Center.

3 Move the New Briefcase to another computer or external hard drive.

4 After you make the changes you want, move the Briefcase back to your original computer. Right-click it and click Update This Item or Update All.

5 Your computer checks for differences between the original files and the Briefcase files, and then it presents the differences.

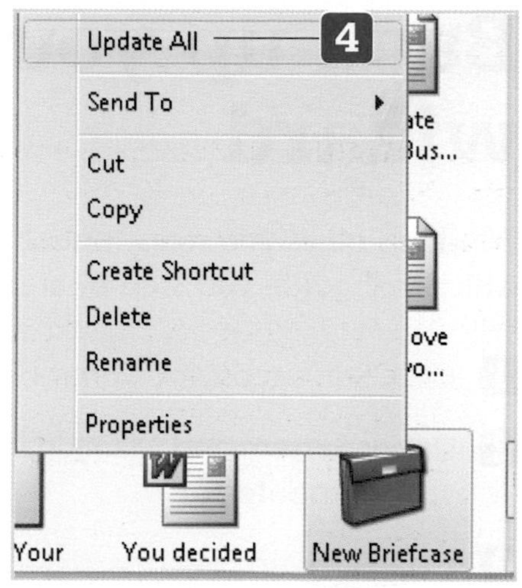

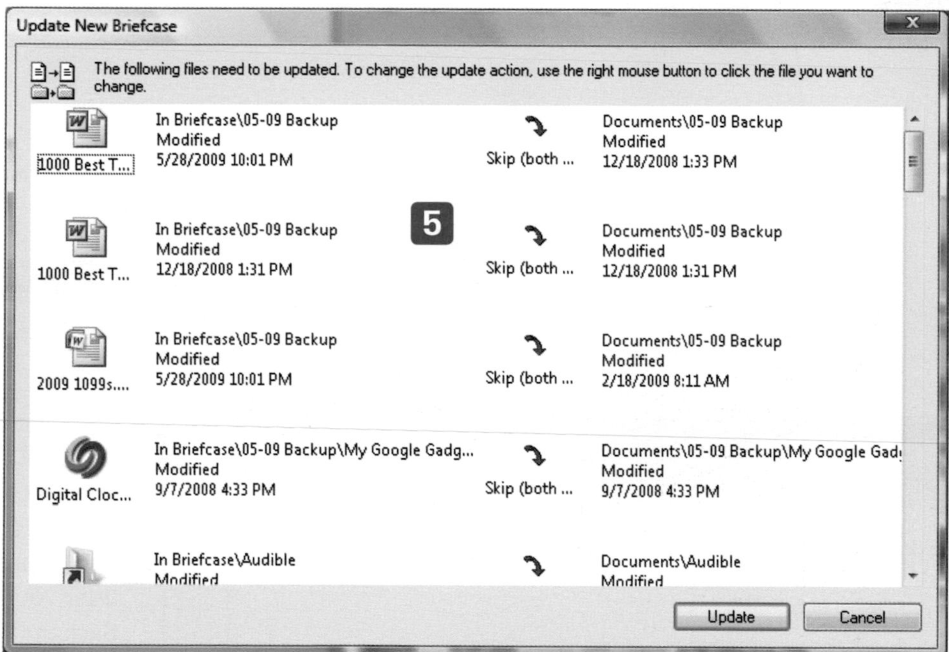

6 Right-click each item to determine whether to keep the original or the new copy. Or you can choose to skip the sync entirely. You can also see the details of the differences between the two files to determine which action you want to take.

DID YOU KNOW?
The files won't disappear from their original locations. The files in the Briefcase are just copies that are linked to your originals.

HOT TIP: If you get worried about what you're working with, the Briefcase will show the original location of your file and its updated status in File view.

Back up your files with a wizard

Windows gives you many options to back up your data. Here's how to use a wizard, which will guide you step by step through the process.

1. Click Start and click Control Panel.
2. Under System and Maintenance, click Back up your computer.
3. Click Back up files.
4. Select the location you want to use.
5. Click Next.

System and Maintenance
Get started with Windows
Back up your computer
2

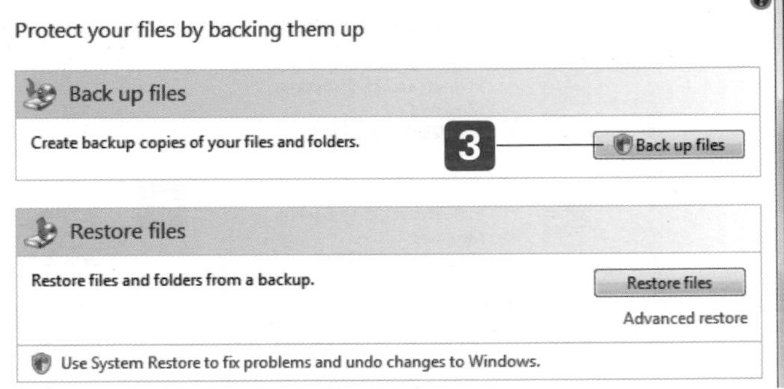

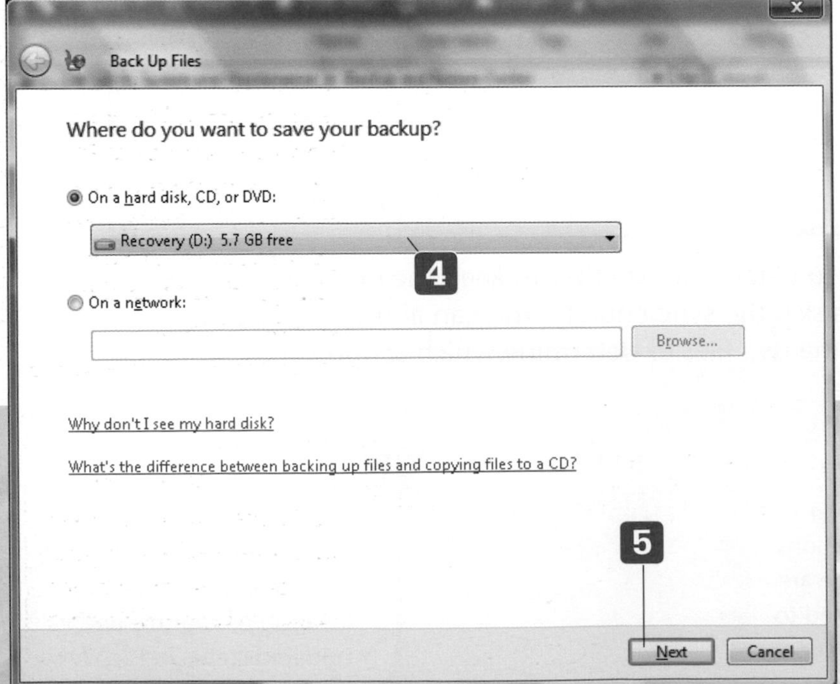

ALERT: If a User Account Control dialogue box appears after you click Back up files, click Continue to move to the next step.

6 Use the tick boxes to select the types of files you want to back up. This process backs up all files of this type in your profile.

7 Click Next.

8 Set the schedule for your backup and click Save settings and start backup.

9 Let the backup run until completed.

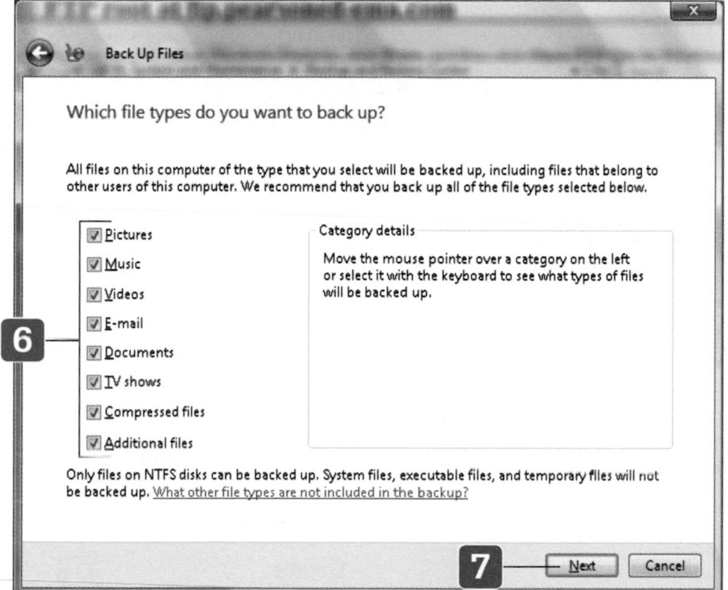

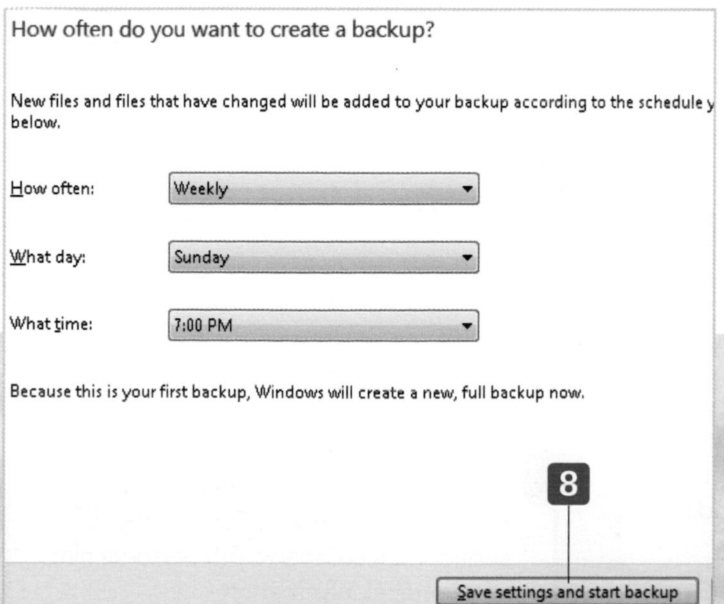

DID YOU KNOW?
The Back Up Files wizard works only when the computer is turned on and connected to your home network or to the device where you want to store files. Make sure your external device is also good to go at the scheduled time.

HOT TIP: Video and audio files can be greedy for space. Make sure your device has ample memory available before you start.

Clean up your laptop before you travel

'Travel light' is advice you often hear. When it comes to your laptop, this suggestion applies both to your data and to your external hardware. Here's what to put on your not-to-pack list.

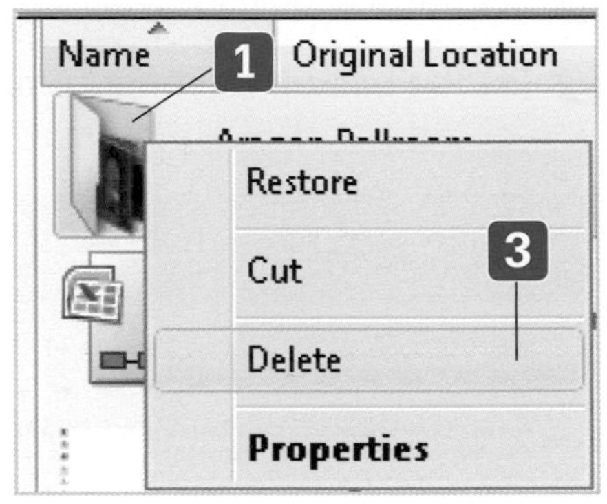

1. Locate a file or folder to delete.
2. Right-click the file.
3. Choose Delete.
4. To completely remove the files, right-click the Recycle Bin on your desktop and choose Empty Recycle Bin.
5. Remove and store in a safe place all unnecessary external hardware, such as webcams, printers, external drives, Ethernet cables and mice.

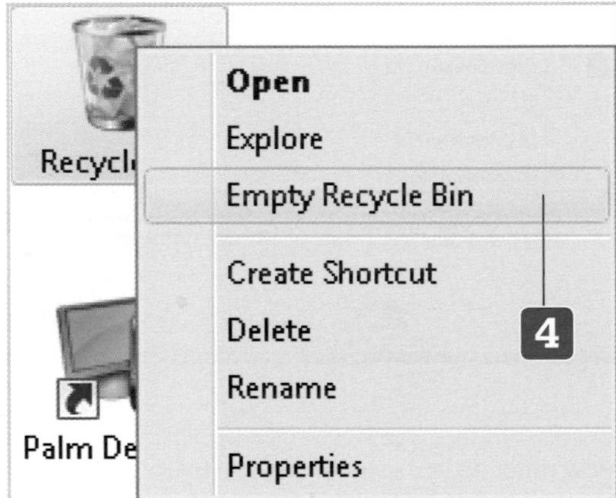

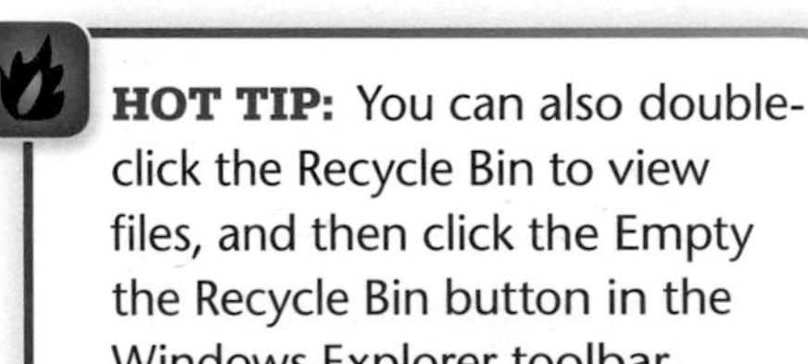

HOT TIP: You can also double-click the Recycle Bin to view files, and then click the Empty the Recycle Bin button in the Windows Explorer toolbar.

HOT TIP: Make sure your backup was successfully completed before you delete anything. When you get back home, you can copy the data from the backup device to the laptop.

ALERT: When you delete files, they are stored in your Recycle Bin until you empty it. (If you need to restore a file, you can drag it out of your Recycle Bin to your desktop.) Get into the habit of emptying your Recycle Bin periodically to free up disk space.

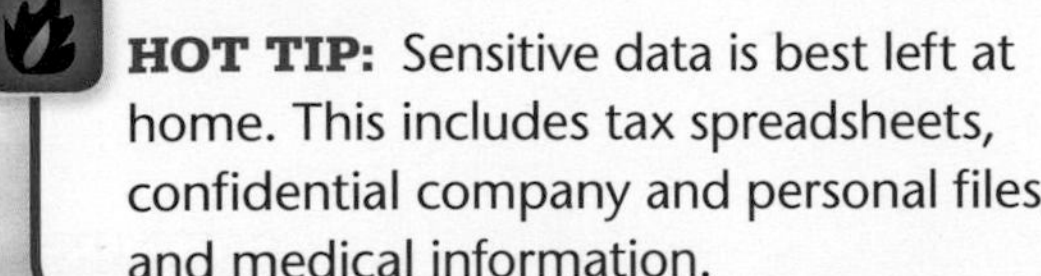

HOT TIP: Sensitive data is best left at home. This includes tax spreadsheets, confidential company and personal files, and medical information.

Remove sensitive data from your laptop

Any information you won't need while travelling is best left at home. But what if you want to work on documents with a business associate, friend or relative at the other end of the line? If you put your information on a USB stick, you might not want to bring your laptop at all and just use their computer. Or you can move data to and from your own computer on a USB stick. Just follow the directions here.

1. Connect a memory stick or external hard disk using one of the laptop's USB ports.
2. Right-click any data you want to move.
3. Click Cut.

4 Browse to the location to move the file.

5 Right-click and choose Paste.

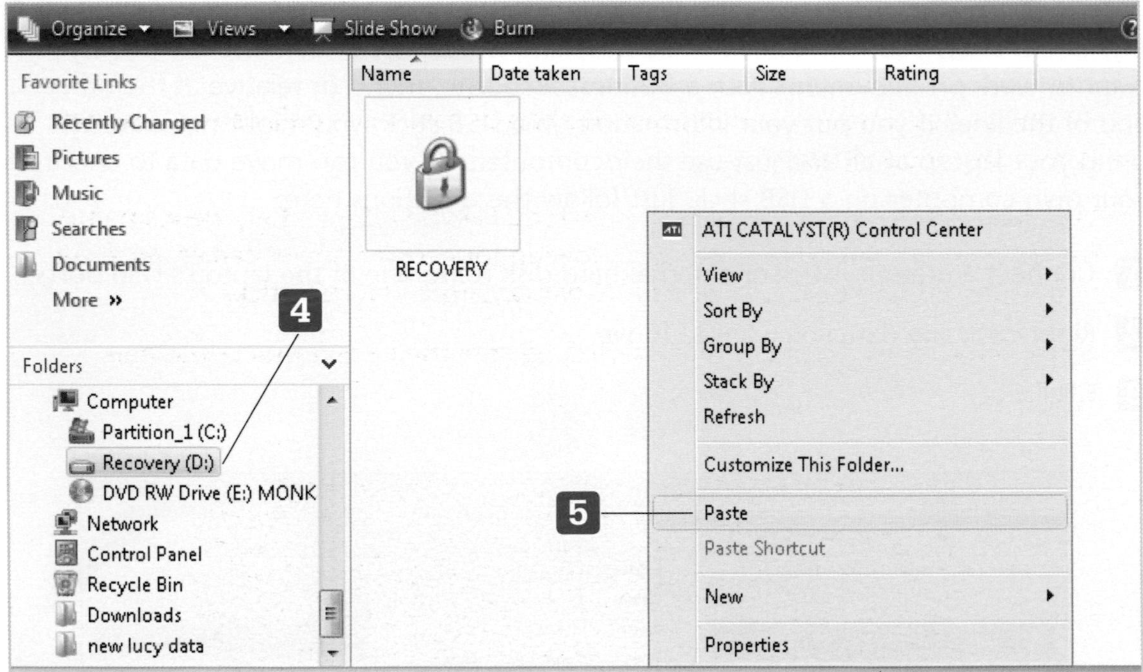

DID YOU KNOW?

If you hold down the Shift key while selecting, you can select contiguous files. To select non-contiguous files, hold down the Ctrl key while selecting.

ALERT: The Paste option only appears in the context menu in Windows Explorer if you have previously cut or copied one or more files or folders.

Pack your laptop with care

I do a lot of selling on eBay, and sometimes it seems I pay more attention to the packing than I do to preparing for the sale itself. If you decide to take your laptop on a trip, you'll want to pack it and the necessary accessories with care.

1. Borrow or buy a heavily padded carrying bag or case that you'll use just for your laptop and accessories.
2. Optional accessories include a mouse, external keyboard, headset, webcam and surge protector. But you'll need the following for certain: power cables, an extra battery, an Ethernet cable, a wireless network card and a USB stick.
3. Arrange the items in compartments, making sure they won't bump into one another.

HOT TIP: Getting through airport security often requires that you take your laptop out of its bag. Choose a carrying case that will make removal a quick and easy process.

HOT TIP: If you're going through high-risk areas, you might want to try to fool potential thieves. A backpack on wheels might disguise the fact that there's a laptop inside.

Taking your laptop on a plane

The effects of 9/11 are still being felt in airline travel. Here are other tips for flying with a laptop suggested by frequent flyers.

1. Carry an extra battery in case you can't get access to a power outlet on the plane. Charge your battery completely before leaving for the airport – or in a waiting area of the airport.
2. Remove disks from disk drives.
3. Call the airline in advance to verify the type of power adapter you'll need so you can pack the right one.
4. Keep your laptop close at all times. Unattended baggage may be confiscated by security personnel or stolen by thieves in the airport. Putting your laptop at your feet during the flight is much better than trusting it to the overhead bin; don't even think about putting it in with luggage that you'll check to go into the hold.

DID YOU KNOW?
It won't hurt your laptop to go through the x-ray machine. But if someone tries to scan it with a metal detector, ask to have it inspected by hand instead.

ALERT: In general, when you travel, it doesn't hurt to have a phone cord for dial-up, an Ethernet cable for wired connections, and a wireless network card for satellite service.

Going through airport security

The trick here is to destress. If you think things out in advance and plan ahead, you won't be flustered when you go through airport security. And you'll be sure to keep your laptop functioning as well. Just follow these procedures.

1. Be prepared to take your laptop out of its case and turn it on to prove that it's a working device.
2. Make sure the battery is fully charged and that your laptop is easily accessible.
3. Have your laptop in Sleep mode so it can be powered up quickly.
4. Keep a careful eye on your laptop when it goes through the x-ray conveyor belt and be there at the other side to collect it as soon as it emerges.

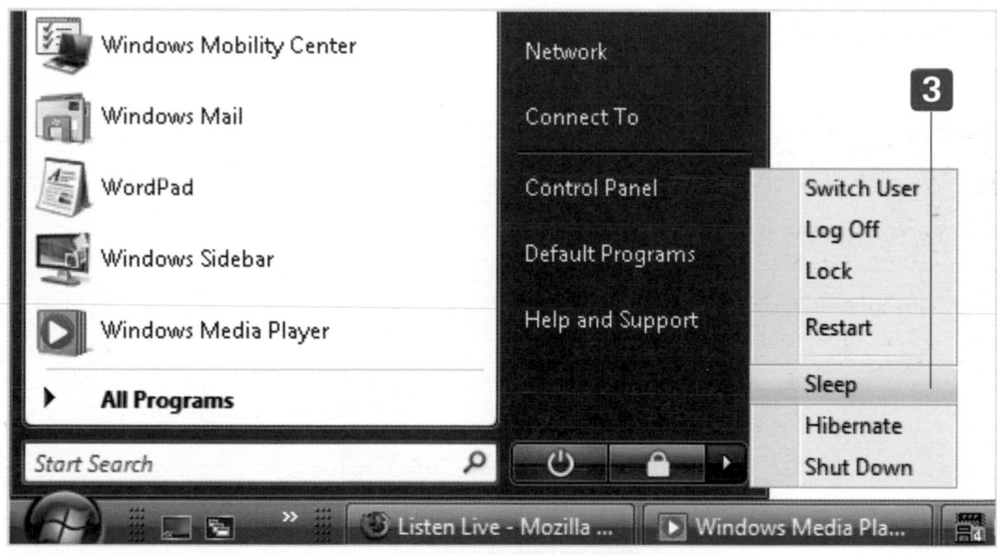

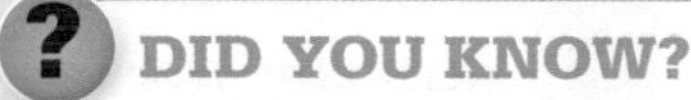

DID YOU KNOW?
Having your laptop pass through the security scanners at the airport will not erase data or damage it.

HOT TIP: If you are uneasy for any reason, ask to have your laptop hand-checked by the security guard instead of being put on the conveyor belt. That will avoid a thief creating a distraction at the security gate while an accomplice takes your laptop from the conveyor belt.

Adjusting to time zone differences

Okay, so now you've made it through airport security yet again, after arriving at your destination. Get a few things unpacked and then you should change the time and time zone settings on your laptop.

1. Click Start.
2. Click Control Panel.
3. Click Clock, Language, and Region.
4. Click Change the time zone.
5. Click Change time zone.
6. Select the time zone from the drop-down list.
7. Click OK.

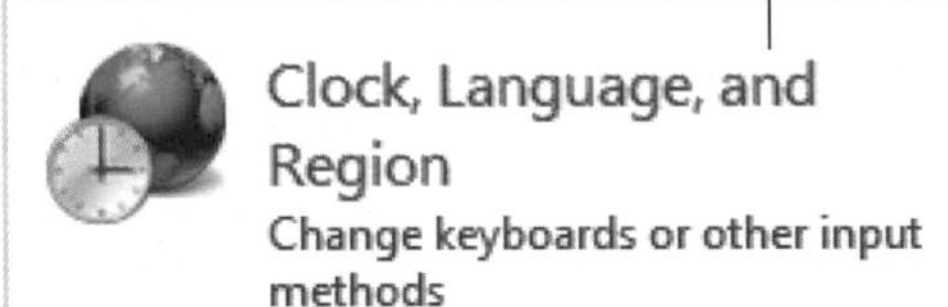

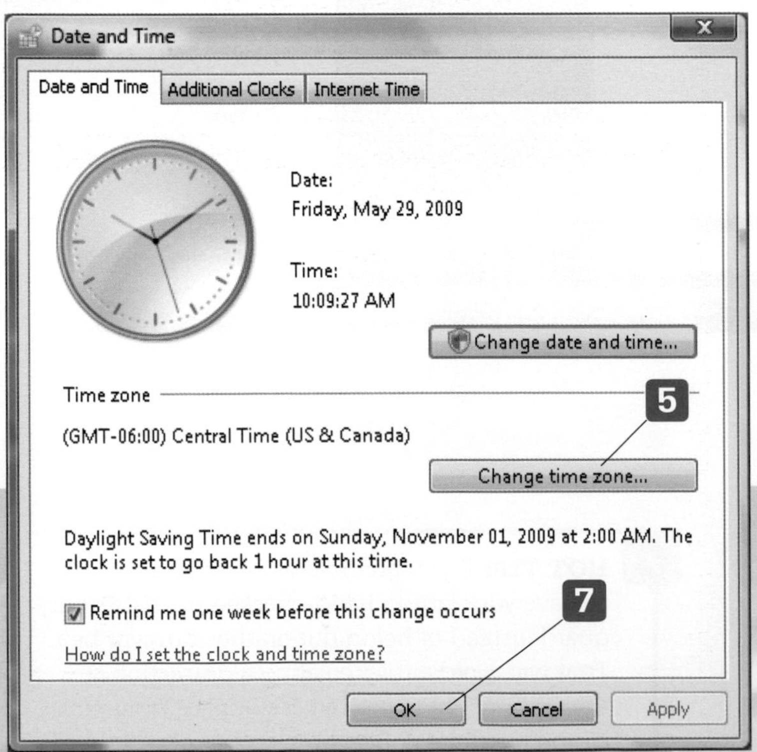

HOT TIP: To add clocks, click the Additional Clocks tab.

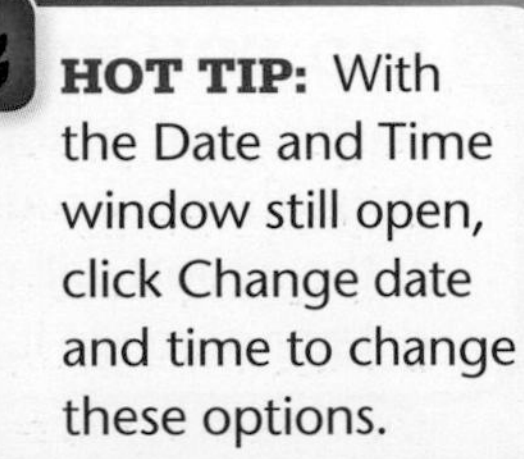

HOT TIP: With the Date and Time window still open, click Change date and time to change these options.

Change your default language

If you're the type who likes to do as the Romans do when you're in Rome, you can make the information you receive online match your current location. Here's how to change the country or region:

1. Open Control Panel.
2. Click Clock, Language, and Region.
3. Click Regional and Language Options.

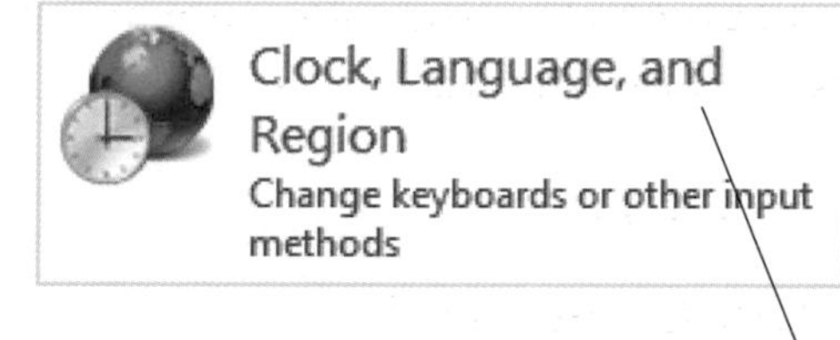

4. From the Formats tab, click Customize this format if you want to change the number, currency, time or date settings.
5. Click Apply.
6. Click the Location tab to select a new location.
7. From the drop-down list, select your present location.
8. Continue configuration as necessary, and click OK.
9. Close the Control Panel by clicking the X in the top right corner.

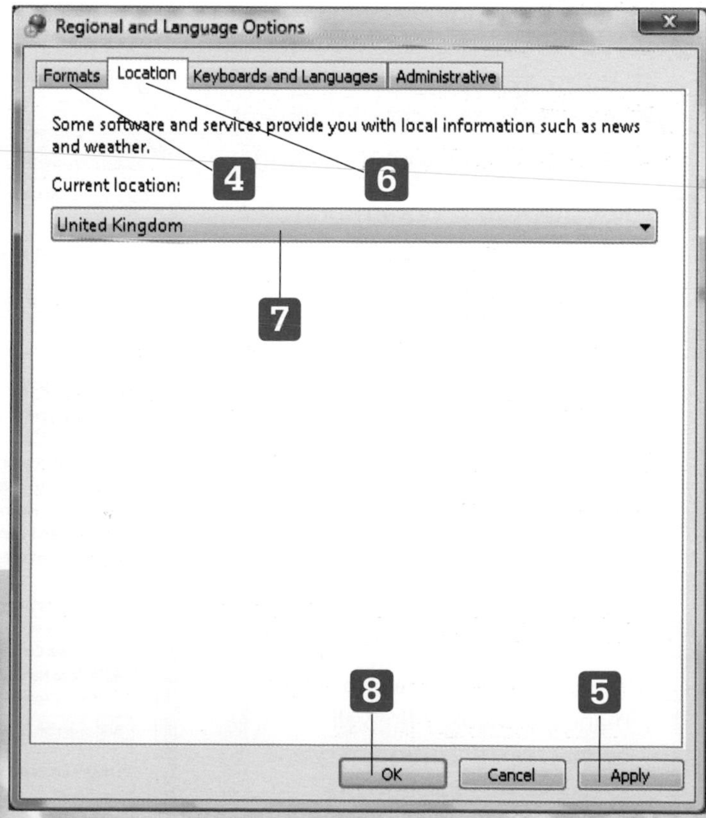

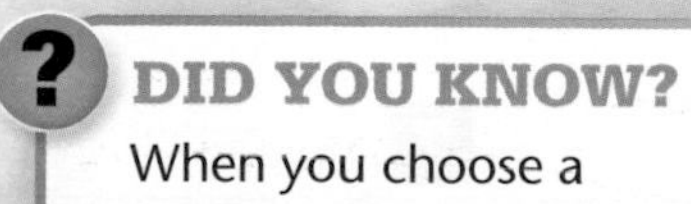

DID YOU KNOW?

When you choose a location, the setting will change computer wide. It's just like you really live in the country you're visiting!

Adjust your Windows Firewall settings

Sometimes you assume that because you're on holiday you've entered a magic place where no harm can befall. When it comes to firewalls, the opposite is true. At home, Firewall provides valuable security because you're behind your router's firewall. But Windows Firewall is an absolute necessity when you're away from your home network. Here's how to make sure your Windows Firewall is always on.

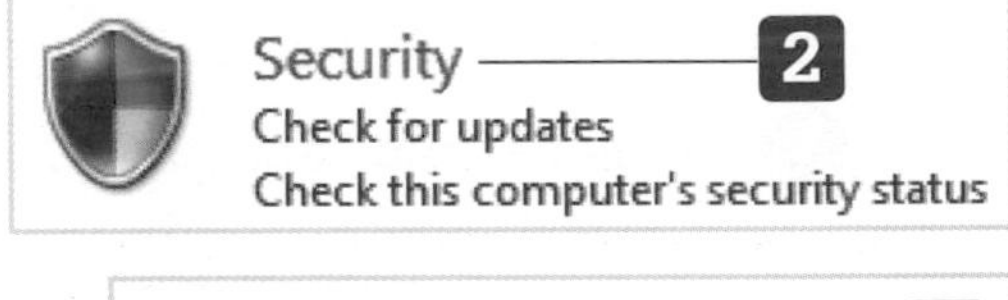

1. Open the Control Panel.
2. Click Security.
3. Click Windows Firewall.
4. Make sure the firewall is turned on. Click Change Settings.
5. Click the Exceptions tab to see the programs that can make connections through the firewall.
6. If you're sure that a program doesn't need a firewall exception (or you no longer use that program), deselect the tick box. If you receive a notification when you weren't expecting it, you should prevent that program from connecting.
7. Click the Add program button and select the program you want to make an exception for.
8. Click the Advanced tab and make sure all your network connections (wired, wireless, Bluetooth) are protected by the firewall.

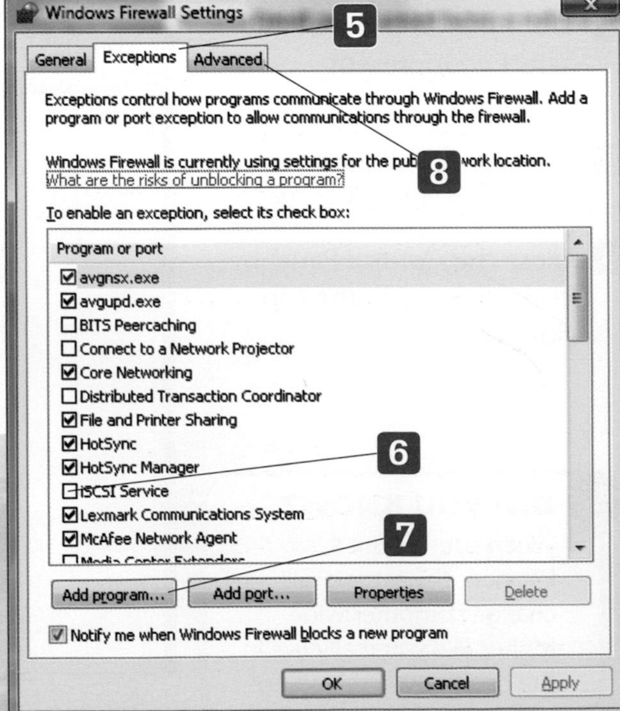

DID YOU KNOW?

You usually don't have to manually enable a firewall connection. If a program needs to gain access through the firewall, it generally asks for it.

Password protect a folder

Again, you probably don't have to use this feature if you're within the comfort and security of your own home network. But you can never be too careful if you're on the road. If your laptop is stolen or if a hotel employee gains access to it, you can still protect important files.

1. Click Start.
2. Click Network.
3. Click Network and Sharing Center.
4. Click the Password protected sharing arrow so that you can choose whether to turn on password-protected sharing.
5. Click the Turn on password protected sharing button.
6. Click Apply.

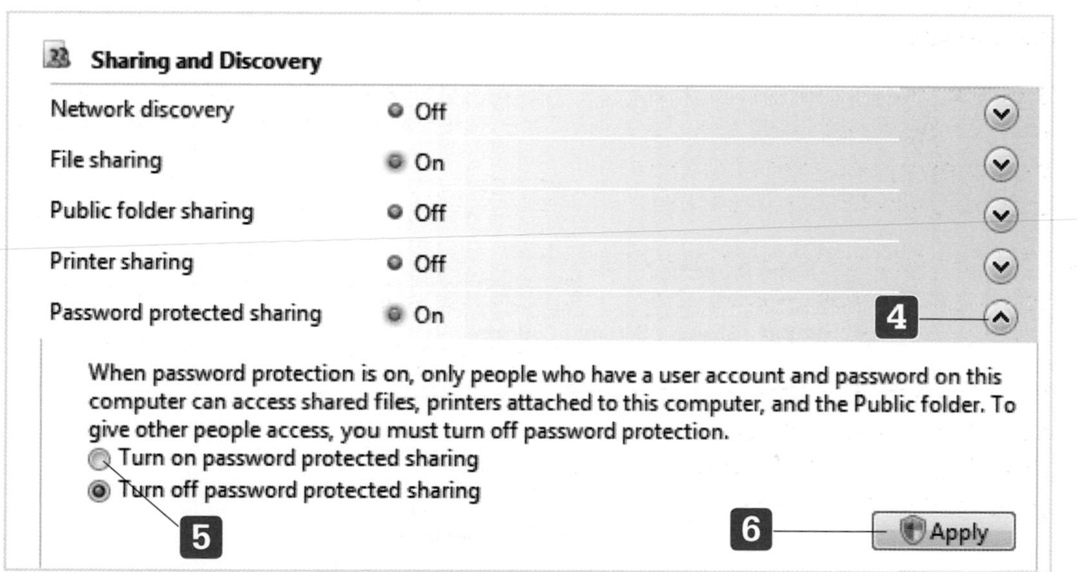

HOT TIP: To add accounts, click Start Control Panel and click the Add or Remove User Accounts link.

ALERT: Be sure to delete any user accounts on your computer that are not being used. That will help reduce access to your computer.

Encrypt a file or folder

You might think this is overkill, but encryption is a useful way to help prevent access to sensitive data even if the files or folders are removed from your computer. In some cases, it's well worth possibly slowing down your access to certain files and folders.

1. Navigate to the file or folder you want to encrypt.
2. Right-click on the file or folder and choose Properties from the context menu.
3. Click the Advanced button to open the Advanced Attributes dialogue box.

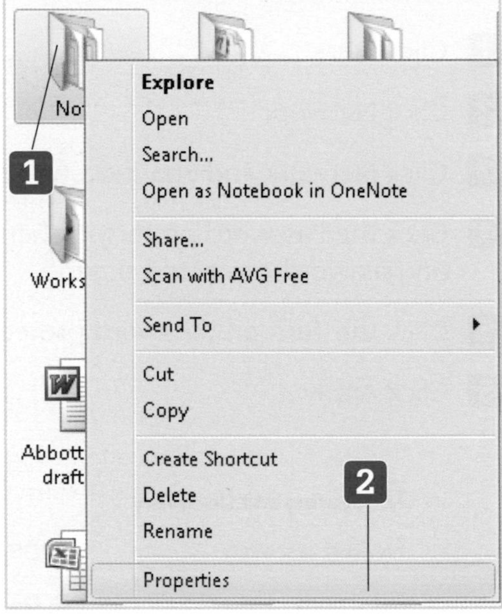

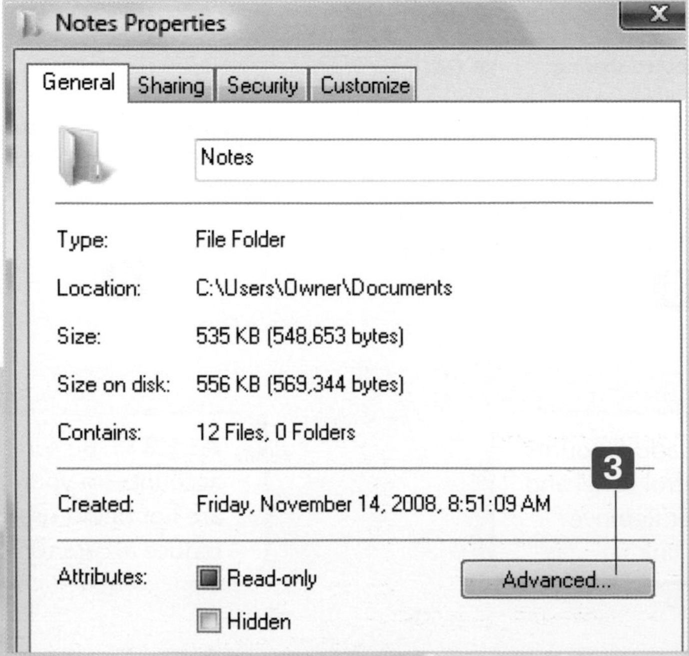

4. Select the Encrypt contents to secure data tick box.
5. If you're encrypting a file, click OK twice. If you're encrypting a folder, click OK twice to open the Confirm Attribute Changes dialogue box, make your choice, and click OK again.
6. Back up your encryption keys, as prompted from the System Tray, in case you have to change the file settings on your laptop.

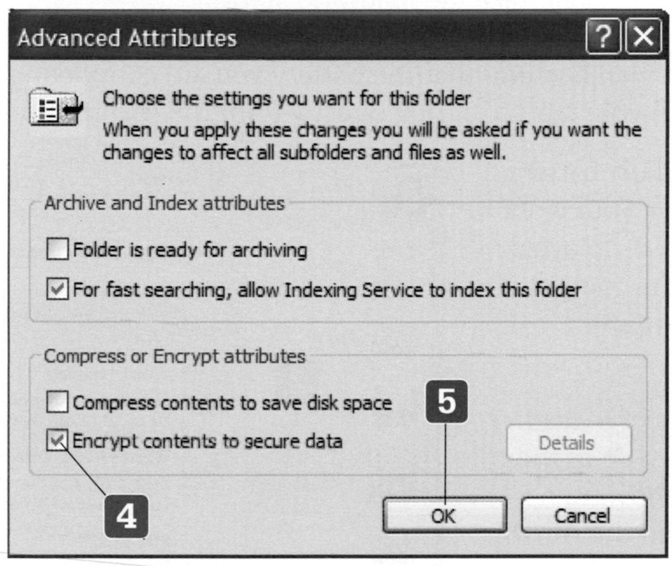

ALERT: Encrypting files and folders isn't fully supported in all versions of Windows. If you are unable to encrypt a file, save it on an external disk and leave it at home.

Take a spare battery

No matter how careful you try to be to save battery power, nothing lasts for ever. This is particularly true if you happen to be in a romantic spot without a source of electricity. You'll notice efficiency on the wane until you won't be able to charge the battery at all. The last thing you want to happen is to be in a remote location with your laptop shutting down unexpectedly or refusing to start. To avoid a frantic search for a battery in an unfamiliar area, take the following steps:

1. Check with the manufacturer that the battery you are considering will be compatible with your laptop, or buy directly from the manufacturer.
2. If you are using just battery power a lot, save your work at regular intervals to avoid losing work if the computer shuts down without warning.
3. Be alert to signs of a dead laptop battery, such as the battery meter showing no movement when the AC/DC adapter is connected. In this case, the battery meter will remain at 1 per cent.

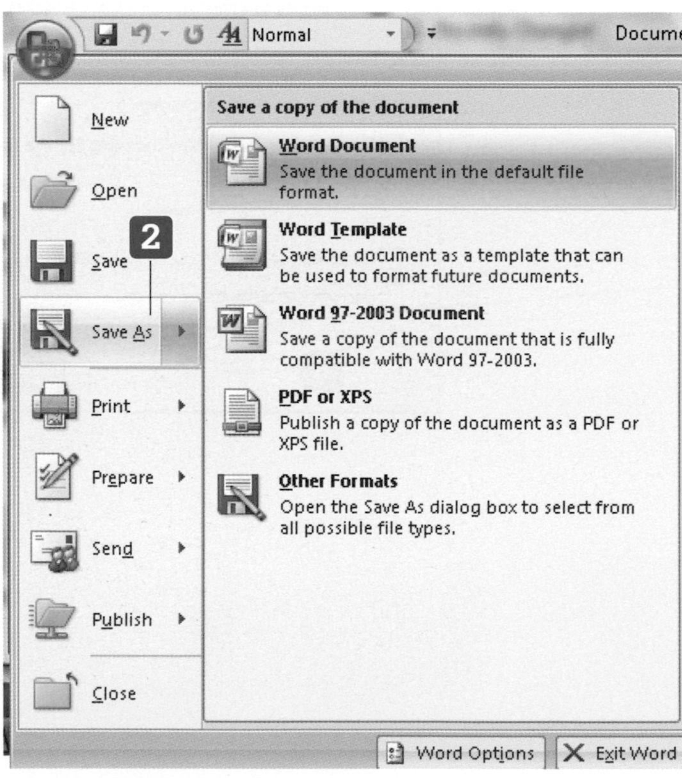

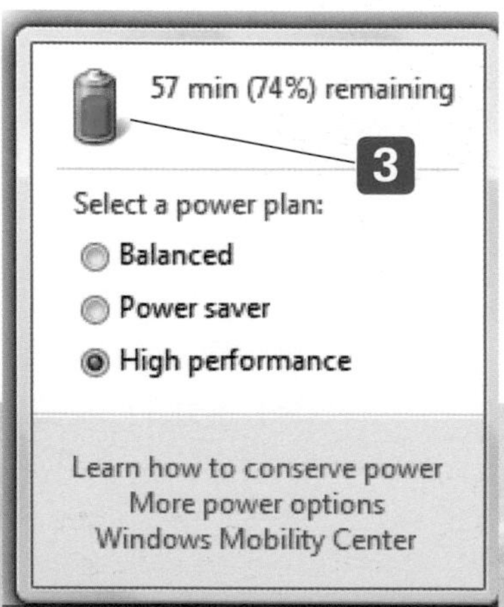

DID YOU KNOW?

Batteries can last as long as five years, but performance will be affected before they are totally dead. Although a spare is not cheap, having the peace of mind is well worth the investment.

Avoid temperature extremes

You may choose to visit exotic locations and prepare for your own creature comforts, but don't forget about your loyal laptop. In particular, don't leave it in the elements while you are in air conditioning or a heated environment. Here's how to prevent damage to your machine and its contents.

1. Wrap your laptop in an article of clothing or a towel to insulate it.
2. Avoid exposure to direct cold or heat.
3. Don't leave your laptop in an enclosed space, such as a car, while you take a tour or have dinner.

HOT TIP: It's better to not let your laptop get too hot or cold in the first place. But if it does suffer from extremes of temperature, let it return to normal room temperature before you try to use it. Even a delay of a few hours is better than damaging the delicate computing elements inside.

HOT TIP: Don't forget that the casing of your laptop is made of plastic. Too much heat can make it buckle, and too much cold can make it brittle.

8 Keeping your laptop running smoothly

Introduction

Like anything else, your portable device requires a little maintenance and upkeep. Because a laptop is carried from one location to another, it can easily get dirty, for one thing. And because it is frequently used on battery power when you are travelling, maintaining the battery is important as well.

By taking a few simple steps on a periodic basis, you will be able to keep your laptop running in top shape. You'll also avoid trouble; you won't encounter files or programs that open slowly, and your hard disk won't get clogged with data so that it is difficult to navigate. Look on this chapter as a sort of 'weekly cleaning and upkeep' routine for your laptop that will keep it operating for years to come.

Understand battery types

If you want to know about the battery provided with your laptop, check out the literature that's in the packing materials. Alternatively, the manufacturer's website should tell you what you need to know about its expected lifespan. But when it comes time to buy a replacement here's what you need to know about the next generation.

1. If you already have a battery, remove it from your laptop and read the label to see what type it is.
2. Look for a laptop that uses rechargeable batteries, such as lithium ion ones (as shown here), which are regarded as more stable.

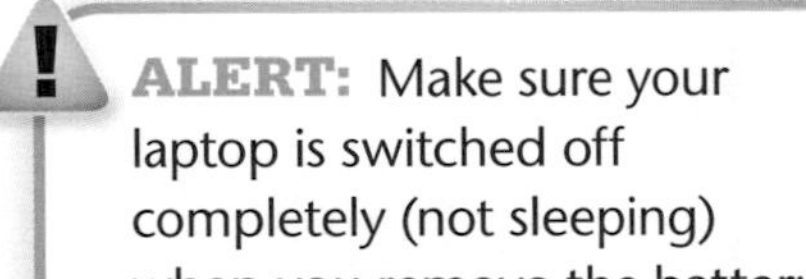

ALERT: Make sure your laptop is switched off completely (not sleeping) when you remove the battery.

ALERT: Although lithium ion and lithium polymer batteries are rechargeable and can be recharged multiple times, no battery lasts for ever. They will have to be replaced eventually.

HOT TIP: If you don't see the battery type listed on your laptop or the battery itself, turn to the laptop manufacturer's website or look in the instructions that came with the laptop.

Minimise power consumption

Conservation is very trendy in this day and age. Your battery plays a vital role in allowing you to use your laptop. So it's in your best interest to follow these tips to make it last as long as possible.

1. Plug your laptop into the power mains when you have the option, rather than using the battery, to conserve power.
2. Monitor power consumption and know how much battery power you have available by passing your mouse pointer over the battery icon in the bottom right area of the taskbar.

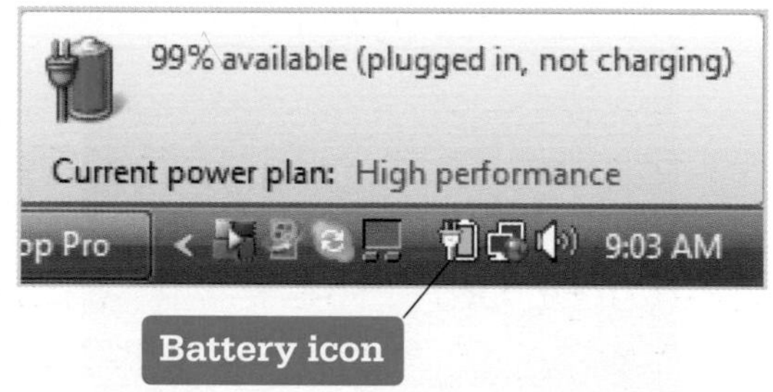

3. Put the laptop to Sleep when you are not using it.
4. Use Window's power management settings to save battery power.
5. Making your computer monitor less bright can help conserve power. Open the Mobility Center and adjust the brightness slider.

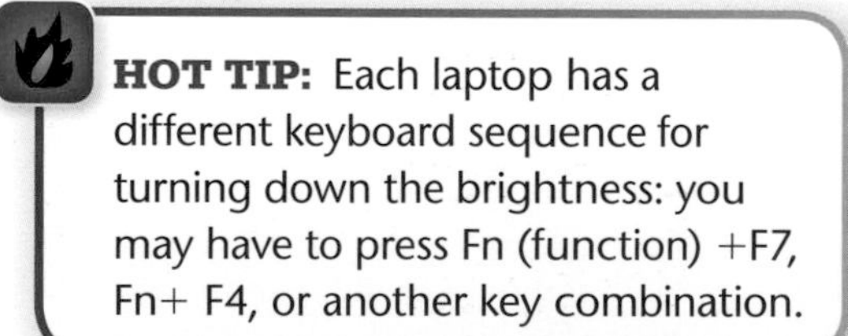

HOT TIP: Each laptop has a different keyboard sequence for turning down the brightness: you may have to press Fn (function) +F7, Fn+ F4, or another key combination.

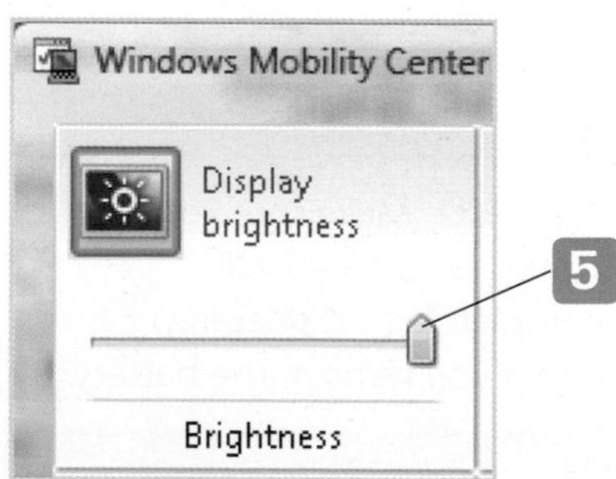

SEE ALSO: Put your laptop to sleep or turn it off, in Chapter 2, will also help you with this aspect of power conservation.

ALERT: Be sure to plug the laptop into the mains when you are performing tasks that consume a good deal of memory, such as listening to music or watching movies.

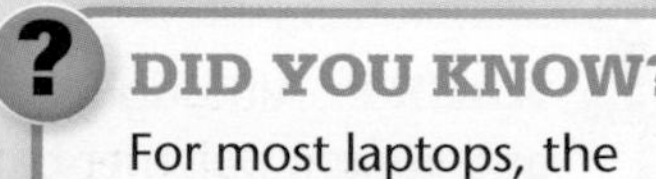

DID YOU KNOW? For most laptops, the battery lasts for an average of three to five hours before it needs to be recharged.

Manage battery power use

In the previous tasks, you learned some behaviours that will help conserve battery power. Your laptop also has battery power routines that you can adjust. Preconfigured power schemes will help you manage your battery life.

1. Click Start.
2. Click Control Panel.
3. Click Hardware and Sound.
4. Click Power Options.

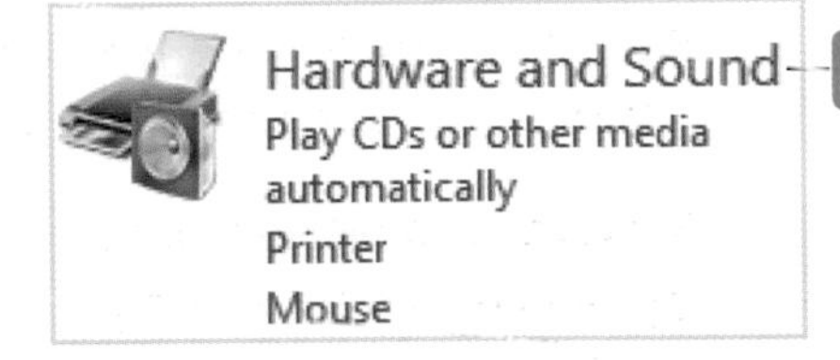

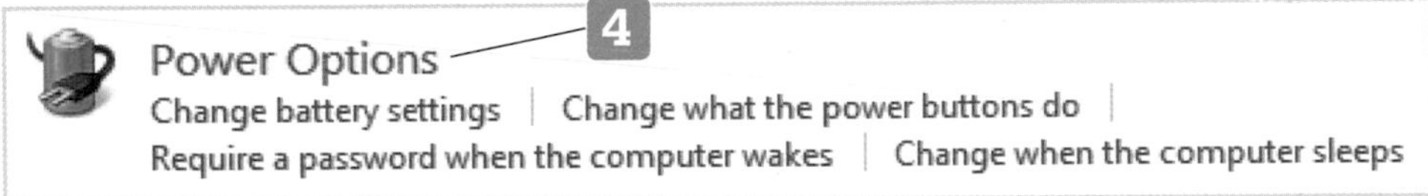

5. Click one of the power schemes, such as Power saver, which will maximise battery life.

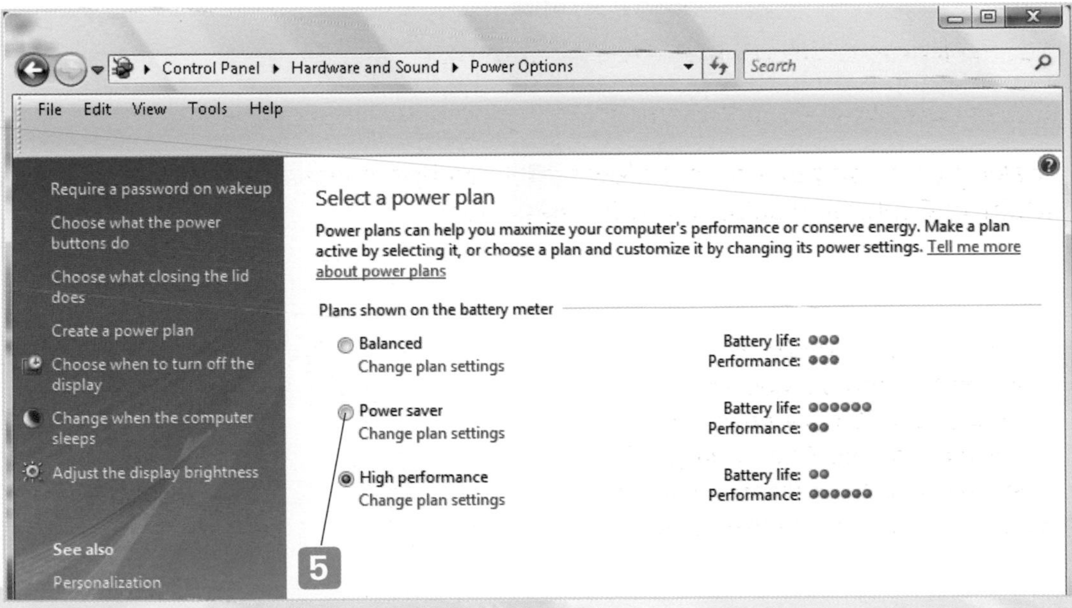

ALERT: Keep in mind that there are trade-offs with power schemes – the routine that gives you the longest battery life will also cause your laptop to go to sleep the quickest when you're not using it.

Keep your battery charged

Just like you used to wind your wristwatch, now you charge your battery. You do the charging not by removing the battery and plugging it into a special charging device, but by keeping it in your laptop and plugging your laptop into the power mains using your AC/DC adapter.

1. Connect the AC/DC adapter to the laptop.
2. Connect the adapter to the mains socket.
3. Turn the laptop on, if necessary.
4. Check the Power Meter icon in the taskbar to make sure the laptop is plugged in. If your laptop is plugged in and charging the icon will appear with a plug.

5. If your laptop is on battery power you'll see the icon below.

HOT TIP: You can also track the amount of battery power remaining, and whether or not the battery is charging, in Windows Mobility Center.

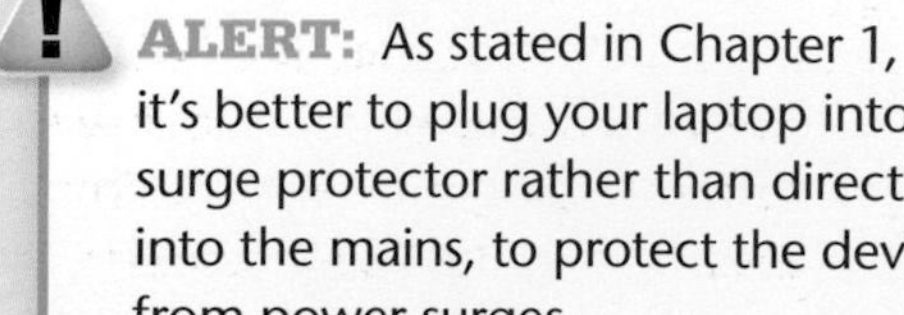

ALERT: As stated in Chapter 1, it's better to plug your laptop into a surge protector rather than directly into the mains, to protect the device from power surges.

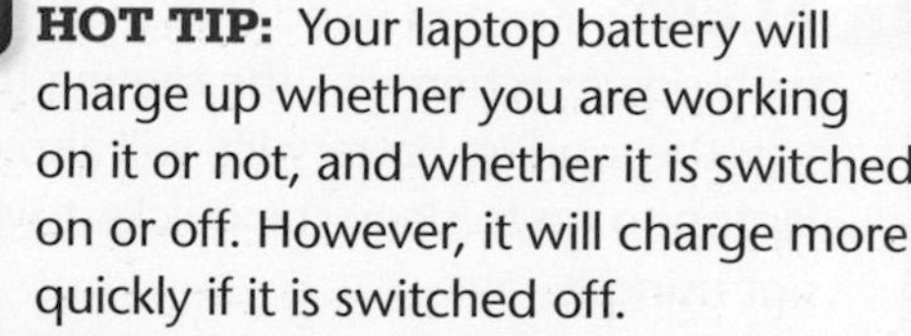

HOT TIP: Your laptop battery will charge up whether you are working on it or not, and whether it is switched on or off. However, it will charge more quickly if it is switched off.

Use the Security Center

If you want the vortex of security, you'll love the Security Center. It's an important tool for keeping your laptop running smoothly. After all, if you block harmful programs and keep unauthorised users out of your file system, you'll head off theft of data and harm to your programs.

1. Open the Control Panel.
2. Click Security.
3. Click Security Center.
4. Check the security settings for your laptop.
5. Click the red or green button or the arrow to view settings for an item.
6. Click this button to turn on specific settings.

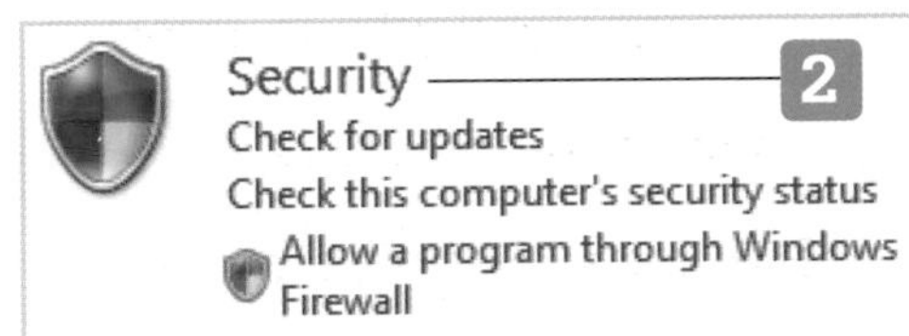

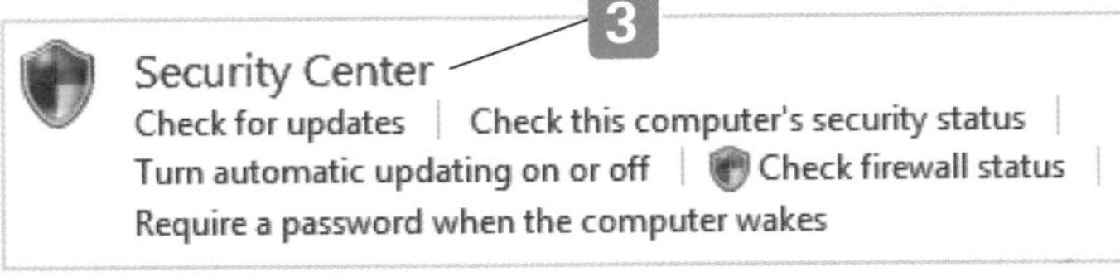

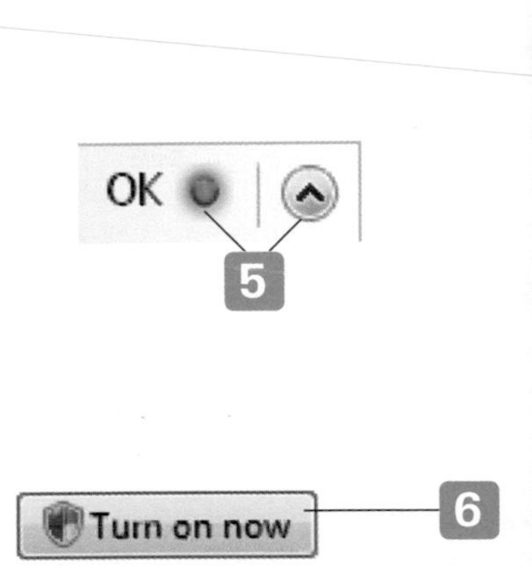

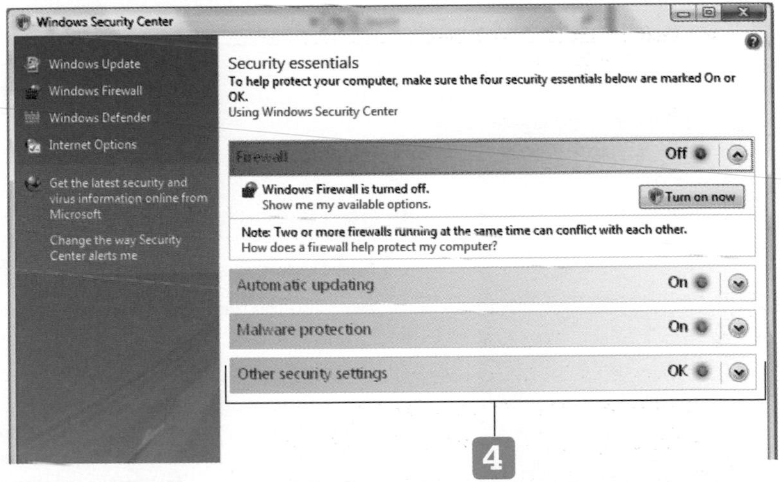

ALERT: A red banner in the Security Center means an item is not up to date and your laptop could be compromised. An amber banner mean there are some issues and you are not fully protected. A green banner means the item is up to date and protecting your system.

HOT TIP: If you are tired of Windows presenting you with the User Account Control dialogue box to confirm instructions, the User Account Control section under Other Security Settings is the place to turn it off.

Keep your software updated

Security is a moving target, so you'll want to take advantage of updates that repair security problems that come to light with the operating system and associated programs. Luckily Windows makes it super easy by allowing you to download and install updates automatically through the use of the Windows Update function.

1. Open the Control Panel.
2. Click either Security or System and Maintenance (both will take you to Windows Update).
3. Click Windows Update.
4. Read about available updates, which are listed in the Windows Update window.
5. Click Install updates to install them.
6. Click Check for updates to look manually for any more available updates.

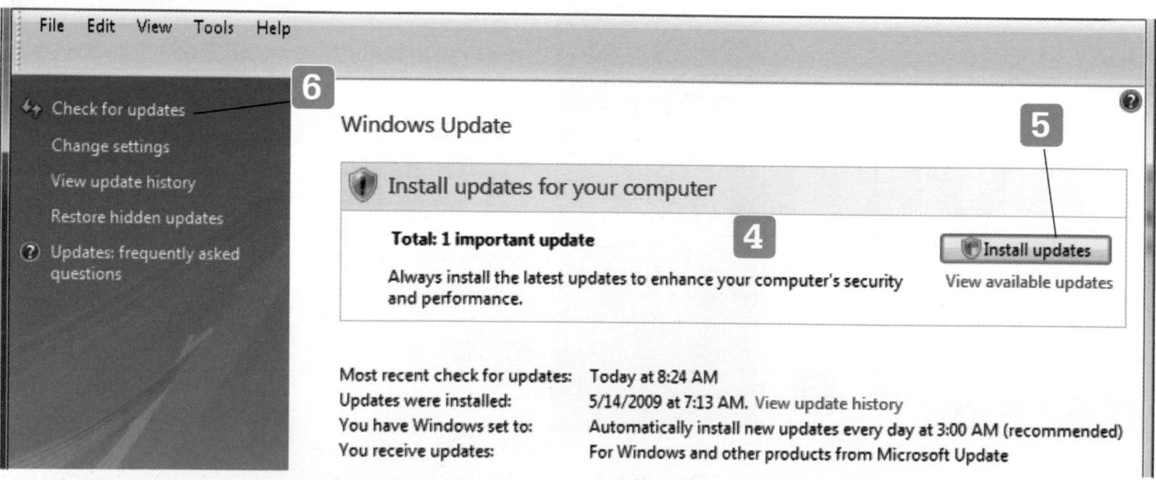

DID YOU KNOW?

The updates you are looking for with Windows Update are new versions and patches to the operating system. Windows periodically updates its operating system software to combat any security threats.

ALERT: Depending on the number of updates you're installing, your computer may run more slowly during the process. You may want to run updates while you aren't working and don't need your laptop.

Configure Windows Update

The preceding section showed you how to use Windows Update to update manually your operating system software. The beauty of Windows Update is that it can run in the background, and even be scheduled to perform updates in the middle of the night while you're asleep.

1. Open Windows Update.
2. Click Change settings on the left side of the Windows Update window.
3. To have Windows Update work automatically, click the Install updates automatically button.
4. Choose how often you want the updates to occur (every day, or one day a week).
5. Choose a time for the update to occur.
6. Click OK.

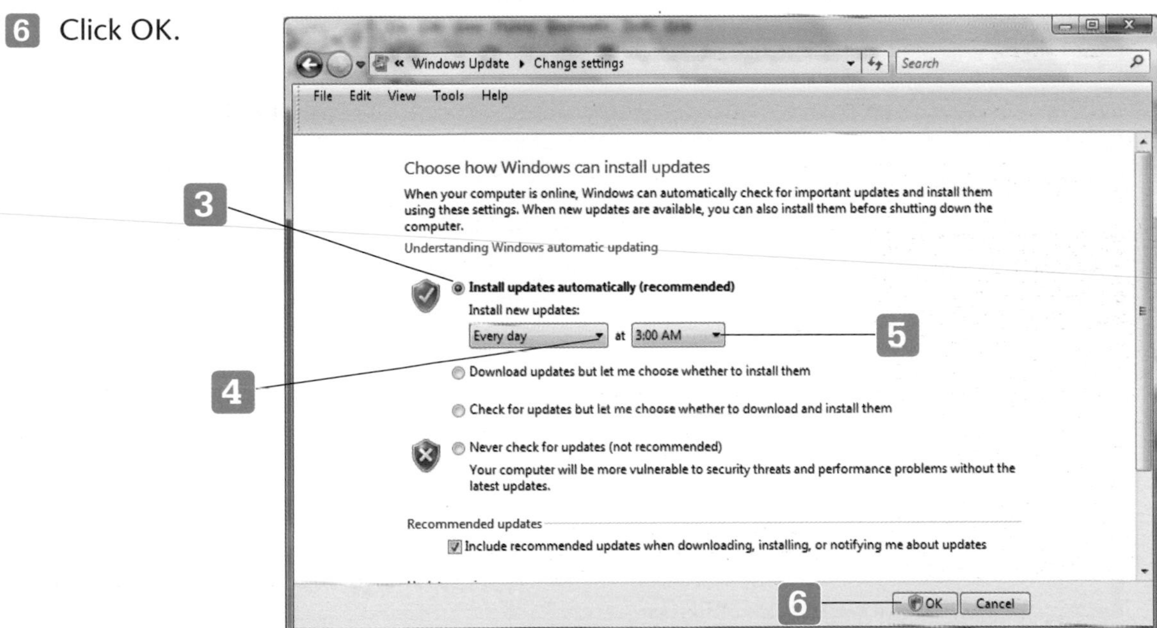

SEE ALSO: See the preceding section for instructions on how to access Windows Update.

HOT TIP: You'll also find a Windows Update icon in the System Tray on the right side of your taskbar. Double-click it to open Windows Update.

Update individual applications

Over time, you'll gather a variety of different software programs, each able to perform a different function. One is for typing, one is for viewing images, one is for listening to audio. These applications need to be updated periodically, and Windows Update can help with this task.

1. Open Windows Update
2. Click View available updates.
3. View the updates available for printer drivers and software used by other hardware devices installed on your laptop.
4. Click the tick box next to the update you want to install.
5. Click Install.

2 Install updates
View available updates

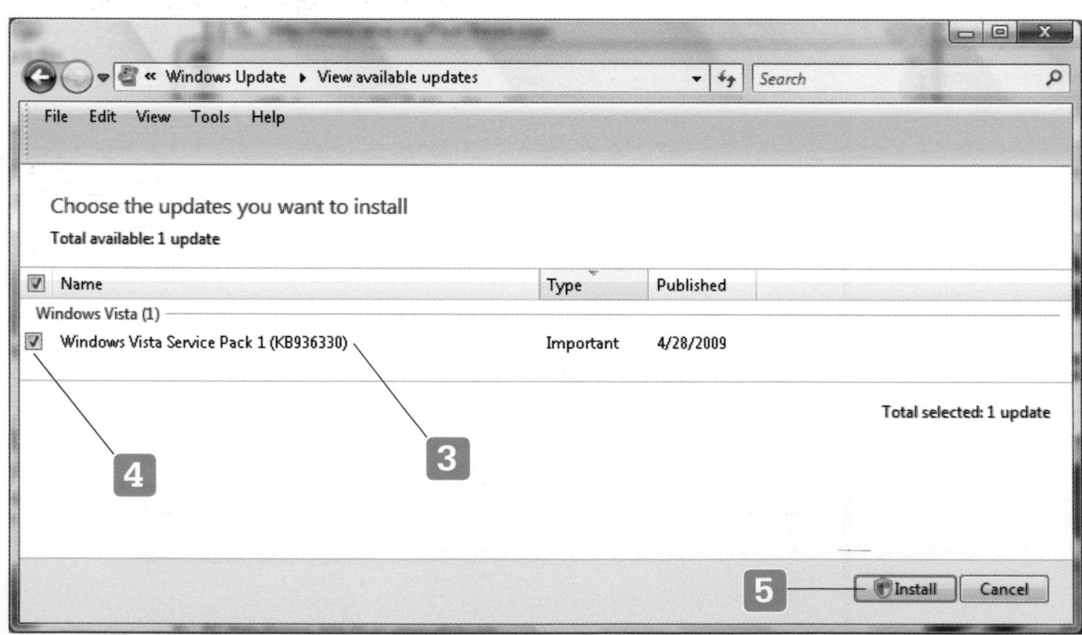

HOT TIP: As you might expect, you can use the Start menu to open Windows Update quickly. Click Start, type update, and click Windows Update when it appears in the Start menu.

SEE ALSO: It's a good idea to check for available software updates, both for Windows and for hardware component software, on at least a weekly basis. This is described in the following section.

Review software updates you have installed

Occasionally, you will read in the media or on the Microsoft website about important patches and updates.

1. Open the Control Panel.
2. Click Programs.
3. Click View installed updates.

4. Review the service packs, security updates and add other updates you have previously installed. If you need to uninstall an update, click it.
5. Click Uninstall.

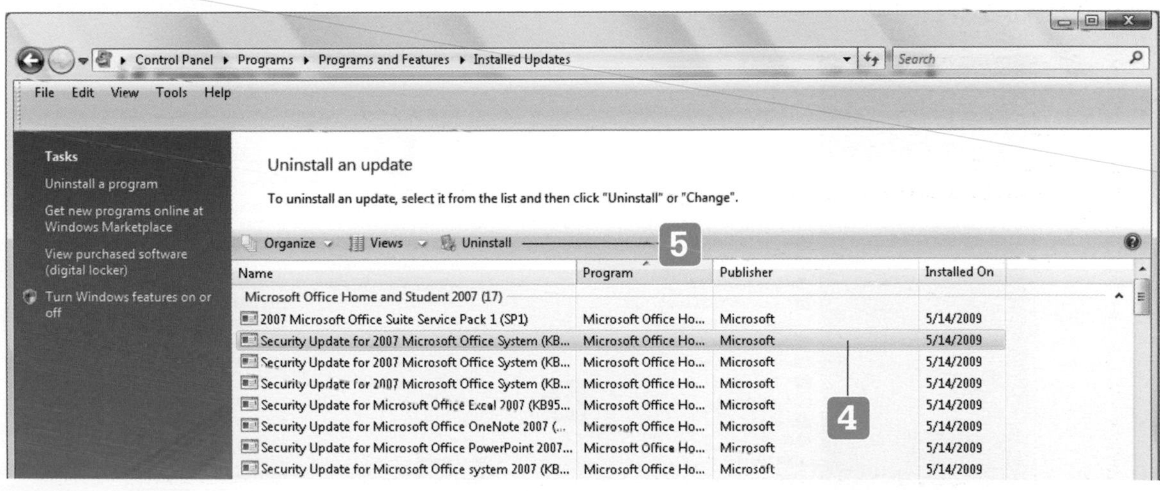

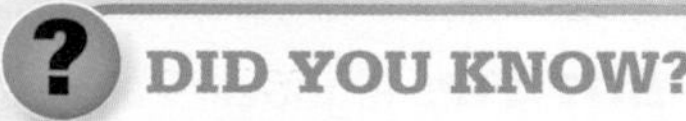

DID YOU KNOW?

Sometimes you need to uninstall an update in order to re-install a new one.

HOT TIP: Open the Control Panel, click Programs, and scan the list of available options for managing your installed software. You can manage Windows Sidebar and use Windows Defender to scan for viruses, for instance.

Uninstall programs you don't need

If you let young people use your laptop for any length of time, you might come back to your computer to find new programs have been installed. It has happened with my daughter, who used my laptop and installed a group of games. To save disk space and keep your Start menu less cluttered, you should uninstall such applications (unless you want your young relatives to use them, of course).

Programs — 2
Uninstall a program
Change startup programs

1. Open the Control Panel.
2. Click Programs.
3. Under Programs and Features, click Uninstall a program.

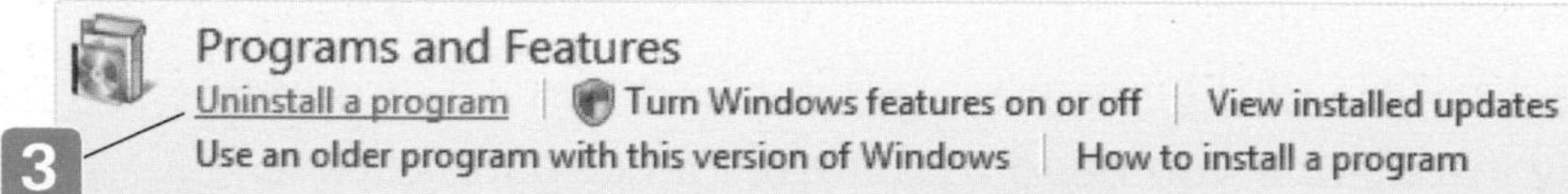

4. Scan the list of installed applications and select the one you want to remove.
5. Click Uninstall.

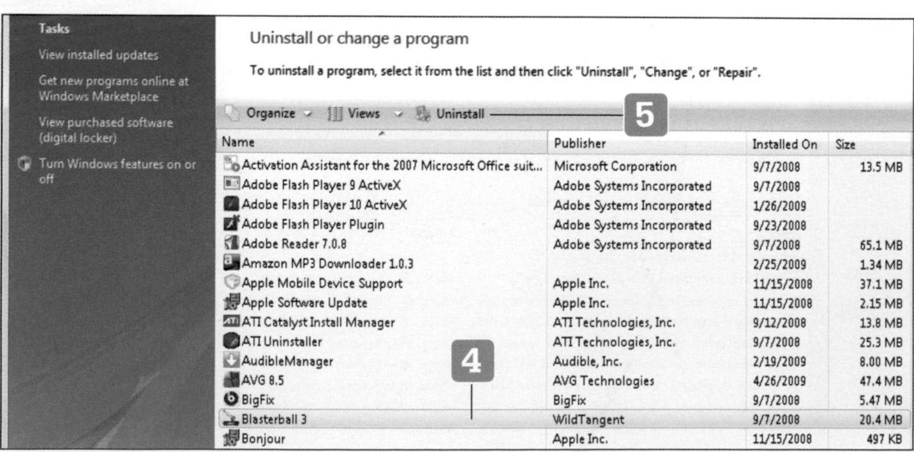

DID YOU KNOW?

When you select a program in the list, a set of details appears beneath it, including the amount of disk space consumed by the application. If you start to run out of hard disk space, turn to this list and remove programs you don't need to free up more space.

HOT TIP: Right-click an application and you may see two options in the context menu: Uninstall and Change. If you see the Change option, click it to update the application.

Back up your files

One of the nice features of Windows is the presence of safeguards that keep you from losing data in case your system suddenly stops working (or in the language of computers, 'crashes'). Nevertheless, it's always a good idea to back up your files. You learned how to do so in preceding chapters by dragging files to an external drive. You can also use Windows' own Backup and Restore Center.

1. Open the Control Panel.
2. Click System and Maintenance.
3. Click Backup and Restore Center.
4. Click Back up files.
5. Select the location where you want to back up your files.
6. Click Next.

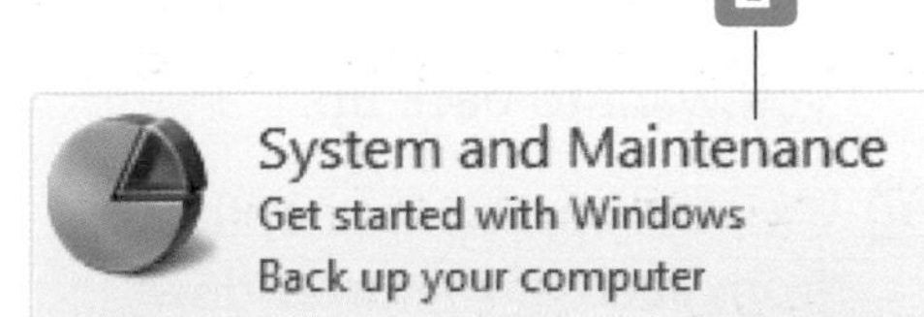

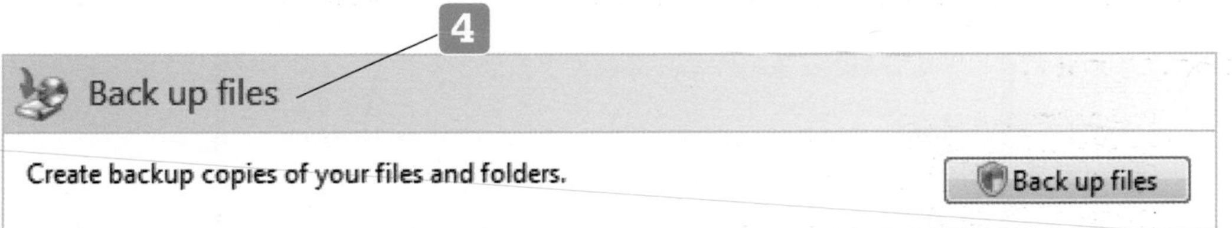

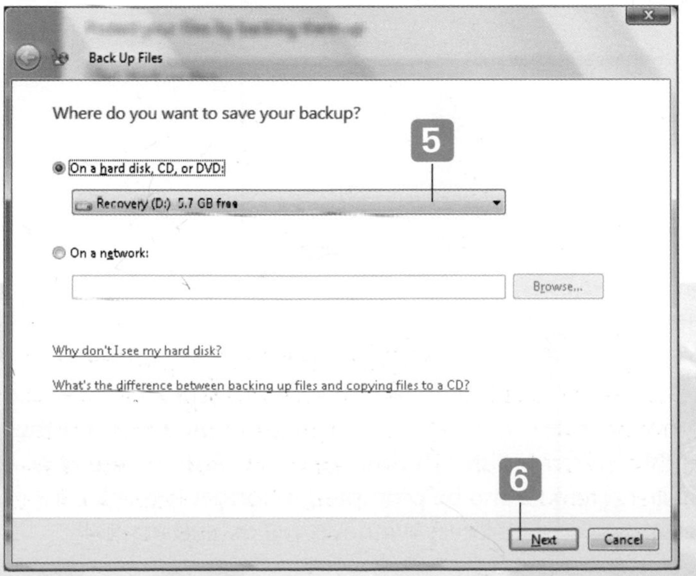

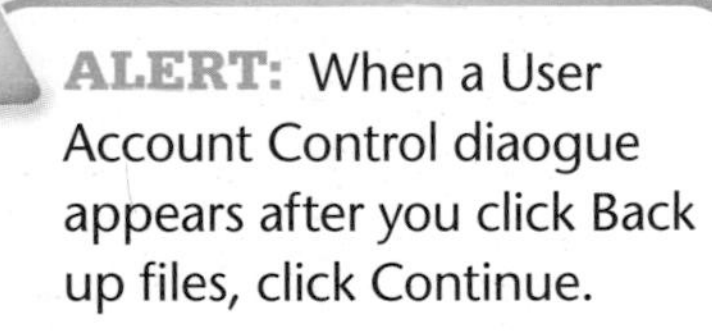

ALERT: When a User Account Control diaogue appears after you click Back up files, click Continue.

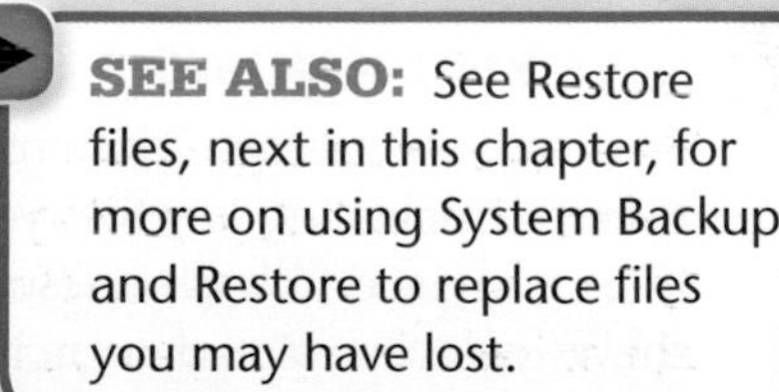

SEE ALSO: See Restore files, next in this chapter, for more on using System Backup and Restore to replace files you may have lost.

7 If you chose the CD drive option, you are asked to choose which disks you want to include in the backup. Tick the box next to the options you want to include.

8 Click Next.

9 Select the types of files that you want to back up.

10 Tick the appropriate options from each of the drop-down lists for how often you want to back up your files.

11 Click Save settings and start backup.

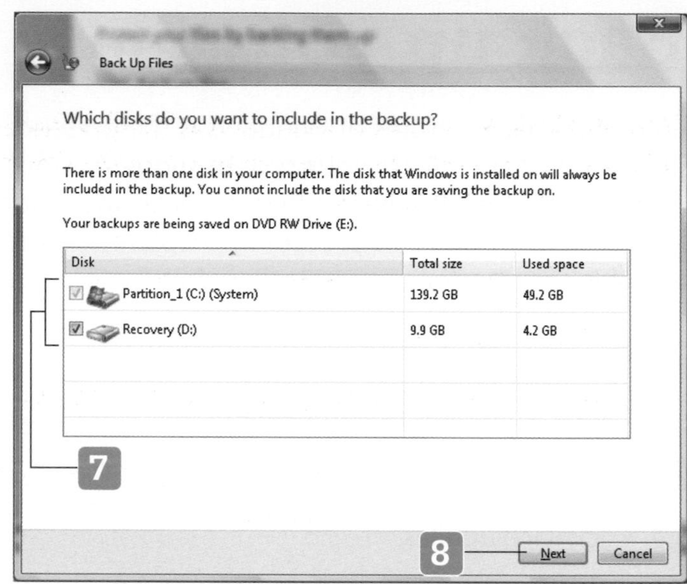

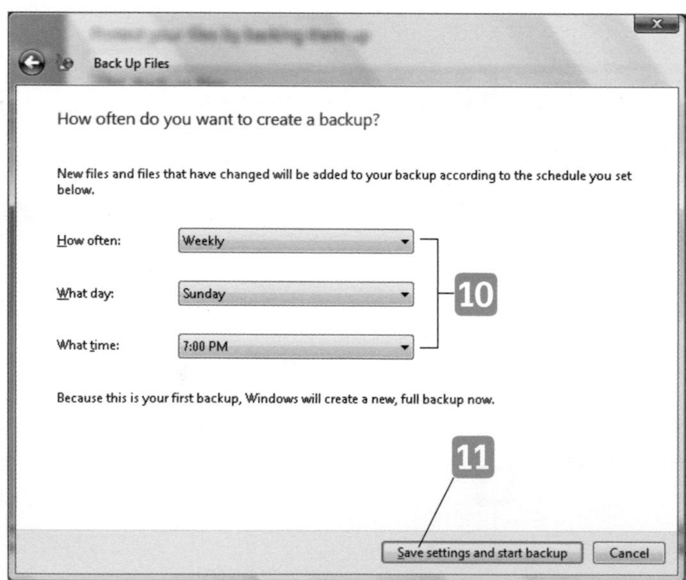

? DID YOU KNOW?

By default, all file type options are ticked. Deselecting any files you don't think you need to back up (such as TV shows you have already watched) will save disk space and make your backup go more quickly.

? DID YOU KNOW?

If you chose the option to back up on a CD or DVD, you will be prompted to insert the disk into your laptop's disk drive. You may also be prompted to format the disk – a process Windows will do automatically.

Restore files

With any luck, you'll never have to restore files. But it should give you peace of mind to know it's possible to do the following using the files you earlier backed up with the Backup and Restore Center.

1. Open the Backup and Restore Center.
2. Click Restore files.
3. Choose one of the backup options – the latest backup or a previous one.
4. Click Next.

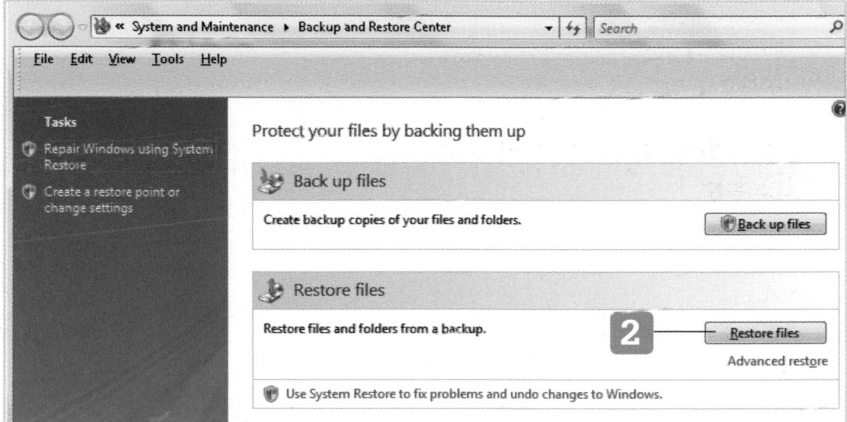

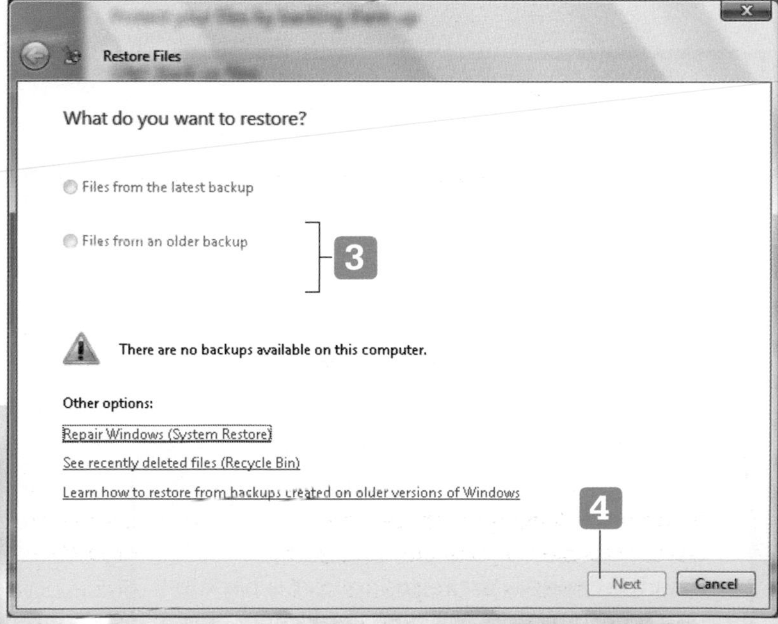

HOT TIP: As you might expect, you can click Start, type Backup and Restore Center, and press Enter to open this Windows application.

5 When the Restore Files window appears, click Add files next to the items you want to restore.

6 Click Next.

7 Select specific folders or files you want to restore.

8 Click Add.

9 When the files to be restored are displayed in the subsequent window, click Next.

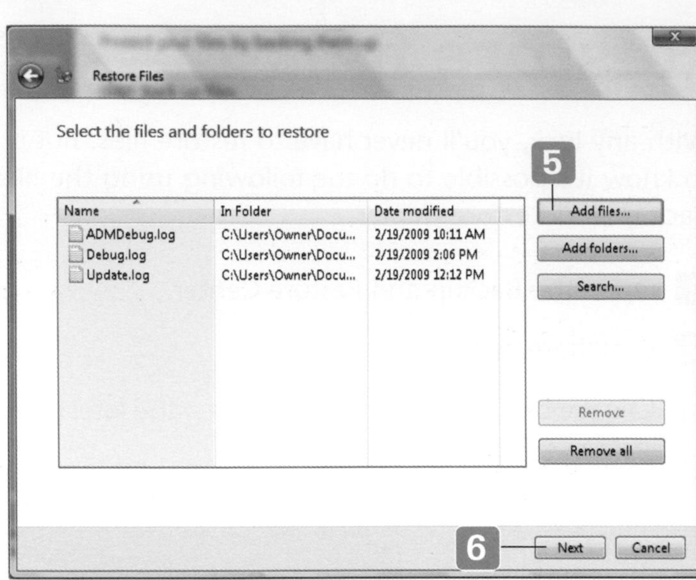

10 Choose the destination for where you want to restore the files – the original location or a new one. If you choose a new location, subsequent screens will prompt you to choose it.

11 Choose Start restore.

12 When restoration is complete, click Finish.

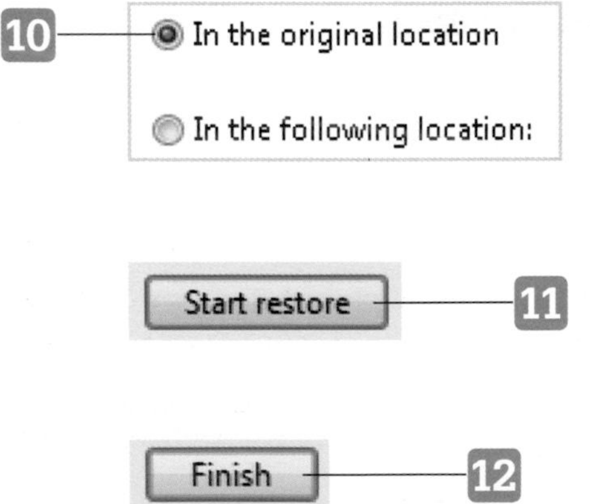

ALERT: If you are not sure whether you want to restore over existing files – for instance, if you aren't sure the existing files are actually older than the ones you are restoring from a backup – by all means restore in a different location, even if it is a folder you create in your file system.

SEE ALSO: The preceding section describes how to open the Backup and Restore Center from the Control Panel.

Save power by turning off your monitor

One way to keep your computer running smoothly and save battery power is to turn off your laptop's monitor when you're not using it. Laptop monitors don't have on–off switches like lamps or TVs, however. You configure when the monitor switches off using the Control Panel.

1. Click Start.
2. Click Control Panel.
3. Click Hardware and Sound.
4. Click Power Options.

3
Hardware and Sound
Play CDs or other media automatically
Printer
Mouse

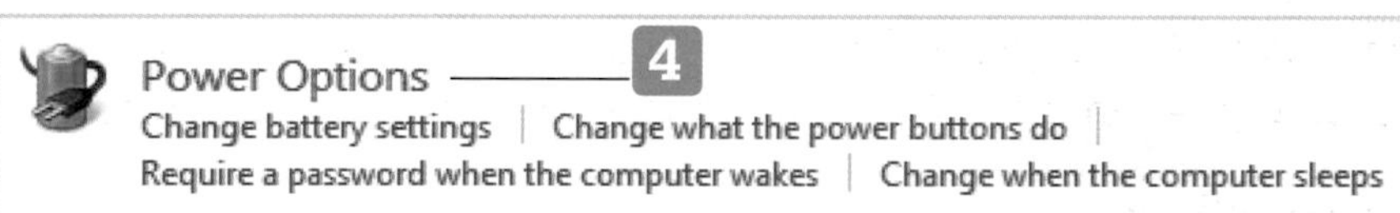

5. Click Choose when to turn off the display in the left-hand column.
6. To improve power consumption, decrease the time that passes for the display to turn off when the laptop is on its battery.
7. Click Save changes.

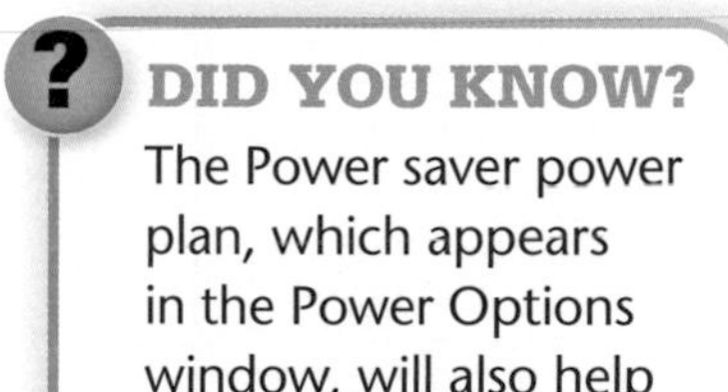

DID YOU KNOW? The Power saver power plan, which appears in the Power Options window, will also help maximise battery life.

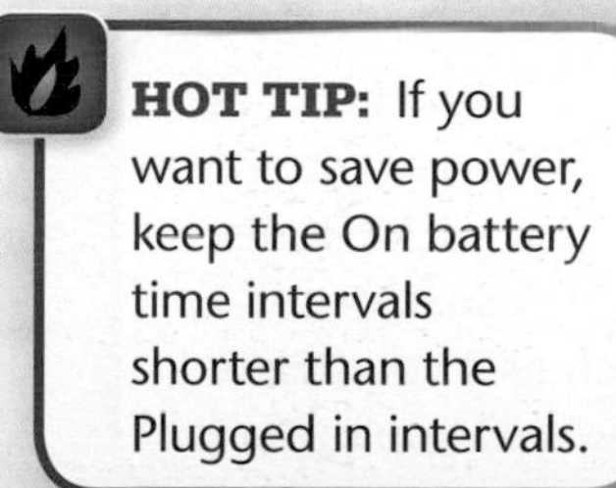

HOT TIP: If you want to save power, keep the On battery time intervals shorter than the Plugged in intervals.

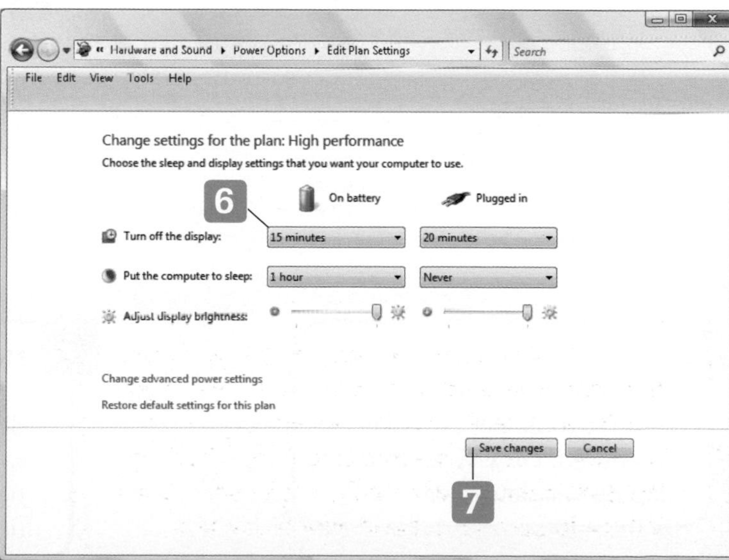

Check available hard disk space

If your computer begins to slow down, or if applications or files open slowly, it's a good idea to check available disk space. If your hard disk is almost full and files are fragmented, processes will take longer to complete. Assessing how much space you have left enables you to decide when to clean up your disk.

1. Click Start.
2. Click Computer.
3. Click the disk you want to check.
4. Click Properties.
5. Review the graphical representation of how much space remains.
6. Click OK.

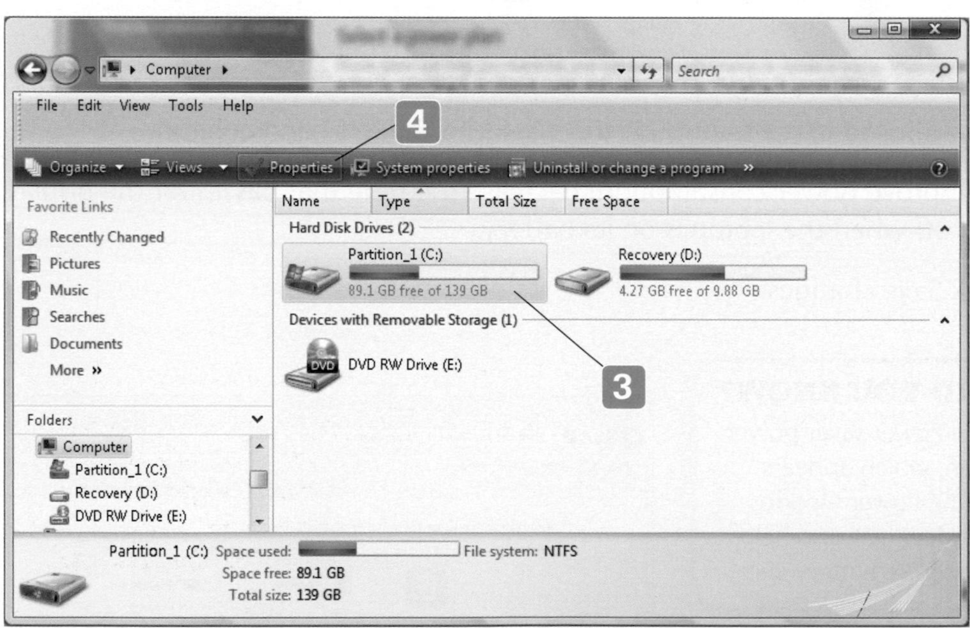

ALERT: To ensure that your hard disk runs smoothly, make sure 15 to 20 per cent of it is unused. Otherwise, your laptop will slow down.

HOT TIP: Tick the box next to Compress this drive to save disk space, and click OK, to save some disk space – but not as much as if you deleted unused files and applications.

Clean up your hard disk

As you work and surf the Internet, your hard disk compiles lots of files you don't need, and don't even know you have. For instance, website images and text files are stored in an area of your disk called disk cache so the same sites can appear more quickly on subsequent visits. You can use Windows' Disk Cleanup routine to delete such files.

1. Follow steps 1 to 5 as described in the preceding section.
2. Click Disk Cleanup.

3. Choose whether you want to clean up only your files or those created by others who have accounts on this computer.
4. A dialogue box appears briefly as your disk is inspected. When the Disk Cleanup dialogue box appears, tick the boxes next to the items you want to delete.
5. Click OK to start cleanup.

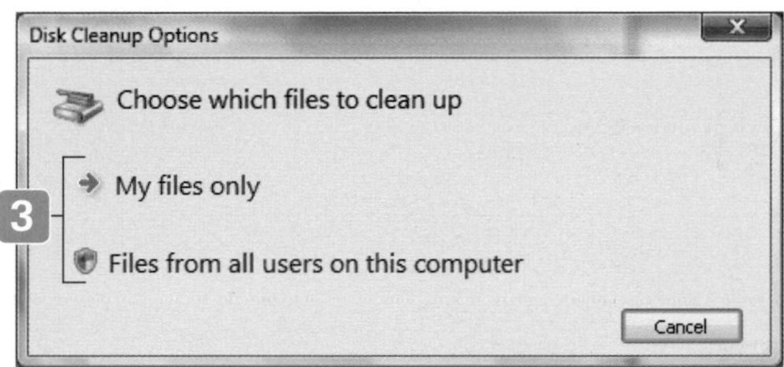

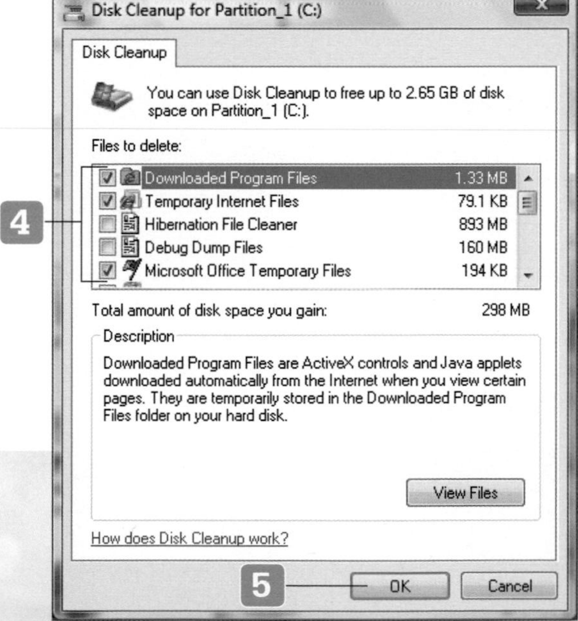

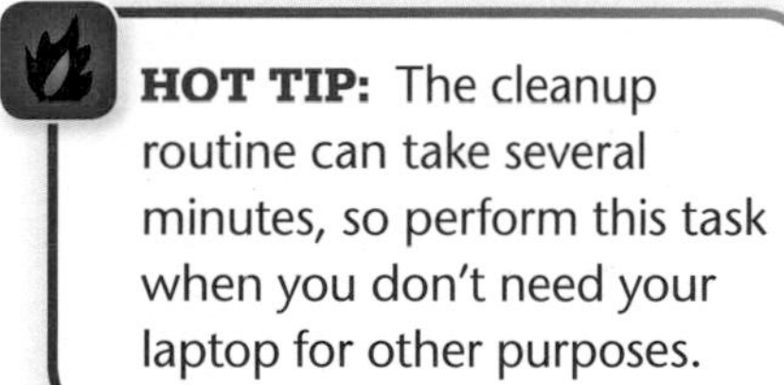

HOT TIP: The cleanup routine can take several minutes, so perform this task when you don't need your laptop for other purposes.

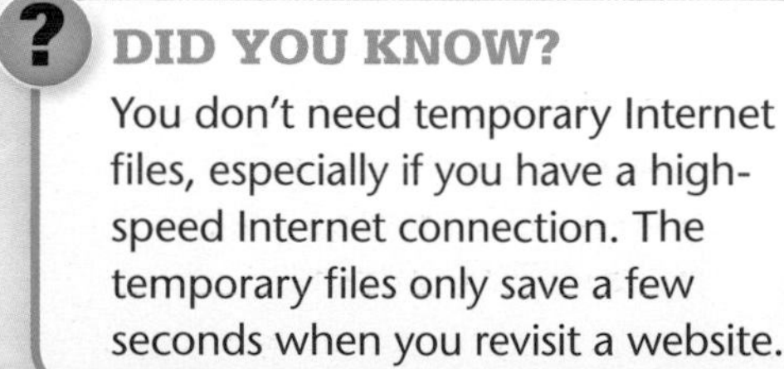

DID YOU KNOW?

You don't need temporary Internet files, especially if you have a high-speed Internet connection. The temporary files only save a few seconds when you revisit a website.

9 Networking and creating user accounts

Introduction

Laptops let you do computing in more than one location. They also allow more than one person to use your computer or access your files. If you live in a household where you want to share your music, photos or other documents with your companions, you need to take advantage of your laptop's networking capabilities.

Networking is a term you hear a lot when you're looking for a job. But in computer language, a network is two or more computers that are connected together to share data or an Internet connection. That way they can swap files without an external storage device and print off the same printer. In this chapter you'll learn about the advantages of sharing and how to make it happen.

Directly connect two computers

Playing telephone with tin cans is a favourite childhood game. You can do the same thing with computers, except that you use an Ethernet cable instead of a string. That way you can share files with your desktop computer:

1. Obtain a length of Ethernet cable and use it to connect your laptop to another computer.

2. Click Start and click Network.

3. When the Network window opens, click Network and Sharing Center.

SEE ALSO: You have to have Network Discovery turned on in the Network and Sharing Center to view connected computers. See the next section for more.

HOT TIP: To view the networked computers, click on View computers and devices. To view its accessible folders and files, double-click on one of the networked computers.

HOT TIP: You can also open the Network and Sharing Center by clicking Start, typing Network and Sharing Center in the start box, and clicking Network and Sharing Center from the Start menu.

4 If your laptop is already connected to the Internet, Network and Sharing Center indicates that you are connected to multiple networks – your Internet connection and the new Local Area Connection.

5 Click View computers and devices.

6 The networked computers are displayed in the Network window. Double-click one to view printers or files you are sharing.

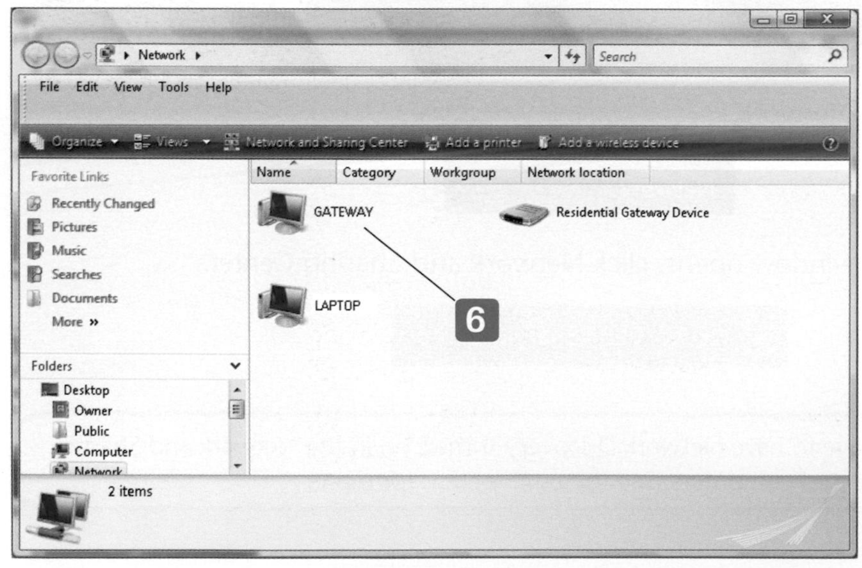

ALERT: Firewalls can also prevent network access. Check the firewall settings if you can't get to the contents of a computer that has been networked.

WHAT DOES THIS MEAN?

Local Area Network (LAN): this refers to a network of two or more computers that is created in a single location such as a house or office.

Ethernet: a high-speed system used for transferring information from one digital device to another using a cable.

Turn on network discovery

Computers only do what you tell them. The Network and Sharing Center is where you tell Windows what you want to share with others on your network and others who have access to your laptop. And in order to view printers, computers and other network devices, you have to turn on network discovery.

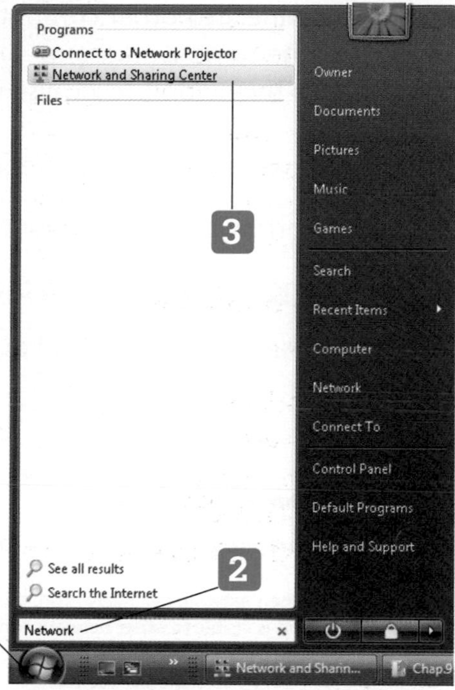

1. Click Start.
2. Type Network.
3. Choose Network and Sharing Center.
4. Click the arrow to the right of Network discovery.
5. Click Turn on network discovery.
6. Click Apply.

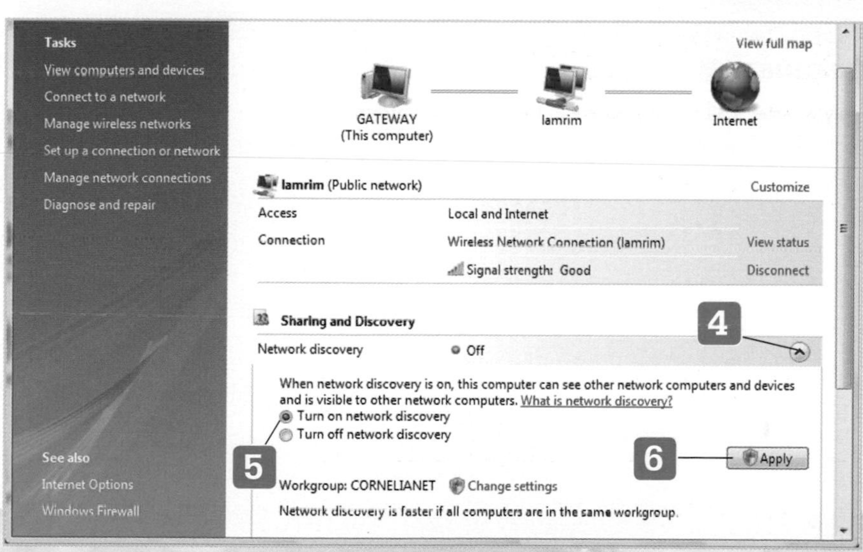

HOT TIP: A shortcut for this process is simply to type Network in the Start Search window.

DID YOU KNOW?

If you click on one of the down arrows in the list you'll get more information about each section.

Change your workgroup name

In order to connect to other computers on your local network, they all need to be members of the same workgroup. The workgroup name must match exactly for all computers, or they won't recognise one another.

1. Open Network and Sharing Center.
2. Click the arrow next to Network discovery.
3. Click Change settings next to the current name of your workgroup.
4. When a User Account Control dialogue box appears, click Continue.

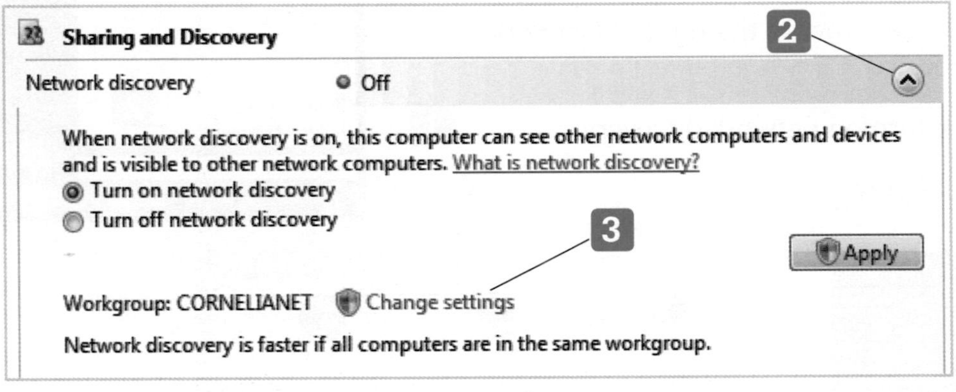

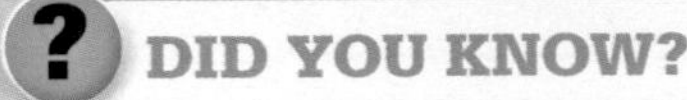

DID YOU KNOW?
You can also click the link Set up a connection or network in the left-hand column of the Network and Sharing Center to set up workgroup names for your laptops or other computers.

HOT TIP: Make your computer names easy to recognise. It's also helpful, if you have more than one computer at home, to identify the computer's location in the name, for example Kitchen or 3rdFloorComputer.

5 Click Change.

6 Type the new workgroup name.

7 Change your computer name, if you wish.

8 Click OK.

9 Click OK.

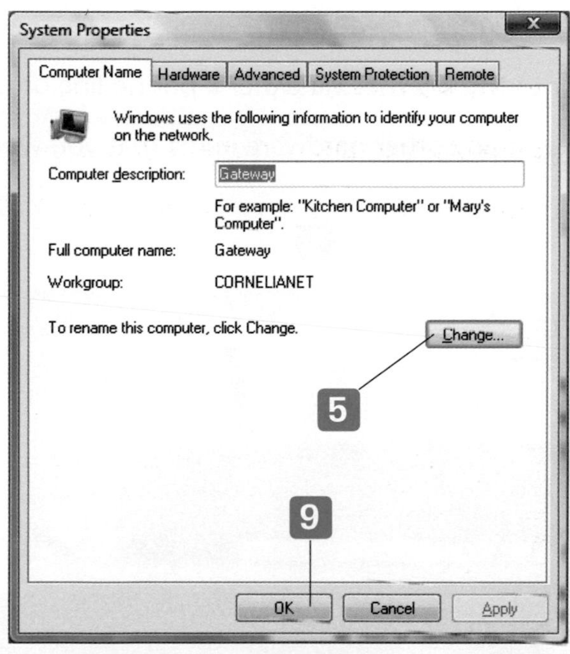

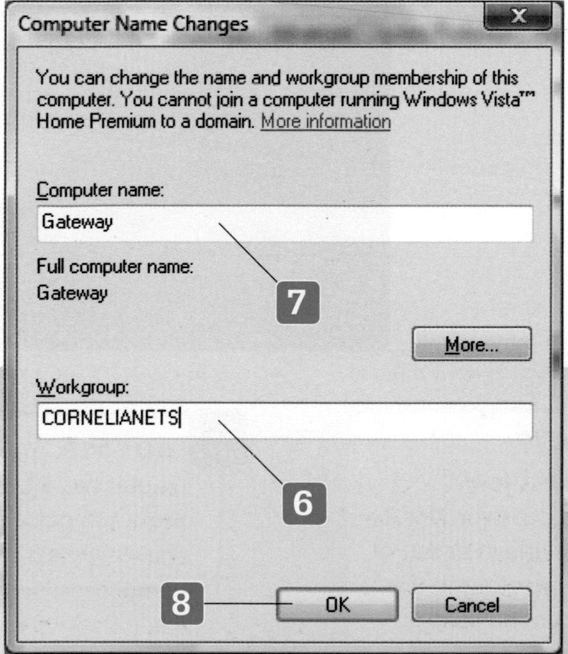

Connect a router

I have an aunt who knows what's happening with all my family members. All the information goes through her. Like my aunt, a router is the device through which all the elements of the network will communicate. Here's how to start the process.

1. Plug your router into the mains electricity.
2. Connect your router to the Internet via either a phone line or cable.
3. Connect your printer or any other hardware items that you want to include in your network.

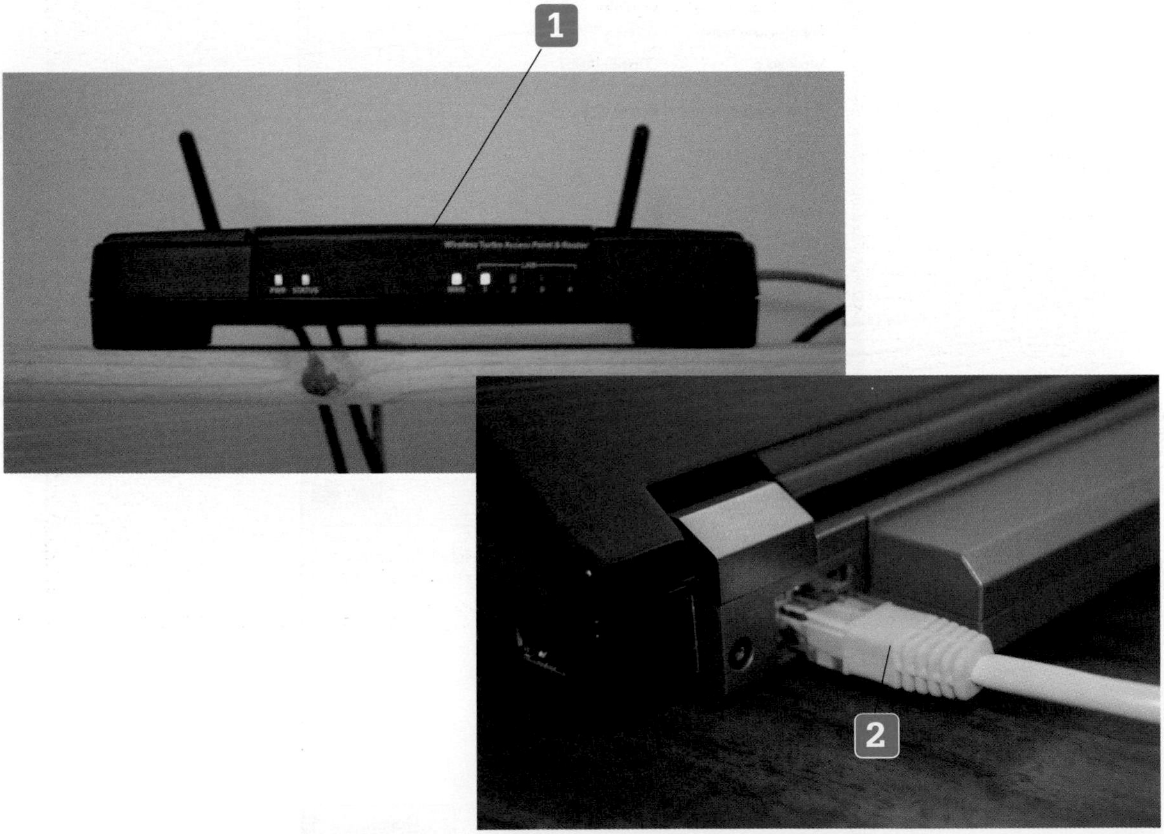

DID YOU KNOW?
When you first connect your wireless router, set a password for it. That will prevent anyone in or out of your house from connecting to the network without your knowledge.

HOT TIP: You can use a cable if your router has a USB connection, but it's easier to get a laptop and printer that have wireless connectivity.

View your network map

It's a good feeling to be master of all you survey. It's fun to view all the elements of the network after you've set it up and computers have been connected to it, so here's what to do.

1. Open the Network and Sharing Center.
2. To see the whole network, click on the link called View full map.

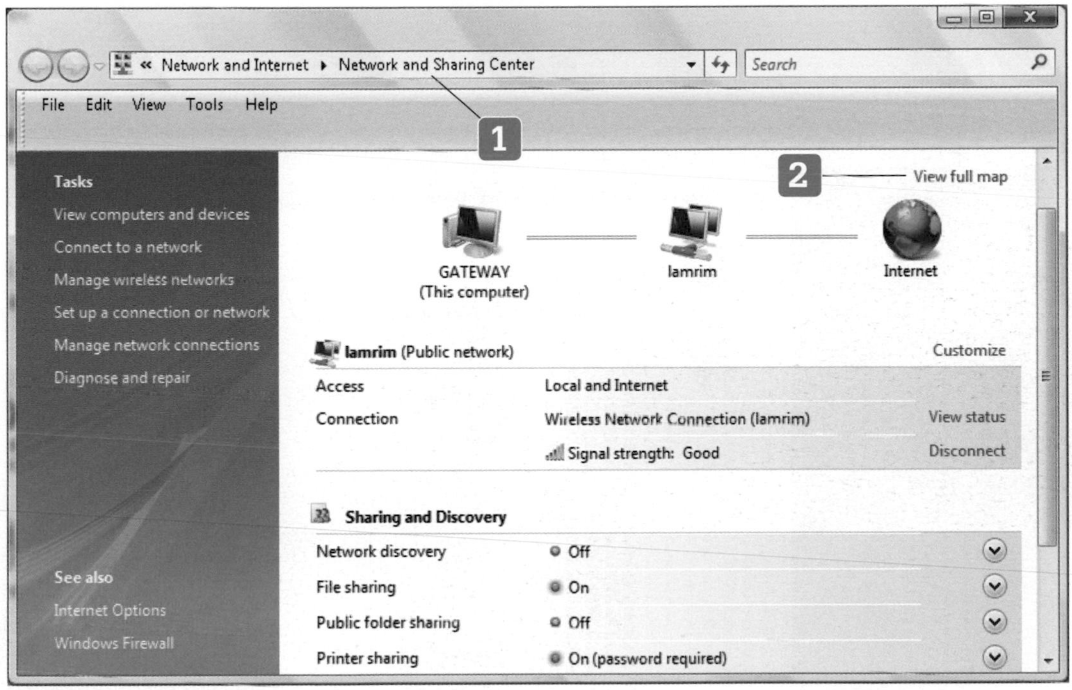

DID YOU KNOW?

In order to be able to view a full map of a network, it has to be a private network.

3 If you are also connected to the Internet, you'll be prompted to choose your network. Click the network you want.

4 Networked computers running the same version of Windows as yours will be displayed in the full network map. Other computers on the network will be shown beneath them.

Network map of
Wireless Network Connection - lamrim
Windows cannot cr
Wireless Network Connection - lamrim
Local Area Connection
3

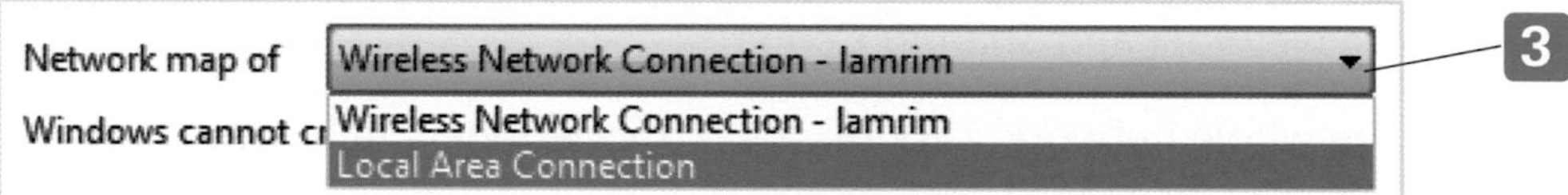

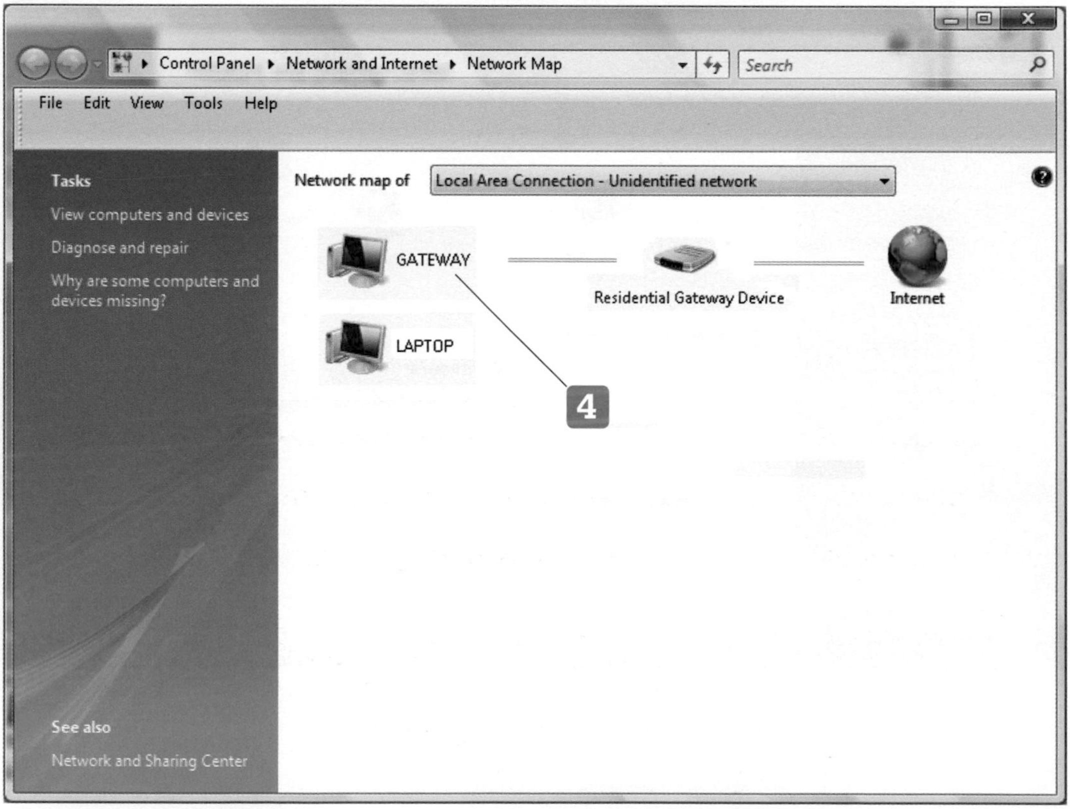

Control Panel ▸ Network and Internet ▸ Network Map
Search
File Edit View Tools Help
Tasks
View computers and devices
Diagnose and repair
Why are some computers and devices missing?
See also
Network and Sharing Center
Network map of
Local Area Connection - Unidentified network
GATEWAY
Residential Gateway Device
Internet
LAPTOP
4

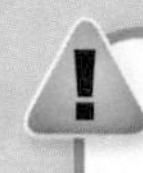

ALERT: If you connect computers while they are still on, they may not show up on the network map. You may need to restart them.

View networked computers

It seems like magic. From one computer to the other, you can look at anything from photos to documents – as long as the computer's owner has decided to share those resources with you. Here's how to view contents of a computer that can be shared over a network.

1 Open Network and Sharing Center.

2 Click View computers and devices.

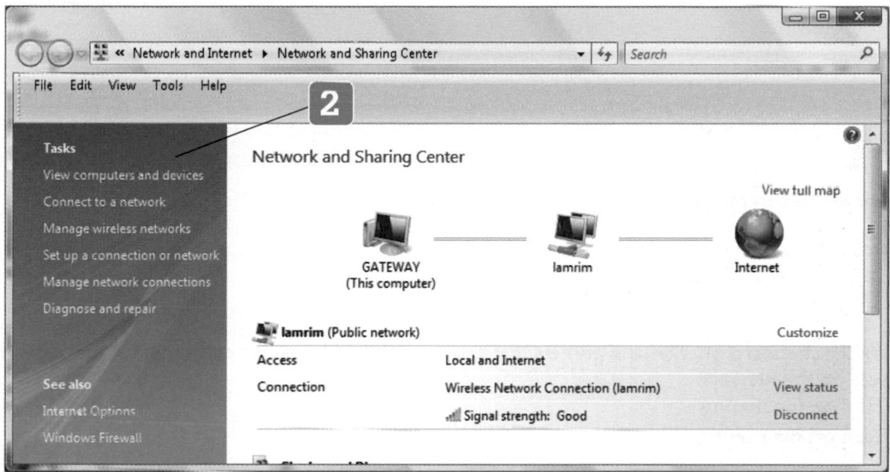

3 All computers and devices connected to the network are displayed.

4 Select the computer you want to use and double click it to view available items.

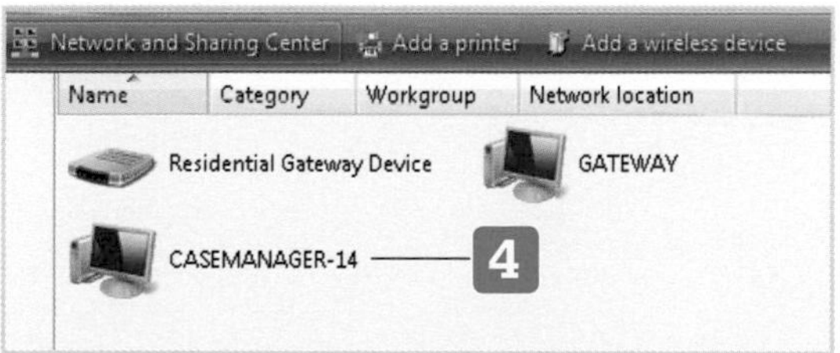

DID YOU KNOW?
In order to see resources such as folders or printers, you need to have file sharing activated. You also have to have a resource that you have designated as shared.

SEE ALSO: The next section, Activate file sharing, explains how to set up sharing on your laptop. Share a printer, and Share a folder, later in this chapter, tell how to share these resources.

Activate file sharing

To make your data accessible to others on your local network you need to turn on file sharing. Here's what to do when you're ready for prime time.

1. Open Network and Sharing Center.
2. Click the down arrow to the right of File sharing.
3. Click Turn on file sharing.
4. Click Apply.

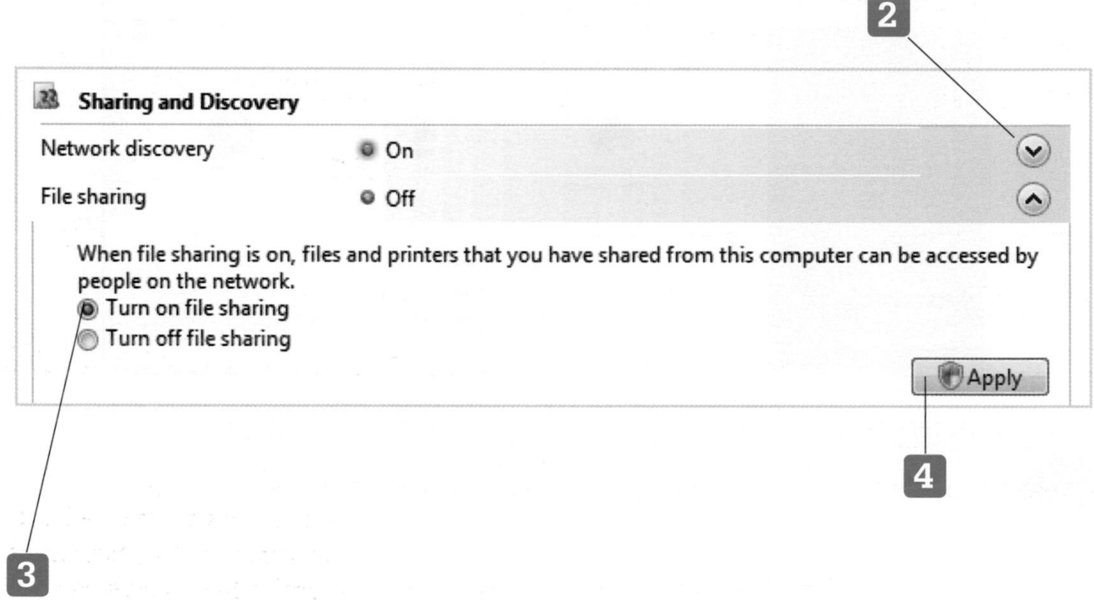

HOT TIP: Network discovery must be enabled for you to join a network.

DID YOU KNOW?

When you turn on file sharing, public folder sharing is also enabled in read-only mode.

Make your network private

In order to connect computers so they can access shared resources, you have to set up the network. One requirement is to make sure the network is private.

1. Click Customize next to the name of your local network – the network that has Local Area Connection listed in the middle column.
2. Click Private.
3. Name your local network if you wish.
4. Click Next.
5. When the User Account Control dialogue box appears, click Continue.
6. Click Close.

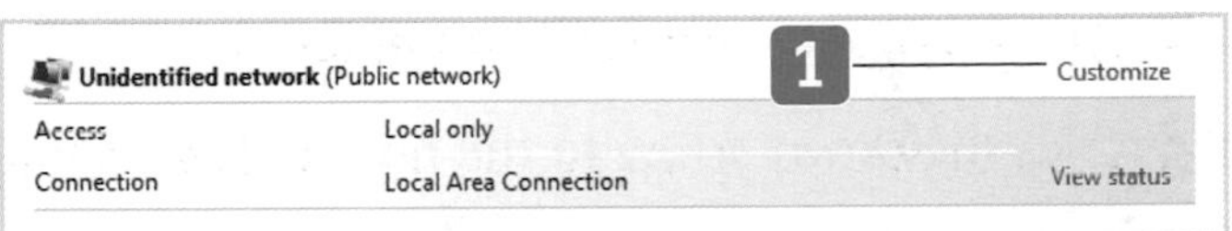

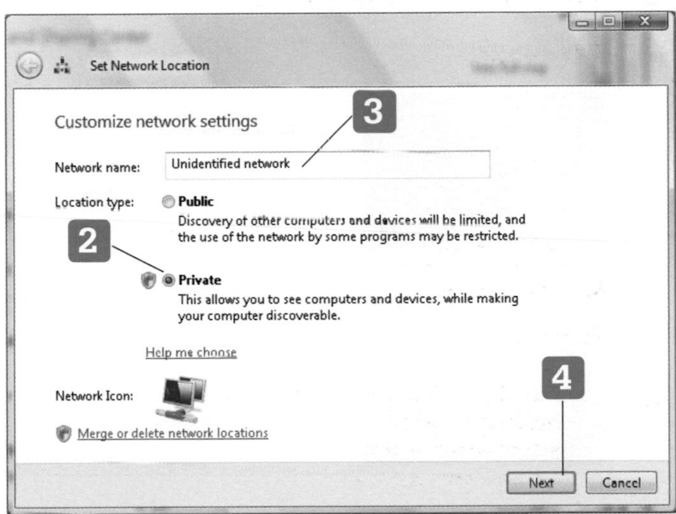

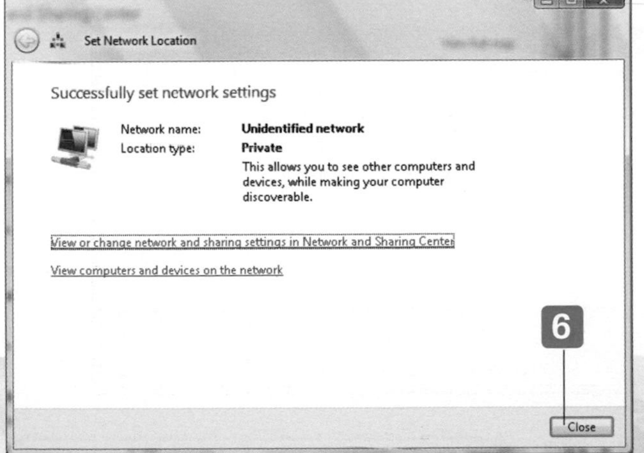

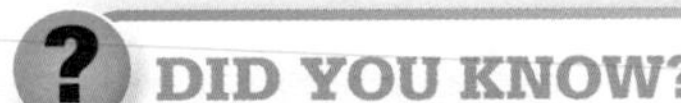

DID YOU KNOW?

You can designate your local network as public, but private is preferable because you gain more flexibility and additional security.

SEE ALSO: Make sure you have Network Discovery turned on, as described in Turn on Network Discovery, earlier in this chapter.

Share a printer

Just because you've shared a printer doesn't mean other PCs can obtain access to it. First you have to turn on printer sharing.

1. Open the Network and Sharing Center.
2. Click the down arrow to the right of Printer sharing. (It will become an up arrow.)
3. Click Turn on printer sharing.
4. Click Apply.

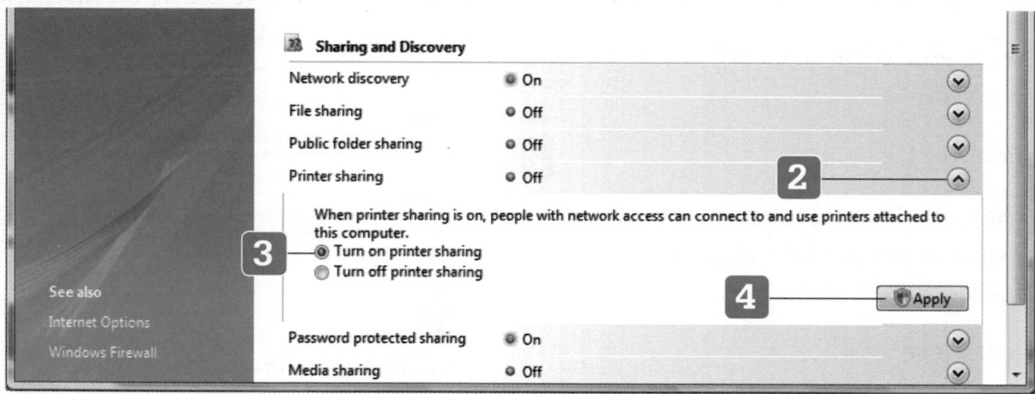

5. When someone else clicks on your computer, any printers you use will be available to them.

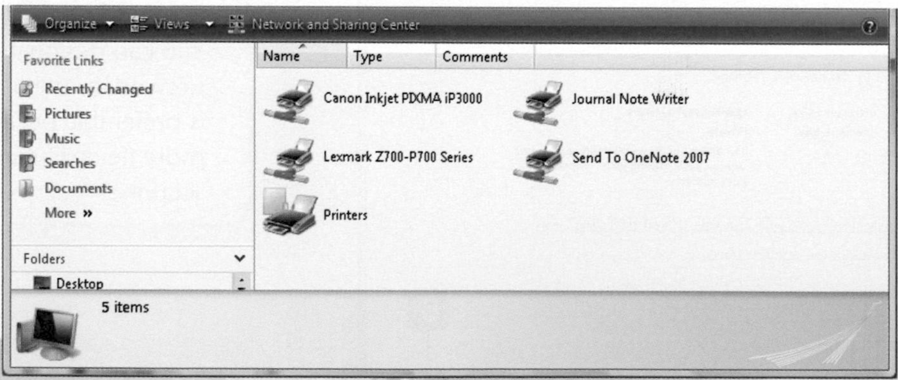

DID YOU KNOW?
If you click Start and then type Printers in the Start Search window, you can then open the Printers folder to manage shared printers.

ALERT: Printers must be turned on and either connected to a router or to a computer that is connected to a router in order to be shared on the network.

Set up password-protected sharing

Sharing is fine up to a point, but it's good to draw a line somewhere. When password-protected sharing is on, only people who have a user account and a password on your laptop can access shared files and printers. If you want all users to input a user name and password, here's how to enable this feature:

1. Open the Network and Sharing Center.
2. Click the down arrow by Password protected sharing. (It will become an up arrow.)
3. Click Turn on password protected sharing.
4. Click Apply.

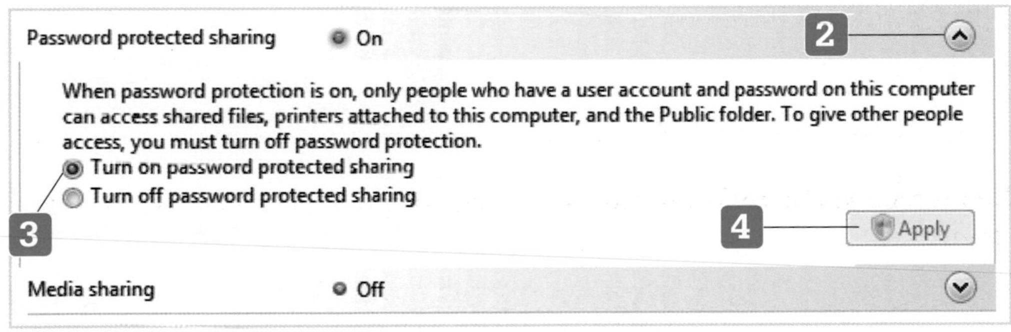

ALERT: Password-protected sharing does not have to be turned on to share files and folders. To view all your shared files, open the Network and Sharing Center and click View all of the files and folders I am sharing.

DID YOU KNOW?
Users who have a user name but not a password will not be able to access files until they apply a password to their account.

Share a folder

Sometimes it pays to be direct. Let's say you don't want to move or copy data into public folders and subfolders. Instead you want to share data directly from your own personal folders. Do the following to share the desired personal folders.

1. Locate the folder to share.
2. Right-click the folder.
3. Choose Share.
4. Click the down arrow and select any user (or Everyone) to share the folder with.
5. Click Add.
6. Click the arrow next to the new user name.
7. Select a sharing option.
8. Click Share.

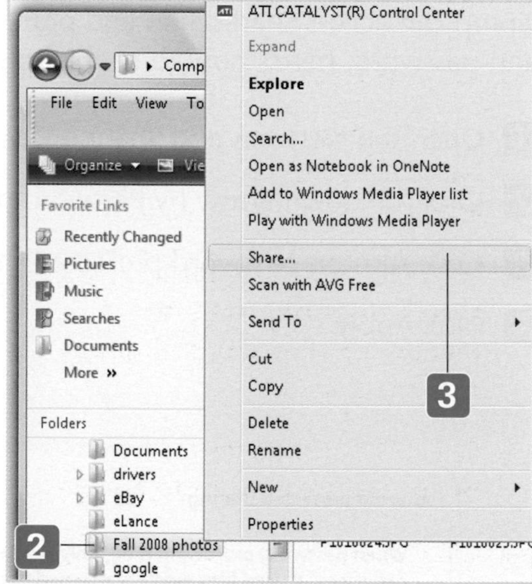

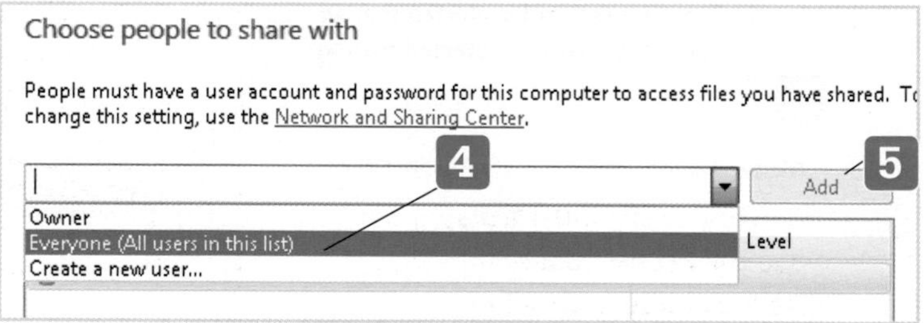

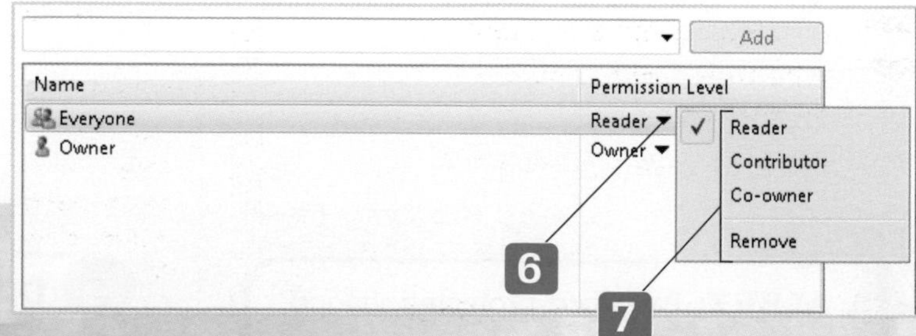

HOT TIP: You may want to share your own Pictures folder instead of copying or moving the files into the Public Pictures folder.

Set security permissions

You get to grant permission for users who truly need it. Limiting users keeps out others.

1. Select the drive, file or folder you want to modify and right-click it.
2. Choose Properties.
3. Select the Security tab in the Properties dialogue box.
4. Click the appropriate group name to see the permissions listed in the bottom section.
5. To edit permissions for a specific user or group, select them in the top section and click the Edit button.
6. Select the tick boxes for the permissions you want to enable.
7. Click close.

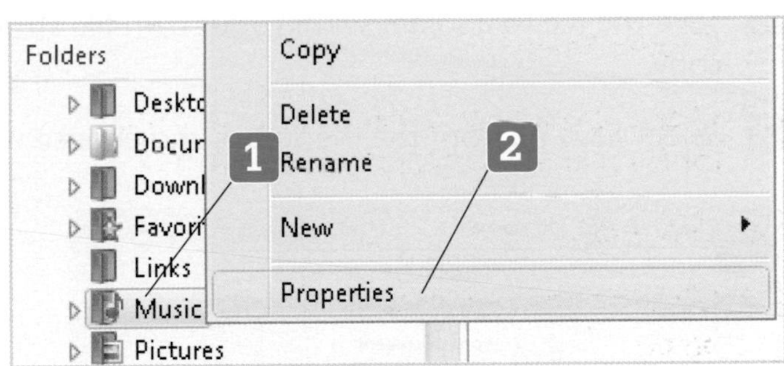

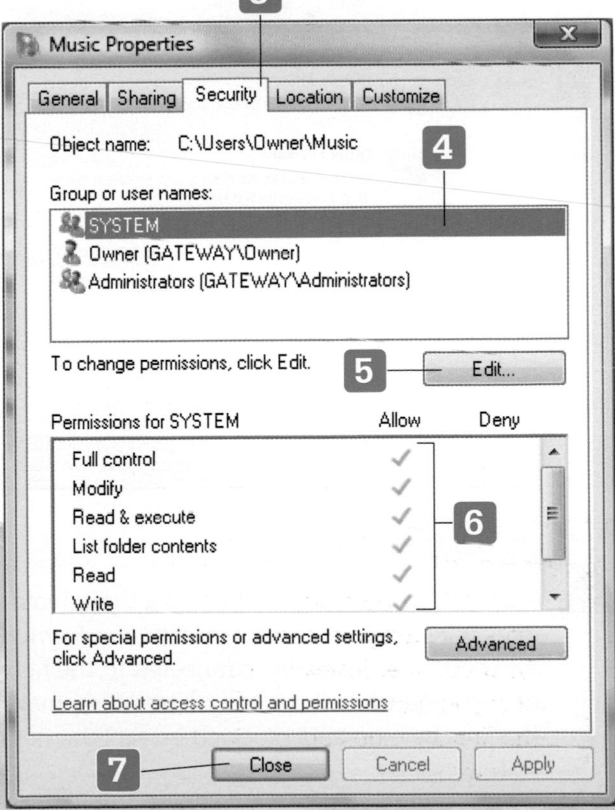

ALERT: Administrators have full access to all files and folders on a file system. Limit the number of administrators to those who truly need to access all resources.

HOT TIP: Write permissions allows other users to add information to a file; Modify allows them to change information in the file; Full control allows them to move or delete the file itself.

Save files in a shared folder

'Open to the Public' is a familiar welcoming sign, and your laptop can send the same message. There are two ways to save files so that other people on your network can access them. Either save them into the Public folder on your own laptop or save them into the Public folder of another computer on your network.

1. Create the file that you want to save onto the network.
2. Save the file to a folder within your own file structure so you'll always have a master copy.
3. Select Save As from the menu bar and choose where to save the file.

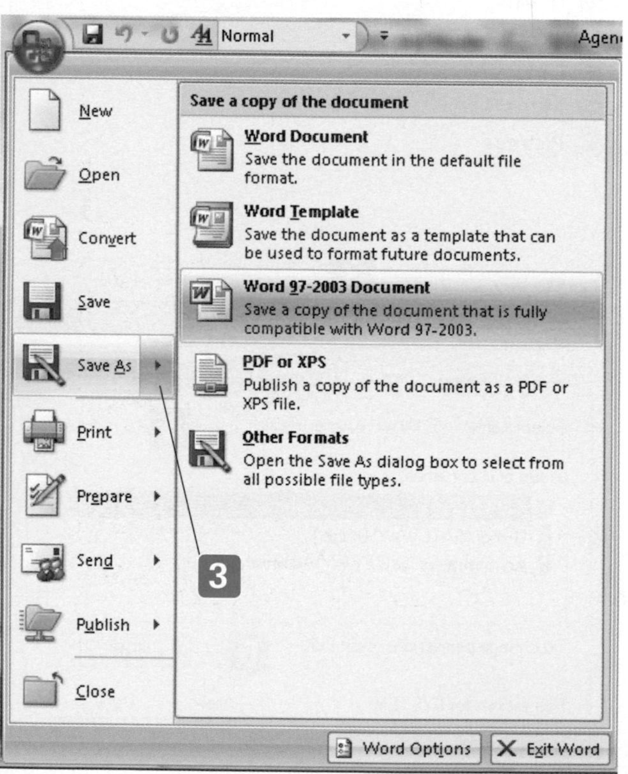

HOT TIP: Files can also be copied to Public folders on the network by dragging and dropping them from within your own file structure. To access this, click on the Start button and then click on the Computer button.

HOT TIP: You can also drag and drop files into shared folders.

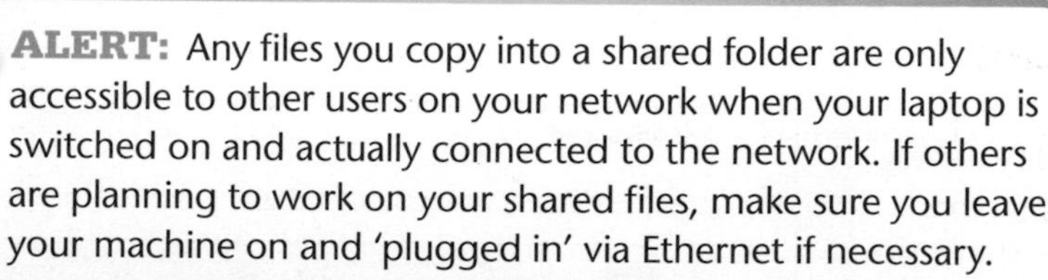

ALERT: Any files you copy into a shared folder are only accessible to other users on your network when your laptop is switched on and actually connected to the network. If others are planning to work on your shared files, make sure you leave your machine on and 'plugged in' via Ethernet if necessary.

4 Click on the Network icon in the left-hand pane.

5 Click the Computer on the network where you want to save the files.

6 Locate the Public folder (or other shared folder) where you want to save the files.

7 Rename the file if necessary.

8 Click Save.

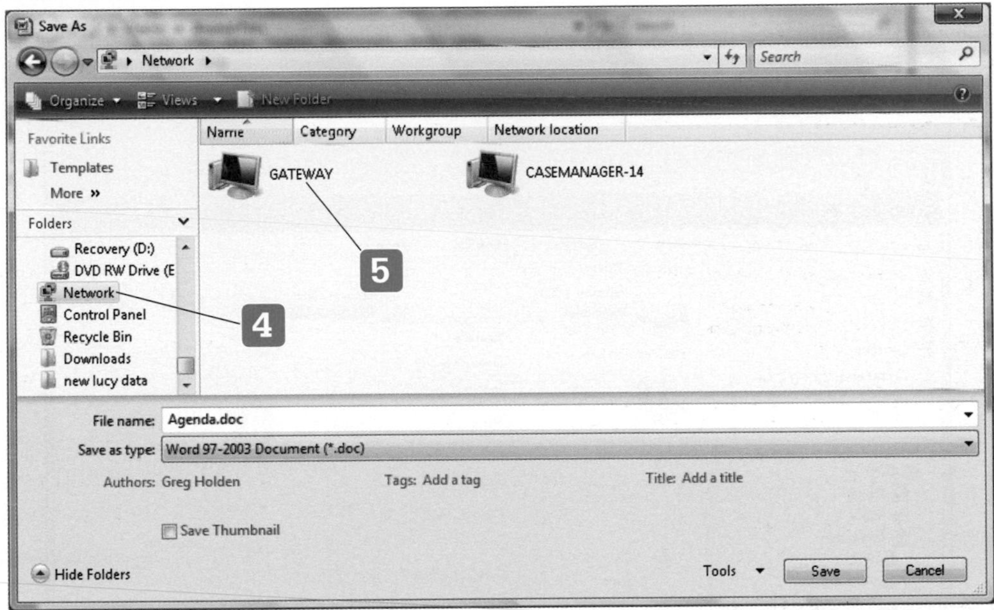

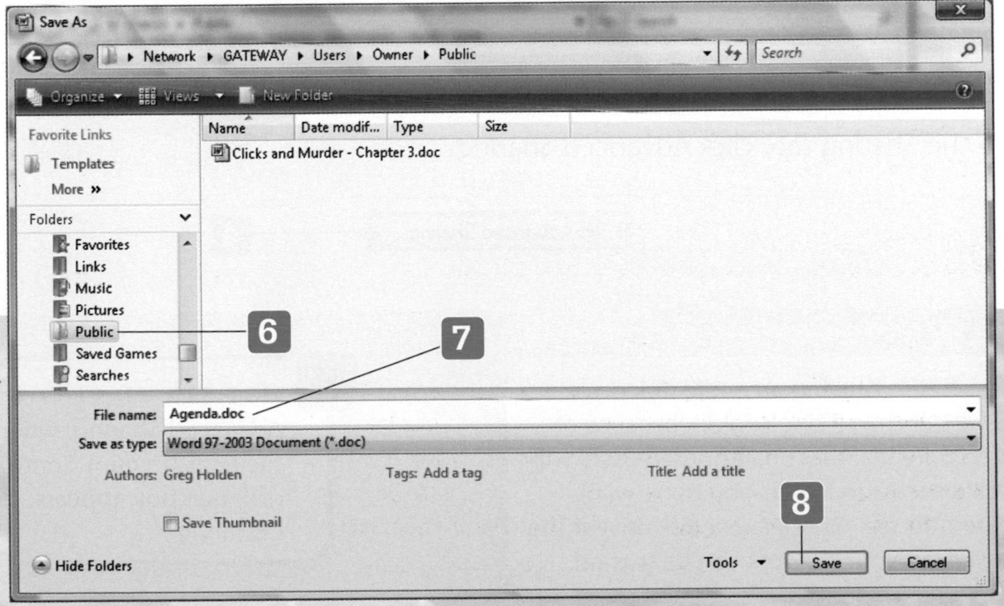

Share a disk drive

If you have nothing to hide and trust the other users on your network, you can make everything on your drive accessible to someone else. Just make sure you specify who should be able to access the share and the level of permissions you want each person to have.

1 Click Start.

2 Click Computer.

2 Computer

3 Right-click the drive you want to share and choose Share.

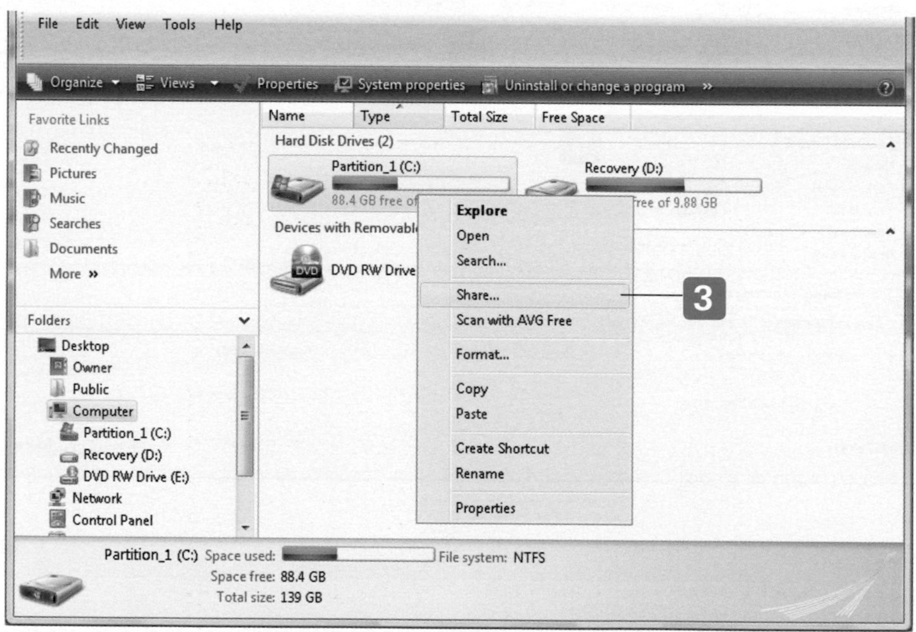

4 On the Sharing tab, click Advanced Sharing.

ALERT: Sharing an entire disk drive is riskier than a single folder because of the potential that unauthorised users will gain access to folders you don't want them to see. Only share a disk drive if the users on your network can be trusted.

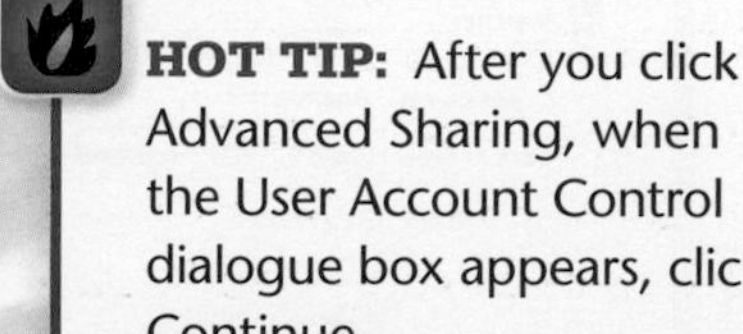

HOT TIP: After you click Advanced Sharing, when the User Account Control dialogue box appears, click Continue.

5 Select the Share this folder tick box.

6 Click the Permissions button.

7 Tick the boxes next to the permissions you want to grant.

8 Click OK.

9 Click OK.

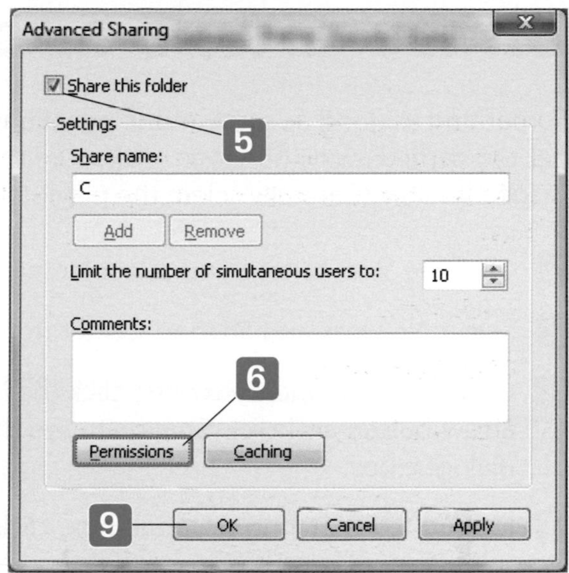

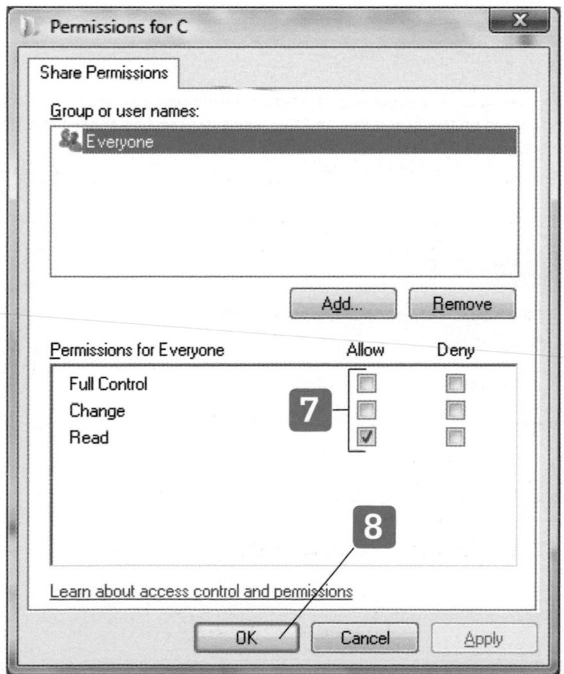

WHAT DOES THIS MEAN?

Full Control: users can create, delete or modify files in any way.

Change: users cannot create or delete files. However, they can edit files.

Read: users can only read files and not make any other changes.

Share music and other media

Something as good as some music selections are just too good to keep to yourself. Don't get too carried away, however. Make sure that only the media you want to share are made available. Carefully select the playlists and ratings you want to share as follows:

1. Click the Start button and select Network.
2. Select Network and Sharing Center from the top menu bar.
3. Under Sharing and Discovery, click the Media sharing arrow button and click Change to see the Media Sharing dialogue box.
4. In the Media Sharing dialogue box, click Share my media.
5. Click OK to share media.

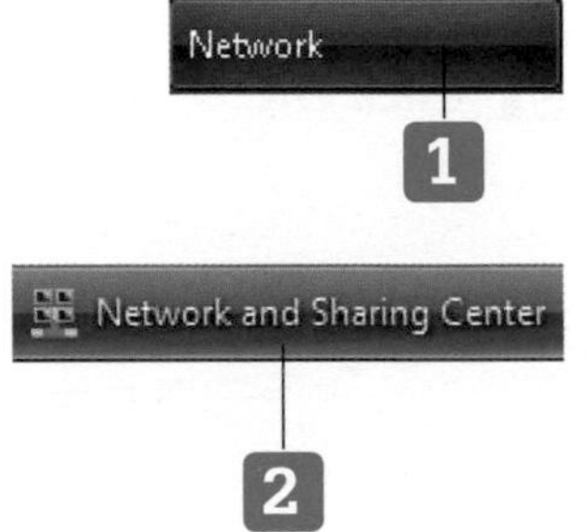

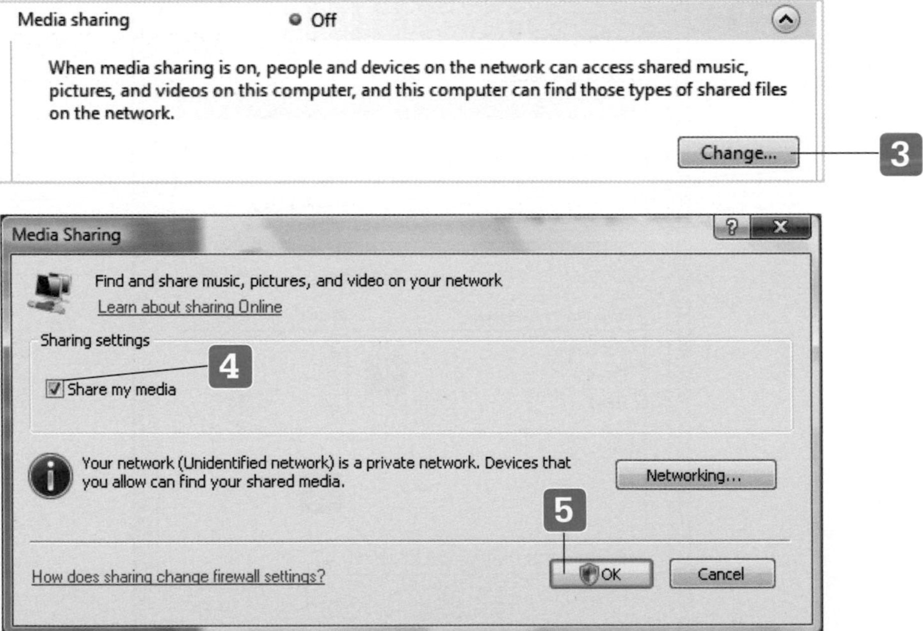

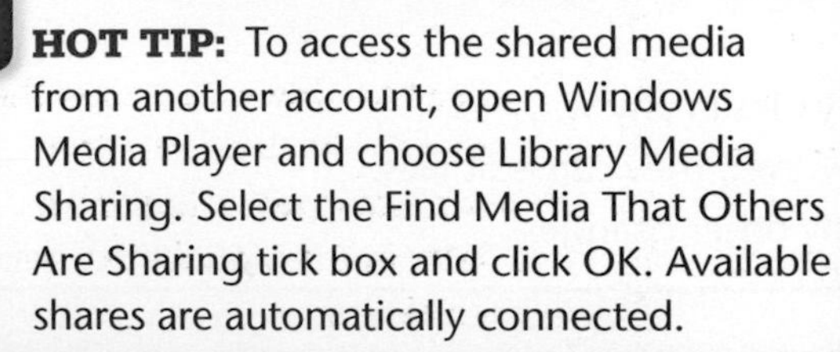

HOT TIP: To access the shared media from another account, open Windows Media Player and choose Library Media Sharing. Select the Find Media That Others Are Sharing tick box and click OK. Available shares are automatically connected.

ALERT: If your network is not private, you won't be able to share media. You'll be prompted to click Networking and change the network to private in the Media Sharing dialogue box.

Connect to a remote server

Before you start this process, make sure that the owner of the drive provides you with the drive letter and location, as well as any web server addresses. If you created the shared drive yourself, you should have received all the necessary information as you completed the process. So here's what you do next.

1 Click the Start button and select Computer.

2 Click the Map network drive button at the top of the menu bar.

3 Enter the drive letter and location of the drive in the Map network drive dialogue box.

4 Click the Finish button. You can access the drive, which should be displayed automatically, by using the Computer icon.

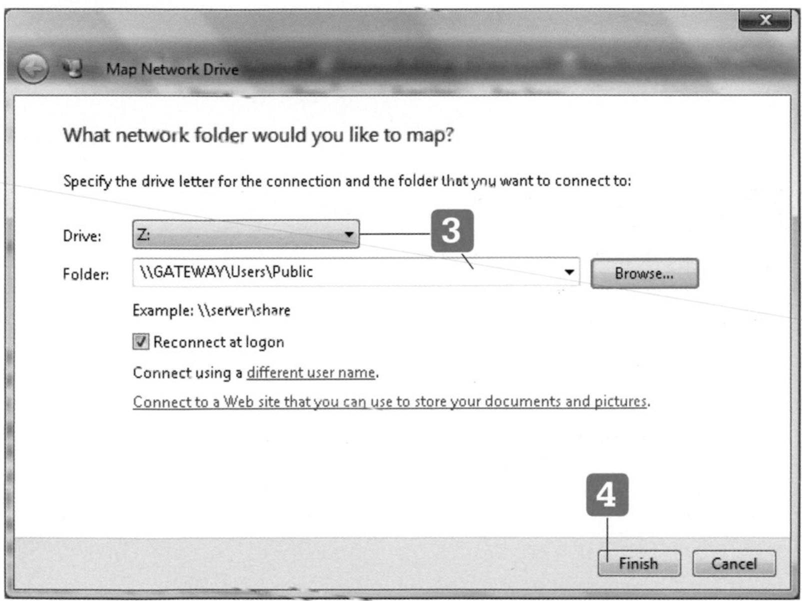

HOT TIP: If the driver requires a higher level of permissions than your current logon identity allows, click the Different User Name link and then enter the appropriate user name and password. You can make the connection permanent by selecting the Reconnect at Logon tick box.

DID YOU KNOW?
No two drives can have the same drive letter. Assign remote drive letters from later in the alphabet to avoid confusion.

10 Managing files and disk drives

Introduction

Sometimes the table next to my front door has archeological layering. That's where stacks of mail collect, waiting for me to dig and delve lest an important letter be lost or a bill become past due. So too the contents of your laptop need some sorting and organising from time to time. In this chapter you'll learn how to figure out what you've got and how to make the most of it.

Explore drive or folder contents with Windows Explorer

Before we get into what to do with your files and folders, you simply need to determine what's there in the first place. Here's how to get started by exploring the contents of your drive or folder with Windows Explorer.

1. Click Start.
2. Type windows explorer and press Enter, or click Windows Explorer in the Start menu.
3. Click the folder you want to explore.
4. If needed, click the arrow to expand a folder.
5. Double-click the folder or files you want to explore.

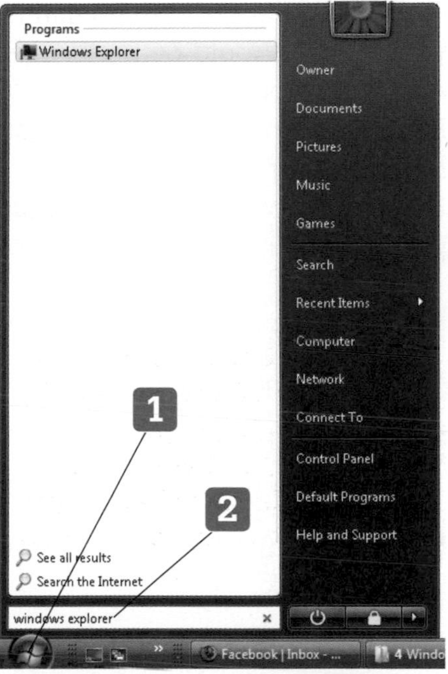

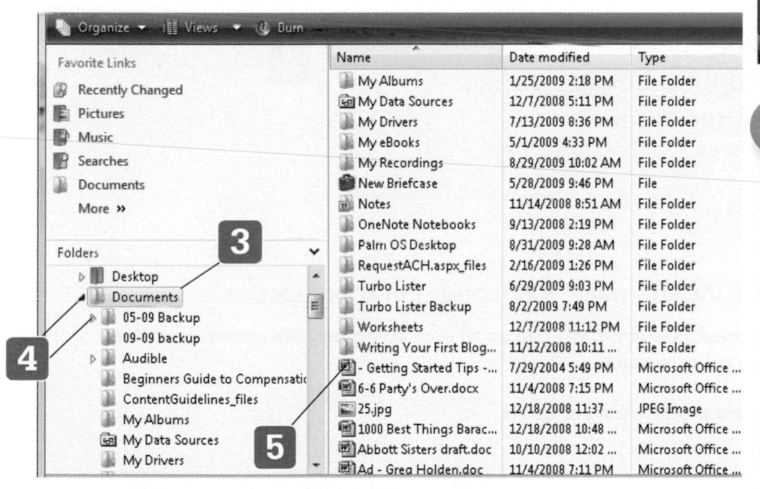

DID YOU KNOW?
Windows Explorer and My Computer (which you access by clicking Start and choosing Computer) look virtually identical. The difference is that Explorer starts by opening your Documents folder, while My Computer starts at the disk drive level.

ALERT: Don't experiment too boldly with the contents of the Windows and Programs folders. They contain files that are essential to the functioning of your laptop. If you don't know what something contains, you might want to leave well enough alone.

DID YOU KNOW?
You can have more than one Explorer window open at a time. Doing so can be useful for comparing the contents of different folders or drives and assisting in transferring files back and forth.

Work with User Account Control

Too much of a good thing can be bad. If you already have antivirus software running, your laptop should be pretty safe from infection from unauthorised programs. That's also the purpose of a feature in Windows called the User Account Control. The problem is that a warning window appears all the time to indicate when a variety of actions is being performed, such as certain programs being run. You might find yourself okaying the window without thinking, just to be rid of it. If this becomes too annoying, it is possible to disable the User Account Control.

1. Click Start.
2. Click Control Panel.
3. Click on the User Accounts and Family Safety link and then the User Accounts link.
4. Click on the Turn User Account Control on or off link.
5. By default, the Use User Account Control (UAC) to help protect your computer box is ticked. Untick it to disable the User Account Control.
6. Click OK.

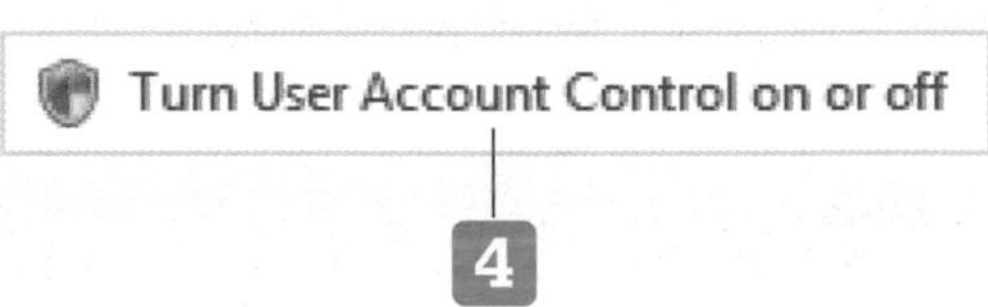

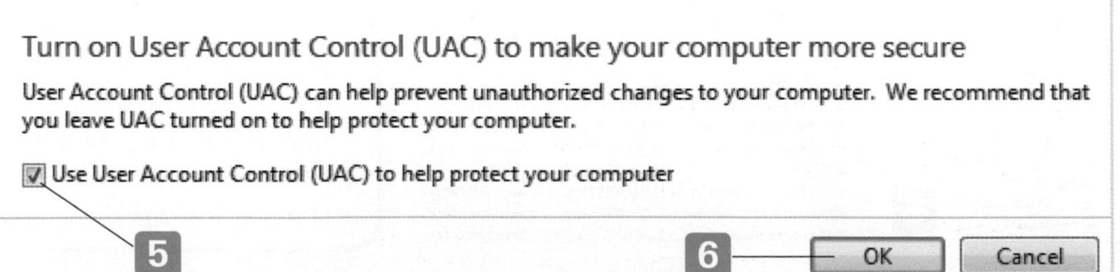

ALERT: After clicking OK, you'll have to restart your computer for the changes to take effect.

DID YOU KNOW?
The User Account Control can also be accessed from within the Other Security Settings section of the Security Center.

Use a default folder

You can store any kind of files in any folder. But most programs save files to the appropriate folder by default, such as Downloads and Documents. Internet bookmarks go into the Favorites folder. Folders such as Music, Pictures and Videos are intended for media files. Items and files on your desktop are shown in the Desktop folder. Here's how to find them.

1. Click Start.
2. Click your user name at the top of the right column of the Start menu.
3. Click your name to display the list of default folders.
4. Navigate the folders as desired.

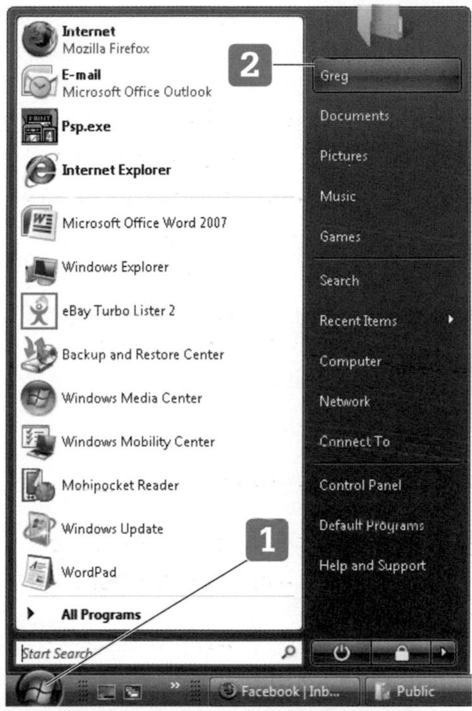

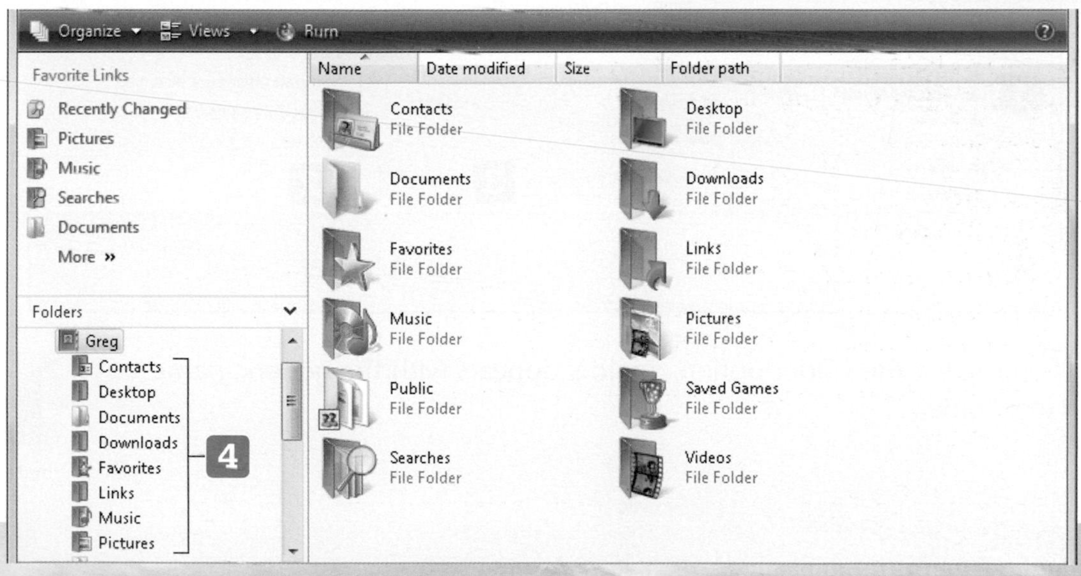

HOT TIP: Creating additional folders inside the Documents folder organises your files. Make a Text folder for text documents and a Budget folder for tax and other finance information.

DID YOU KNOW?

Although this section is all about default, it's always possible to change behaviour through the program if you want something done differently.

Create a new file or folder

It's like shoes: no matter how many pairs you have, you're always on the lookout for new fashion. When it comes to files and folders, making new ones is somewhat intuitive. But just for the record, here's how to get started from the beginning.

1. Navigate to the location where you want to create the new file or folder.
2. Right-click in a blank area of the window to open the menu.
3. Choose New to list the choices.
4. Click the item to open or create it.

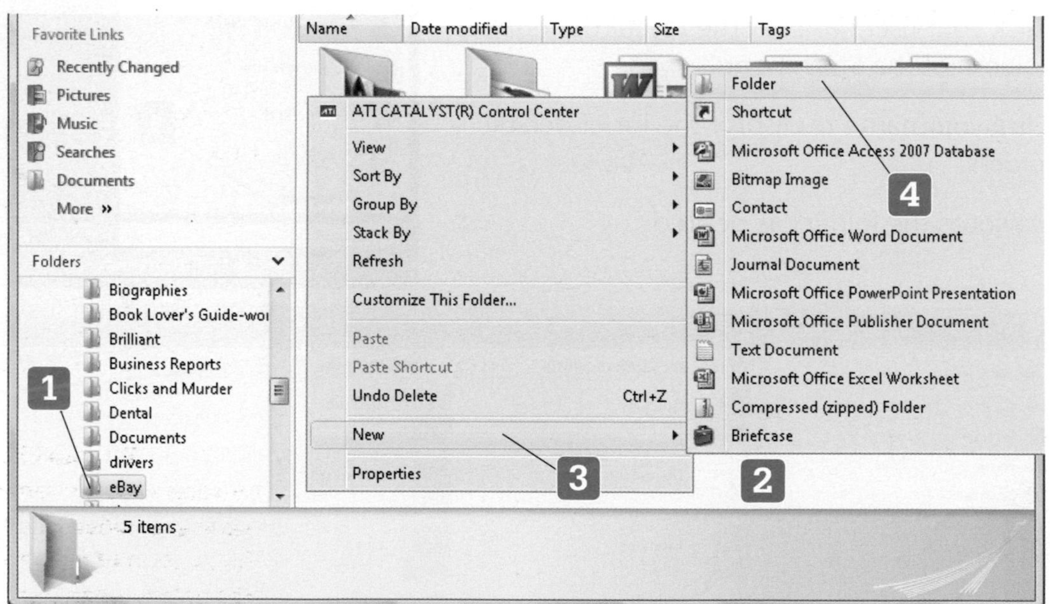

5. If you select the Folder option, a folder appears with the generic name New Folder.

ALERT: If you choose a particular type of document, the application needed to create it launches if it isn't open already.

HOT TIP: Give a little thought to names. Shorter filenames are easier to manage, but at the same time it's good to have names that are as descriptive as possible. You should also stick with only letters and numbers because some special characters cause problems when transferring files from one system to another.

Rename a file or folder

You can always just click the icon of a file or folder, click the name and type the new name. But here's the official way to change a name.

1. Navigate to the location of the file or folder you want to change.
2. Right-click the item.
3. Choose Rename from the pop-up menu.
4. Type the new name.
5. Press Enter.

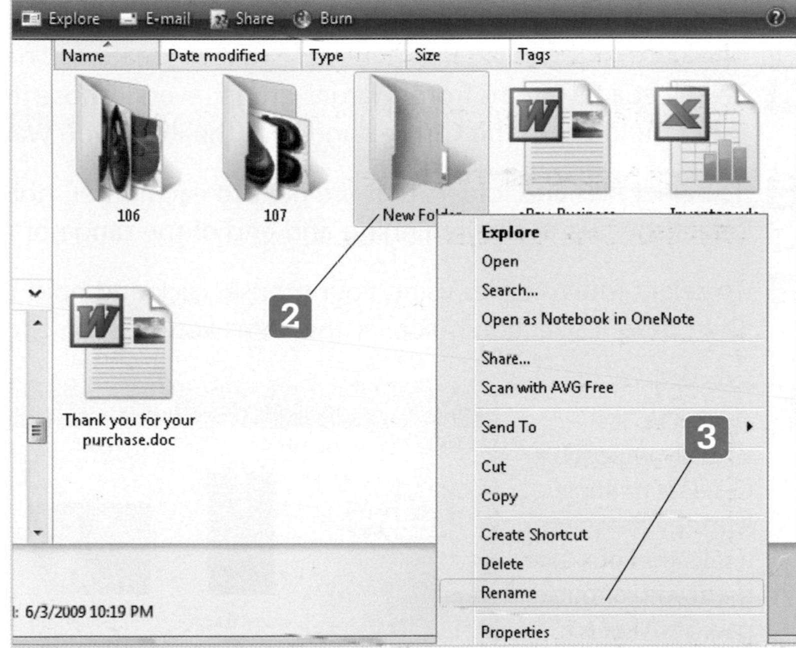

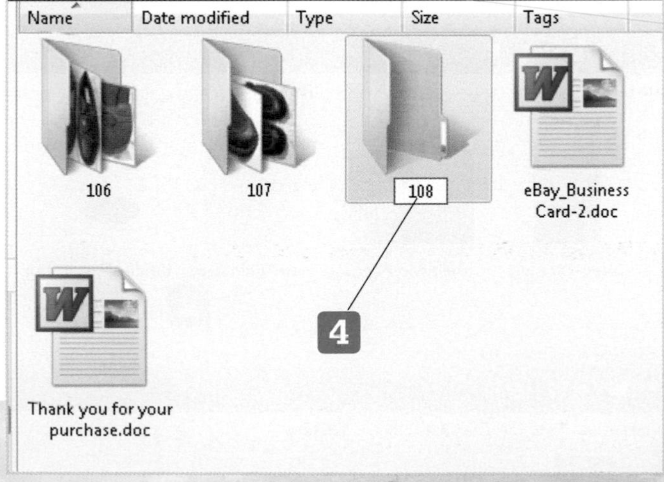

ALERT: You can't have two files with the same name in a folder. Change the location of one of the files before renaming it.

HOT TIP: You can also rename a file by single-clicking its name and waiting a second or two. When the name appears highlighted, you can type the new name to replace the old one.

Select multiple files or folders

You know how to select a single file or folder: you simply click it. You might also know how to select multiple items that are next to one another in a folder or on a disk. But there are some nuances to selecting multiple items on your laptop that will help you save time when you have to perform a function.

1. To select a few items from a larger group, even if those items are not next to each other, hold down the Ctrl key and click the items you want to choose.
2. To select files and folders that are next to each other, hold down the Shift key and select the files at the beginning and end of the range of items you want.
3. To select multiple files using your mouse, click and hold the mouse in a window and then drag a selection box over the items you want to choose.

ALERT: It's virtually impossible to select multiple items by dragging a selection box over them with a touch pad. You'll need to Shift+click or Ctrl+click for that.

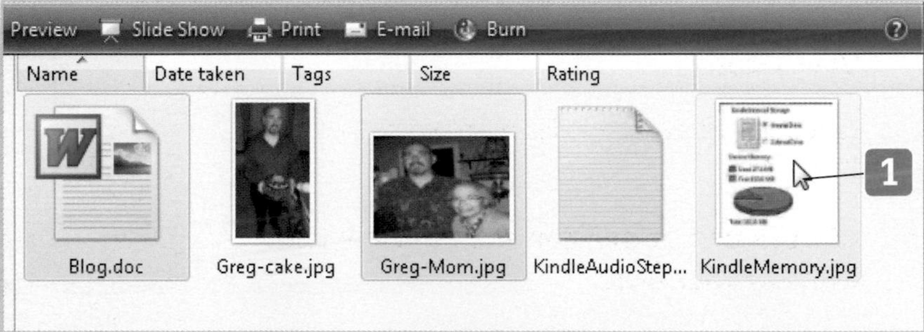

Change your view of files or folders

Choices, choices, choices. When you want a new view of how you see data on your laptop, here are your choices: list (shows you just the names of the files and folders); details (shows you names and other information about your files and folders such as file size and date and time stamps); and tiles (shows an organised display of your icons).

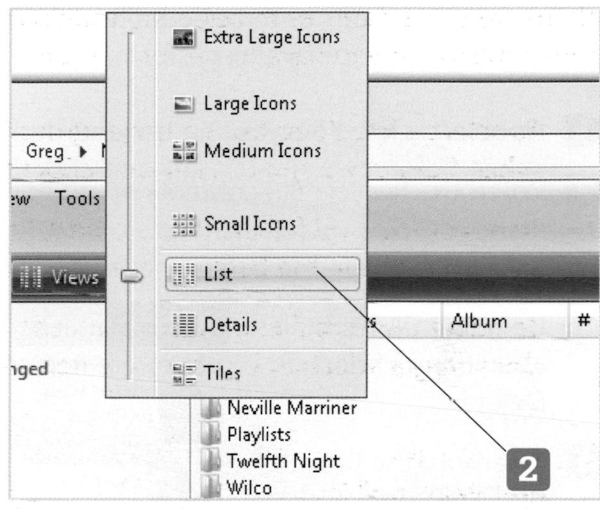

1. At the top of the Explorer window, click the down arrow next to the Views icon.
2. Choose List to see a list of all your files.
3. Choose one of the icon sizes to view visual icons of your files.
4. Choose Details to view creation date, file size and other information.

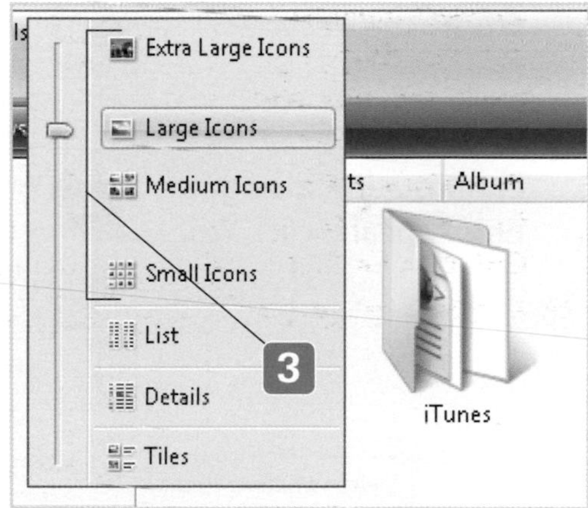

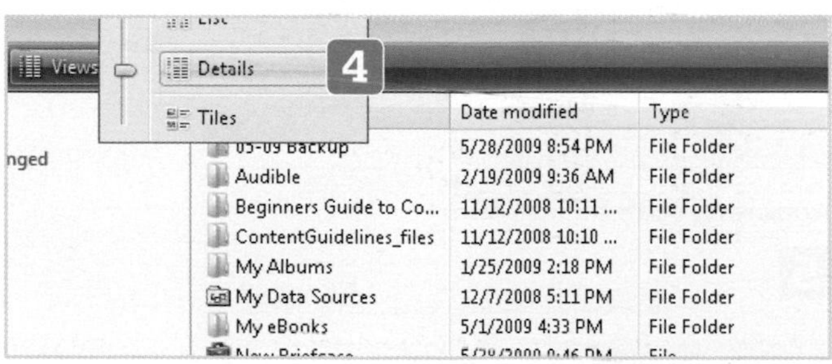

HOT TIP: Click the View button repeatedly to cycle through all four view choices.

DID YOU KNOW?

You can set different views for different locations, depending on your needs.

Clean out your Recycle Bin

When you click a file or folder and choose Delete, it goes away. But not for ever: it sits in your Recycle Bin until, like the rubbish collectors who move up and down your street, you take steps to throw the files out permanently. You can save a substantial amount of disk space by doing so.

1. Double-click the Recycle Bin on your desktop.
2. When the Recycle Bin contents open, scan them to make sure there aren't any files you really need.
3. To delete a single file permanently, right-click it and choose Delete.
4. To empty the Recycle Bin all at once, click Empty the Recycle Bin.
5. When the confirmation dialogue box appears, click Yes.

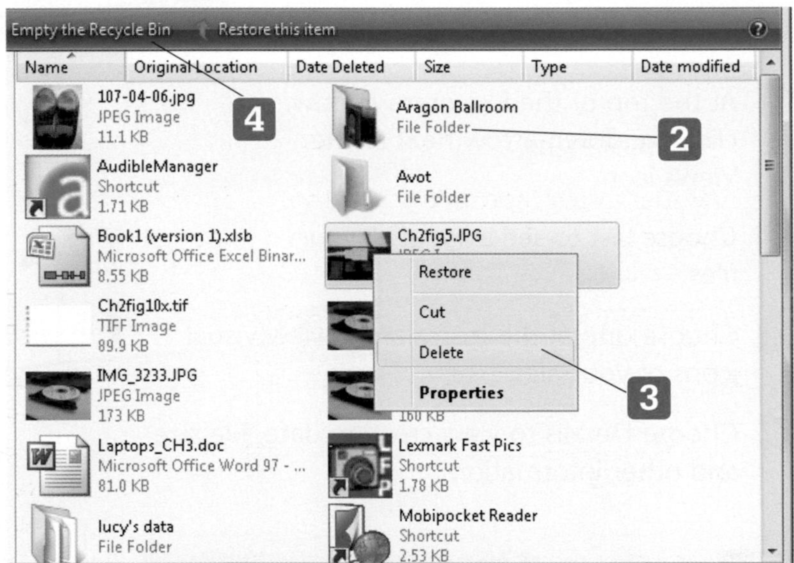

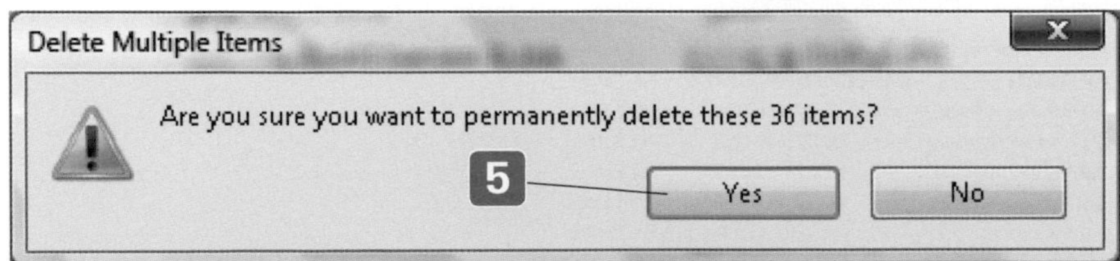

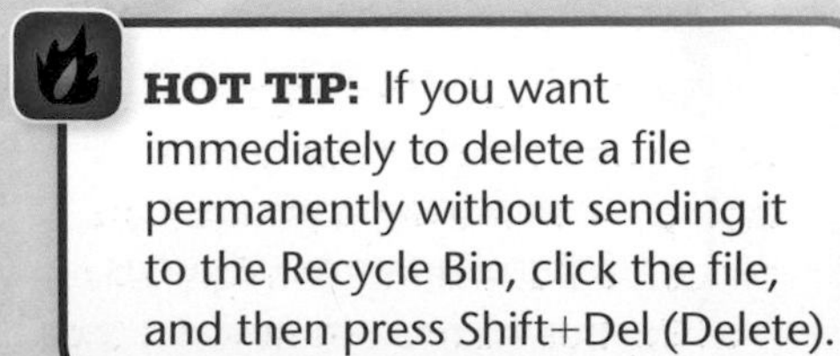

HOT TIP: If you want immediately to delete a file permanently without sending it to the Recycle Bin, click the file, and then press Shift+Del (Delete).

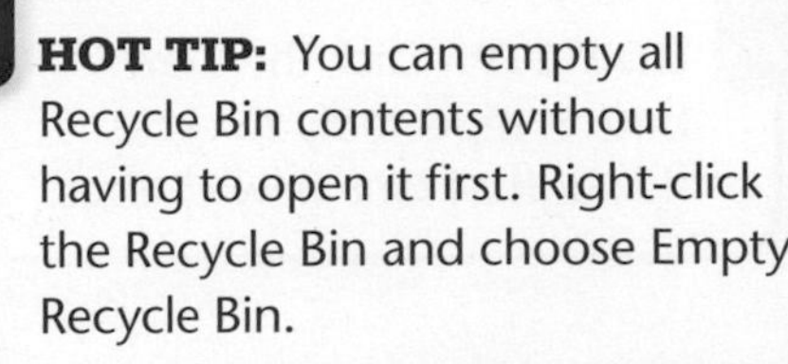

HOT TIP: You can empty all Recycle Bin contents without having to open it first. Right-click the Recycle Bin and choose Empty Recycle Bin.

Defragment your hard disk

When you defragment, you move chunks of data closer together on the hard drive. That makes file retrieval quicker and easier, and it also keeps your system running smoothly.

1. Click Start.
2. Click Computer.
3. Right-click the hard drive you want to defragment.
4. Click Properties.
5. Click the Tools tab.
6. Click the Defragment Now button.
7. Wait until your laptop tells you the process is complete.

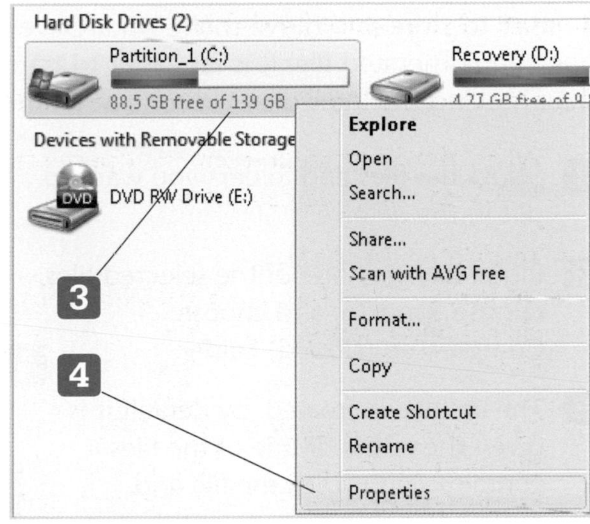

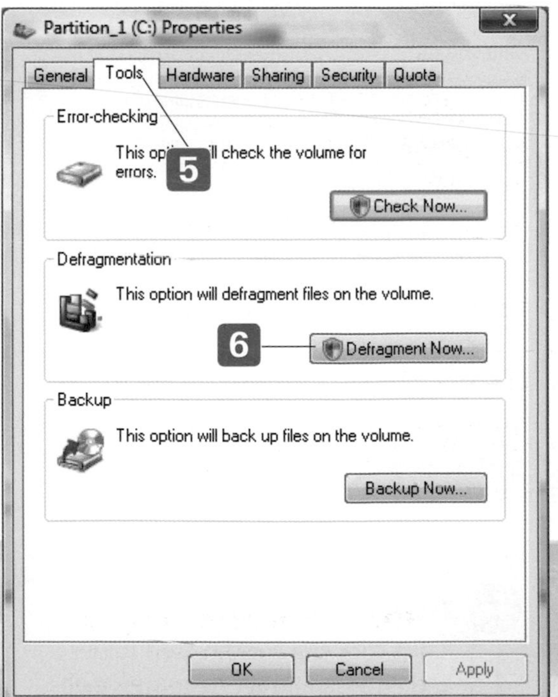

DID YOU KNOW?

It's possible to set up a regularly scheduled defragmentation, but if your laptop isn't on when it kicks in it won't work well. It's better to do it manually at least once a week.

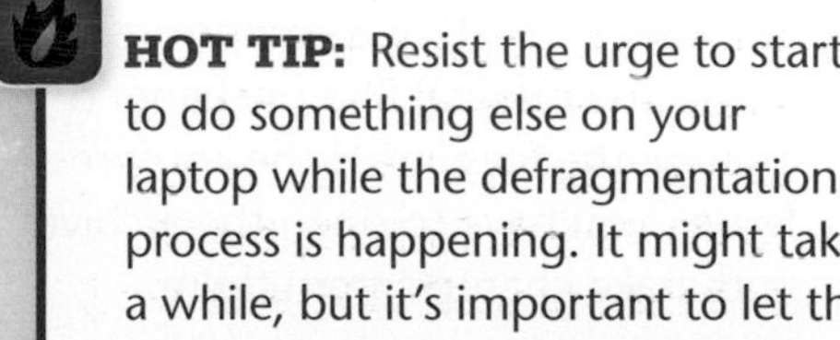

HOT TIP: Resist the urge to start to do something else on your laptop while the defragmentation process is happening. It might take a while, but it's important to let the process run completely on its own.

Create an archive from multiple files or folders

When you have a collection of large files or folders, you can create an archive to make it easier to store and move them. An archive compresses their size and places them in one conglomerated file. It is far easier to transfer or email the single archive file rather than moving the individual files one at a time.

1. Select the files and folders you want to put in the archive.
2. Right-click any one of the selected files, choose Send To, and choose Compressed (zipped) Folder.
3. The archive is created; by default it is given the name of one of the files it contains. Right-click the file and choose Rename, then type the name of the new compressed folder.

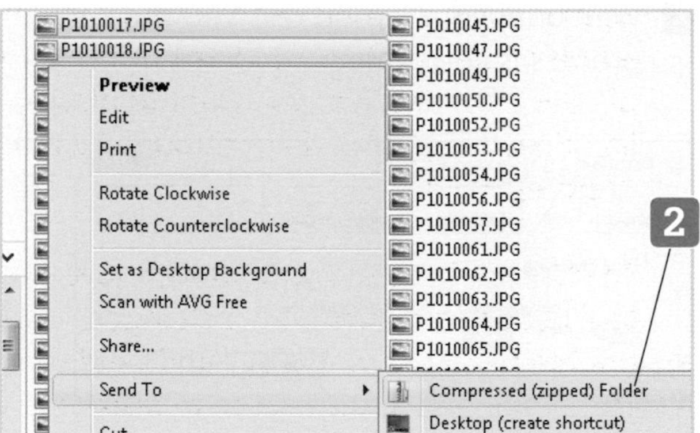

HOT TIP: After you create a compressed folder, you can drag other files to it and double-click on it. That will open it and access its contents.

ALERT: Creating a compressed folder leaves the original files unchanged. To change the files inside the compressed folder, you have to open the archive and make changes from there.

DID YOU KNOW?

Right-click the compressed folder and choose Extract All to move all items from outside the archive. Then the files will appear in the same location as the compressed folder.

Resize an open window

Comparing and contrasting is something you learn how to do when you're researching and writing. So I find it very convenient at times to keep more than one window open on my desktop to refer back and forth from document to document. But then you need to know how to navigate through the open windows, moving one out of your way so you can see another or looking at something in a minimised window.

1. To minimise an open window and remove it from the desktop, click the underscore in the upper right corner of your screen.

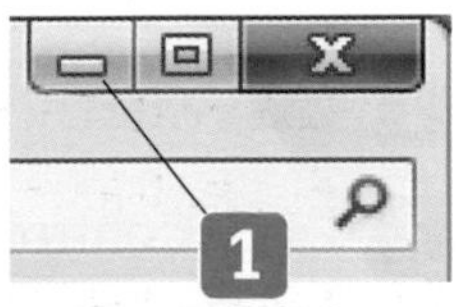

2. When you want to display the window again, click its icon on the taskbar.

3. To maximise an open window and make it fill the entire screen, click the middle button in the upper right corner of your screen. When you want to display the window again in its original size, click that button (which has changed to Restore) again.

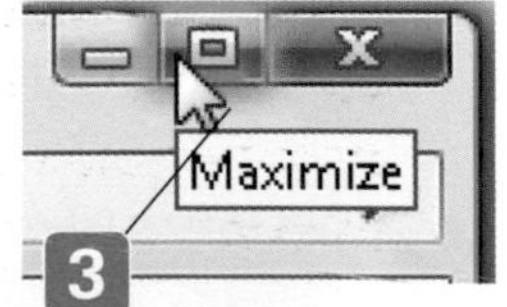

4. To change the size of a window, move the cursor to its edge or corner until it changes to display a double-headed arrow. Click and hold the edge or corner and move the mouse to resize the window, releasing the mouse when the window is the size you want.

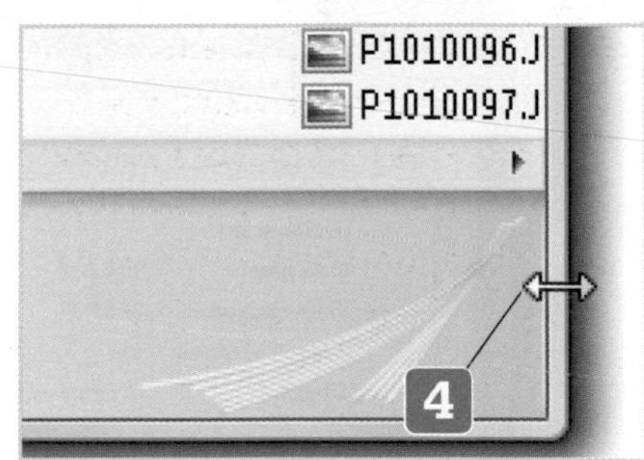

5. Click the X in the upper right corner of your screen to close the window.

ALERT: Don't get so carried away with having multiple windows open on your desktop that you use up too much space and computer resources. Pause from time to time to clean up the clutter.

Clean out viruses with Windows Defender

Most of the time you can rest easy knowing that Windows Defender, which is enabled by default and runs in the background, is protecting your laptop from online threats such as hackers. But you can run a manual scan if you suspect that your laptop has been attacked by malware (a virus, worm or spyware).

1. Click Start.
2. Click Control Panel.
3. Click Security.
4. Click Windows Defender.
5. Click Scan.
6. When the scan is done, click the X in the top right corner to close the Windows Defender window.

4

Windows Defender
Scan for spyware and other potentially unwanted software

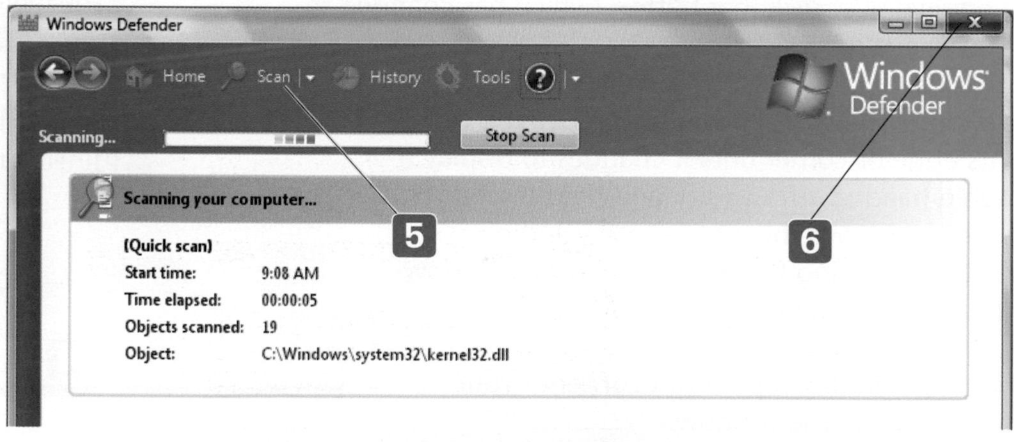

HOT TIP: Click the down arrow next to Scan to scan your entire computer. When you click Scan, you initiate a 'Quick Scan' that does not include all of your resources.

HOT TIP: Click Full Scan if you think the entire contents of your laptop have been infected, but don't click the arrow next to Scan.

Adjust the way AutoPlay works

If you like to mix it up, you can respond to the AutoPlay dialogue box each time you insert a blank CD, a DVD movie or a music CD. But if you want your laptop to do the same thing each time, you can bypass the prompt and get right to your entertainment of choice by performing some simple customisation.

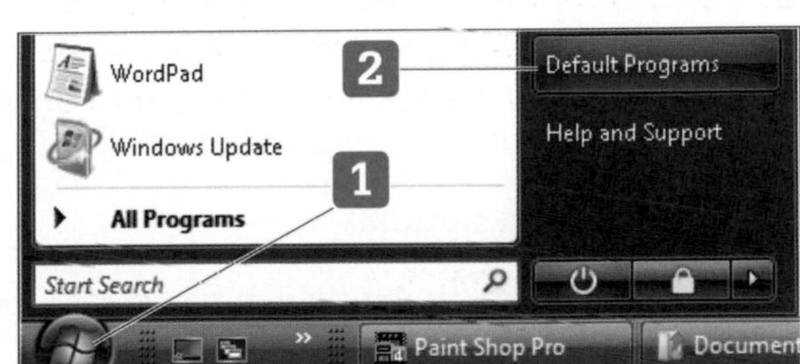

1. Click Start.
2. On the Start menu, click Default Programs.
3. Click Change AutoPlay settings.
4. Use the drop-down lists to select the program to use for the media you want to play.
5. Click Save.

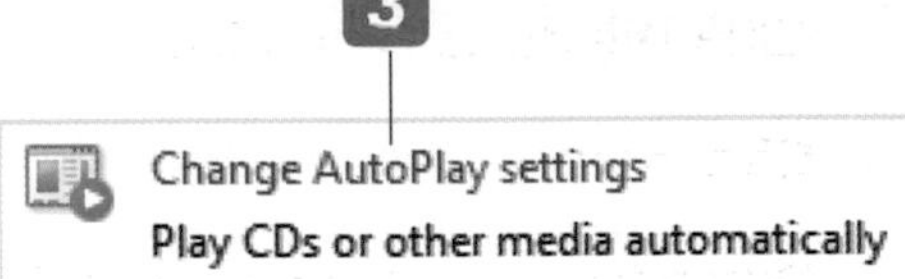

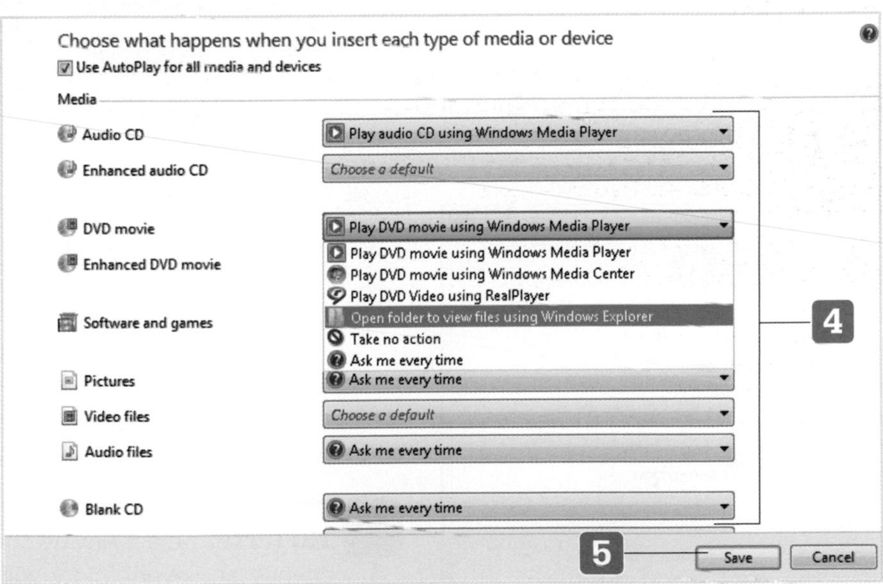

DID YOU KNOW?
For audio CDs, choose Rip music from CD using Windows Media Player. For DVD movies, choose Play DVD movie using Windows Media Center if you're running Home Premium or Ultimate.

HOT TIP: You can change AutoPlay settings to configure what programs should be used to open what types of media.

Change folder options

Some families communicate in public by using a special whistle or hand signal. You can develop your own secret language with your folders by configuring Folder Options. Instead of double-clicking, for example, you can single-click to open a folder, choose to open each folder in its own window, or view hidden files and folders.

1. Click the Start button.
2. In the Start Search window, type Folder Options.
3. Under Programs in the results list, click Folder Options.
4. From the General tab, read the options and make changes as desired.
5. From the View tab, read the options and make changes as desired.
6. From the Search tab, read the options and make changes as desired.

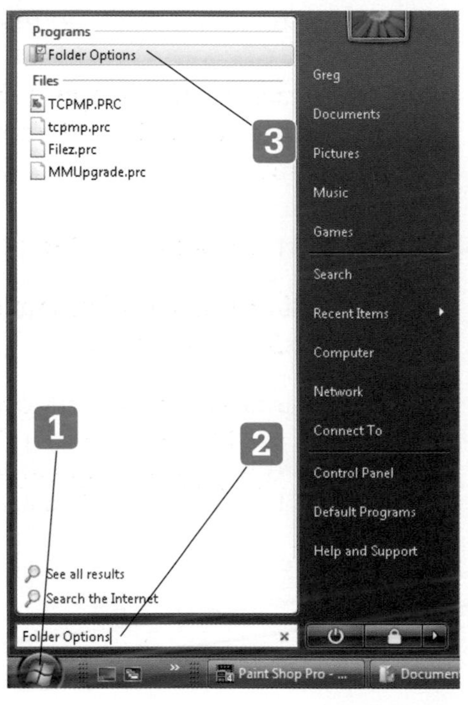

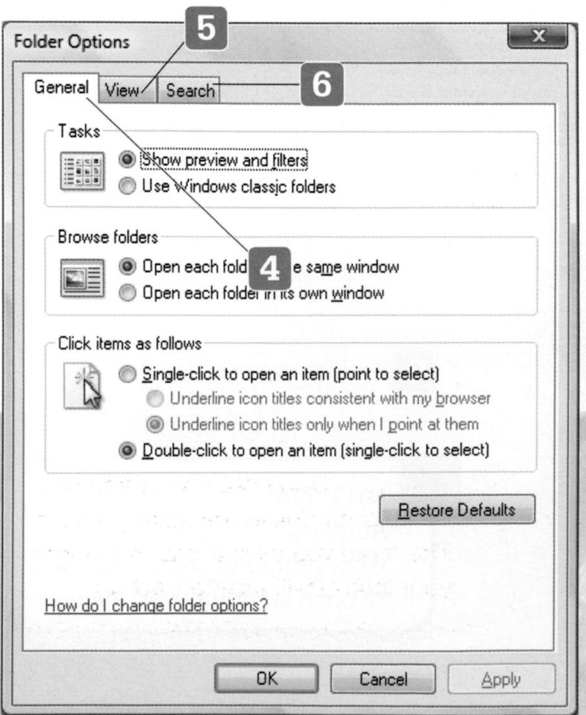

DID YOU KNOW?
To shorten the list of search results, deselect Find partial matches (located in the Search tab of the Folder options dialogue box).

HOT TIP: Select Always show menus, and every folder will offer menus where available.

HOT TIP: If you're more comfortable with older operating systems, choose Use Windows classic folders.

Designate which files or programs launch at start-up

Even if there were other people behind you at the checkout buying a laptop similar to yours, soon they will all be different. One way to individualise your laptop is to control which programs or files launch at start-up.

1. Click the Start button and select All Programs.
2. Right-click the Startup folder and choose Open to open the Startup window.
3. Create a shortcut for the file, folder or program you want to start by right-clicking the right-hand pane, clicking New, and clicking Shortcut.

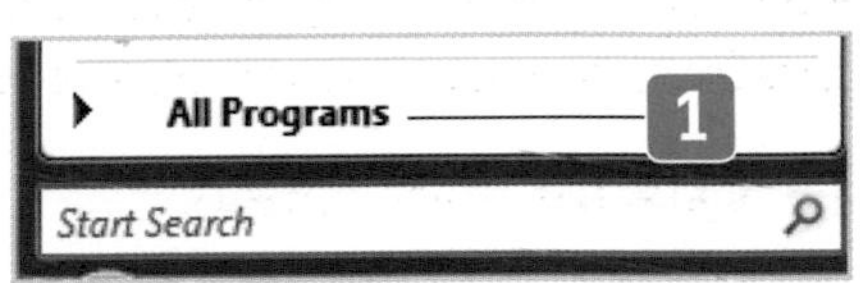

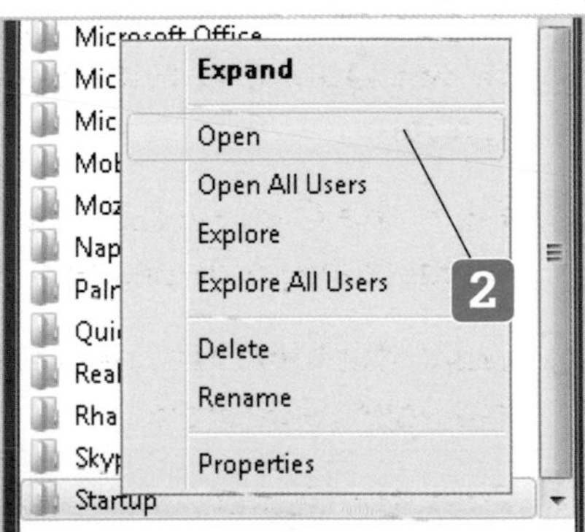

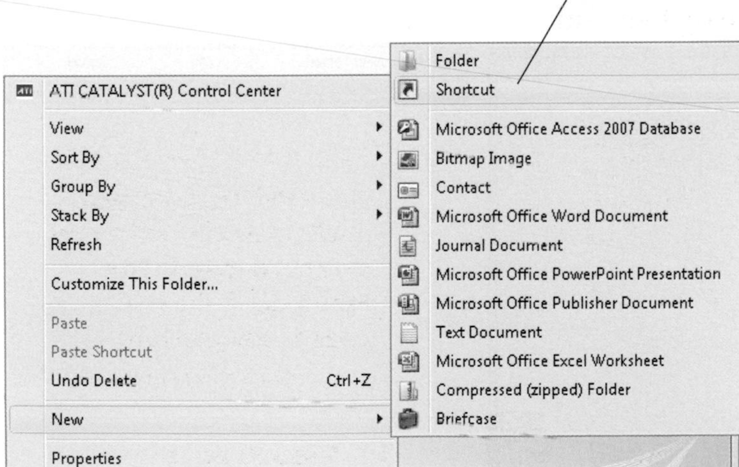

DID YOU KNOW?
The right-hand pane of the Windows Explorer window contains the contents of the Startup folder. You may not have any contents in the folder as yet.

ALERT: Don't put everything but the kitchen sink in the Startup folder. The more you have there, the longer your laptop will take to start up.

4 Click Browse to locate the program.

5 Find the program's icon.

6 Click OK.

7 Click Next.

8 Type a name for the shortcut, if needed.

9 Click Finish.

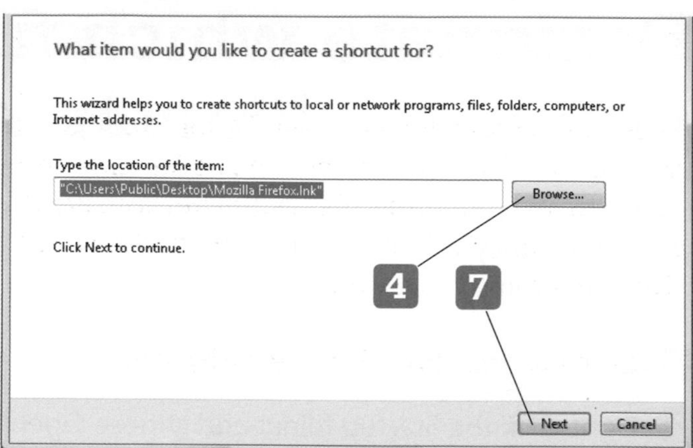

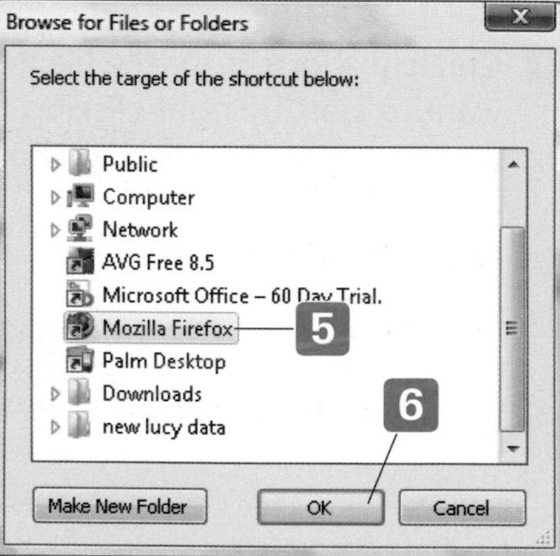

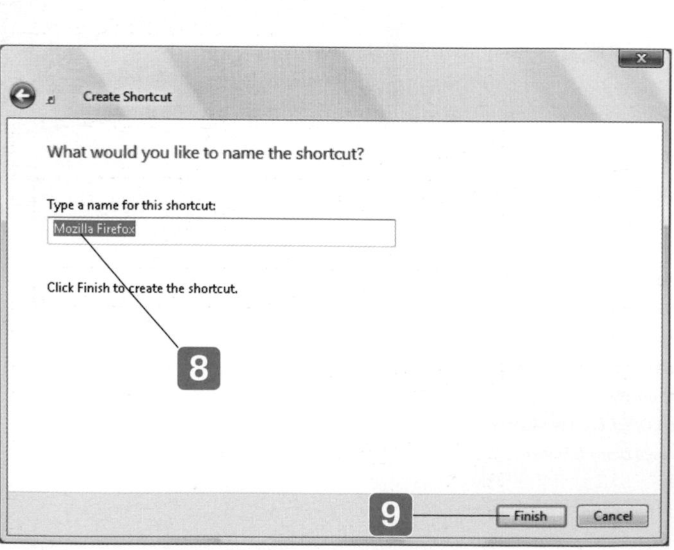

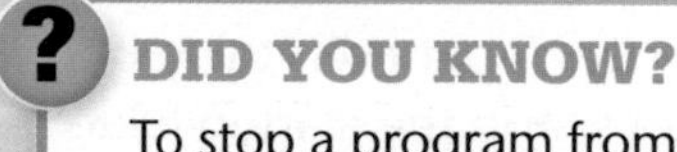

DID YOU KNOW?

To stop a program from opening, delete its shortcut from the Startup folder.

Format a new disk drive

To use a new disk drive on your laptop, you have to format it first using one of two file systems. NTFS should be your choice for larger drives that will stay on the Windows system. Select either the FAT (for drives that are 2 GB or smaller) or the FAT32 (for drives that are 32 GB or smaller) for smaller flash drives or drives you'll use on both Mac and Windows systems.

1. Connect the new drive to your laptop.
2. Click Start.
3. Click Computer.
4. In the Computer window that appears, right-click the drive you want to format and choose Format from the context menu.
5. Name the drive.
6. Select the file system you want to use.
7. Click Start to format the drive.

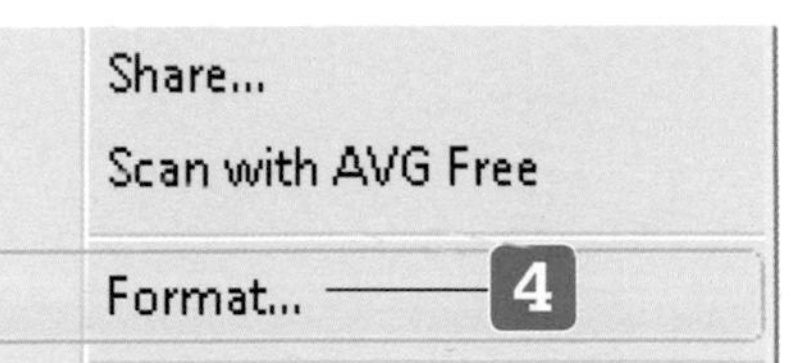

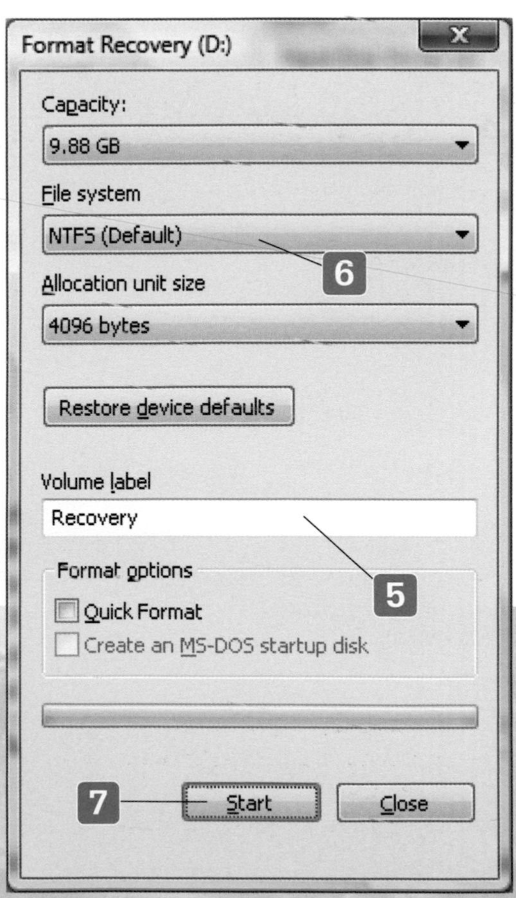

ALERT: First be sure to back up any content you need that's on the drive. The formatting process totally erases the drive.

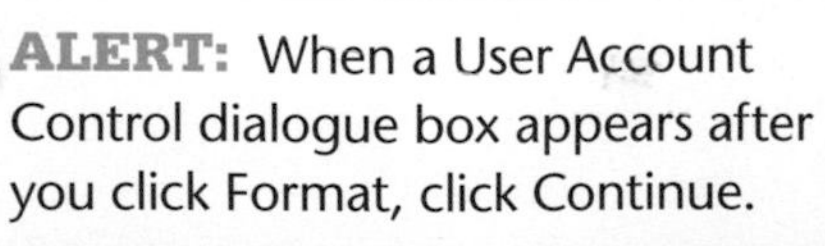

ALERT: When a User Account Control dialogue box appears after you click Format, click Continue.

Top 10 Laptop Problems Solved

Problem 1: I find my laptop screen hard to read. What can I do?

If you are used to reading only on paper, suddenly trying to read text and view lists of files and folders on a computer screen can be disorienting. Not to worry: you have several options available to you for making your laptop's contents more readable.

1. Purchase and install an external flat-screen monitor for use at home.
2. Turn up the brightness: open Mobility Center and move the brightness slider to the right.
3. Change the resolution: open the Control Panel.
4. Under Display, click Adjust screen resolution.
5. Move the slider to the left to make the resolution smaller, which makes contents appear bigger.
6. Click OK.

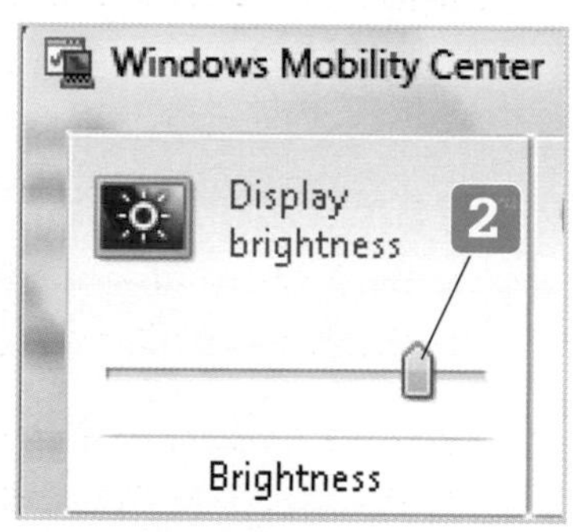

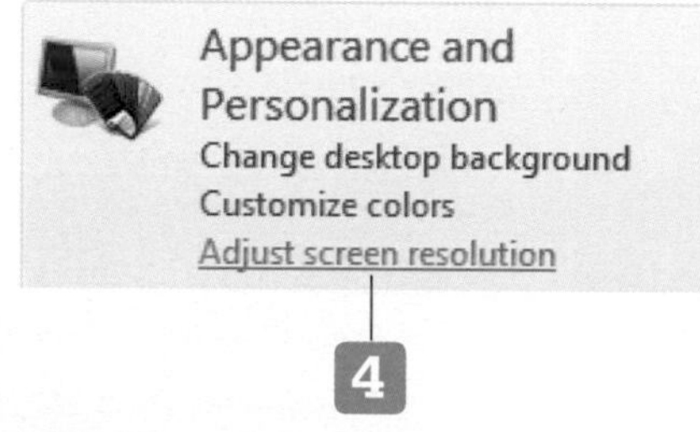

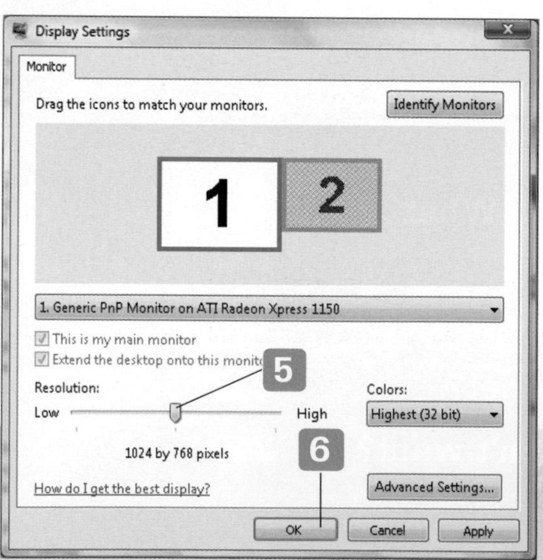

HOT TIP: Flat-screen monitors are becoming more affordable all the time. When this was written, you could find a 17-inch model at eBay UK for £34.99.

ALERT: Changing screen resolution is an option, but if you make icons on your screen too big, you might lose sight of some of them. Before you try the smallest resolution (800 × 600), try an in between resolution such as 1024 × 768.

Problem 2: My laptop crashed and I lost data. What can I do?

This section won't do you a lot of good if you never back up. Or if you've stored backups in the same place as the original files, you're also out of luck. But for the sake of argument, let's say that your original files have been deleted or corrupted. Here's how to get your files off the backup disk or network location.

1. Open the Control Panel, click System and Maintenance, and click Restore files from backup under Backup and Restore Center.

2. In the Restore files section, click on the Restore files button.
3. Select a backup from which you want to restore the files.
4. Click on the Next button.
5. The Restore Files window contains options for selecting which items you want to restore. Click on an Add button.

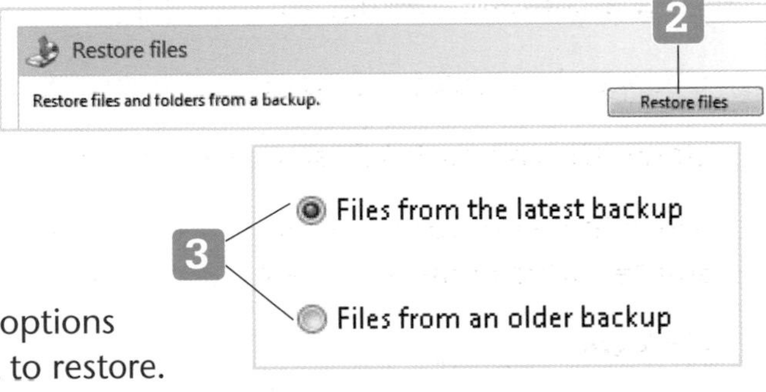

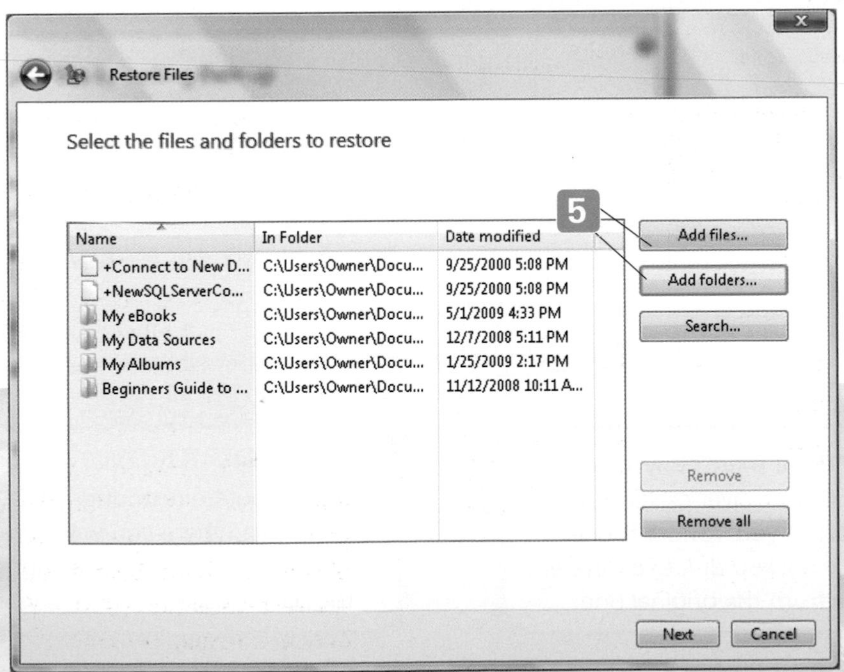

6 Select a folder or file.

7 Click on the Add button, and the selected folder or file is displayed in the Restore Files window. Repeat steps 6 and 7 as needed.

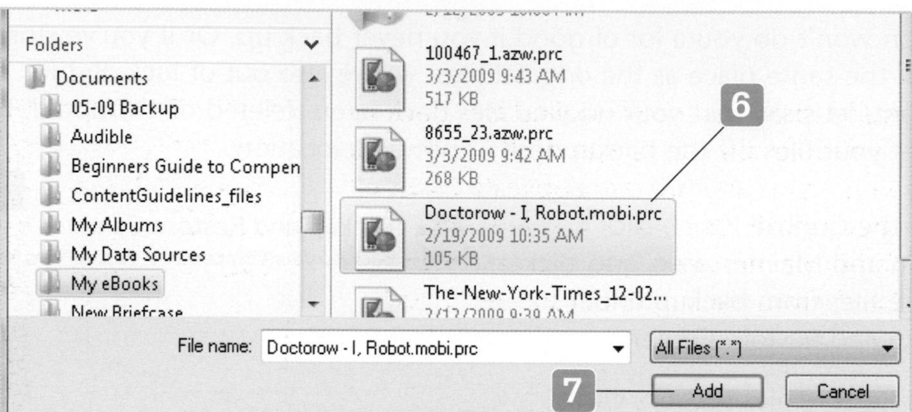

8 Click Next.

9 Click a destination.

10 Click on the Start restore button.

11 Click on the Finish button.

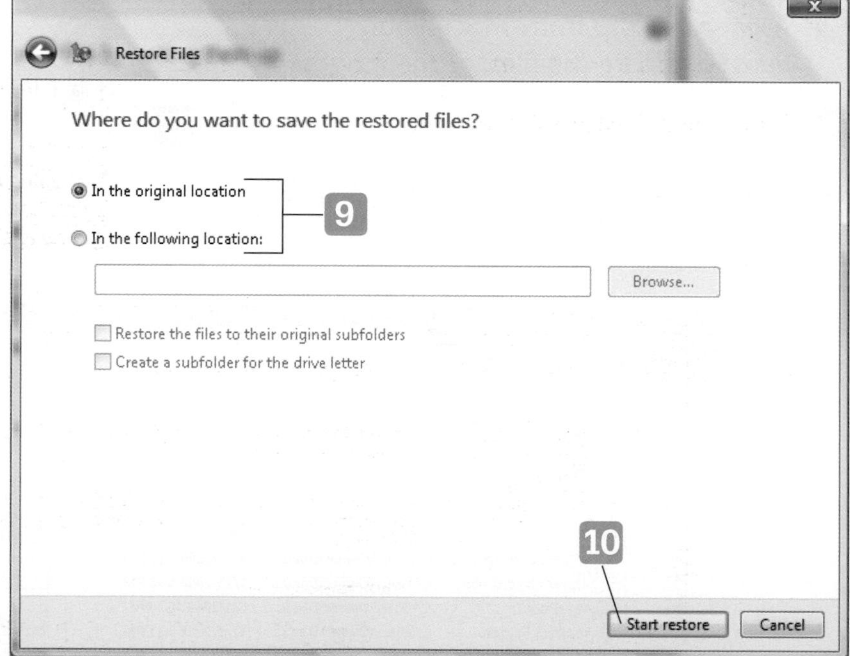

HOT TIP: If there's anything about copying over existing files that worries you, restore the files from the backup disk to a different location from the original one.

DID YOU KNOW?
When you are restoring items, you select a location where you want them to be restored, rather than selecting them from the backup disk.

Problem 3: Windows isn't working correctly. What can I do to fix it?

Have you ever wished you could rewind the clock to go back to a happier time? You can do this with your laptop's operating system. In case applications won't launch, your computer crashes or you are presented with repeated error messages, you can take Windows back to a date before your problem started. First, enable System Restore.

1. Click Start.
2. In the Start Search box, type System Restore.
3. Click System Restore under the Programs results.
4. Click, open System Protection.

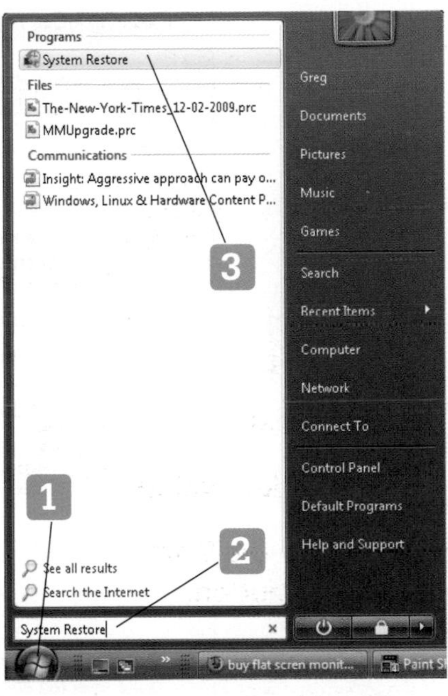

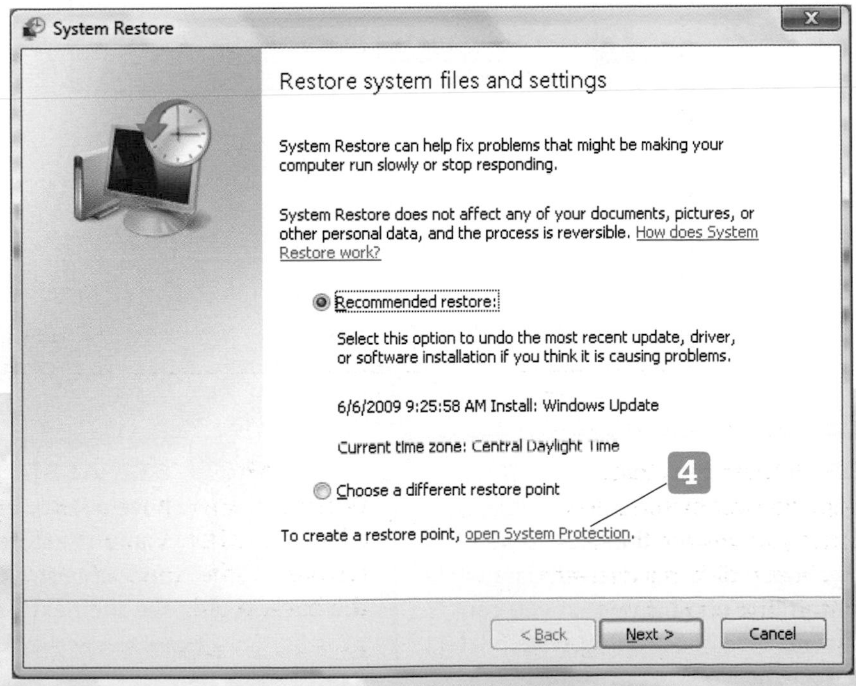

5 Select the C: drive, or the System drive, if it is not already selected.

6 Click OK.

7 In the System Restore window, click Cancel.

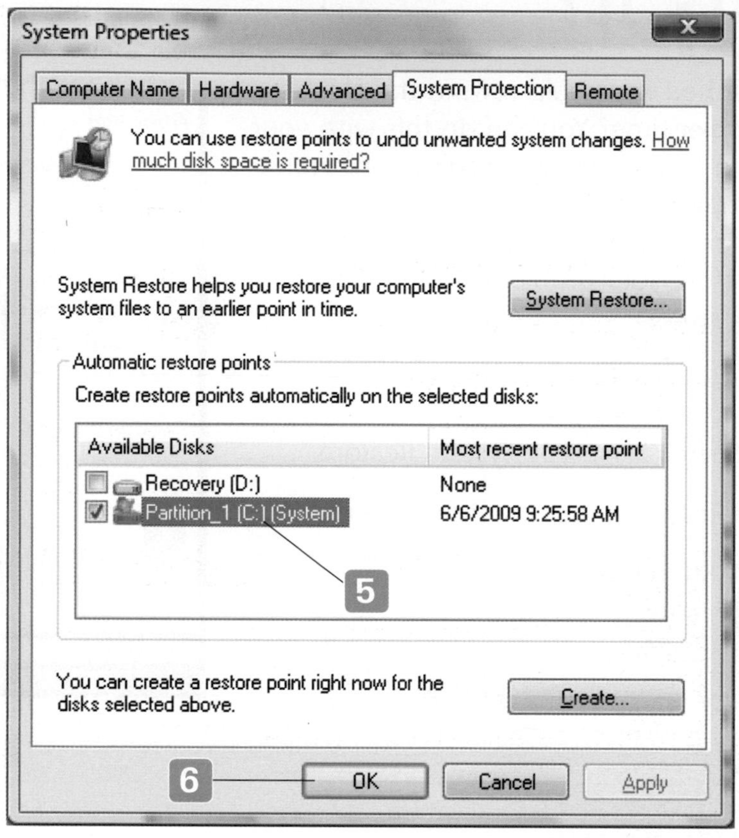

ALERT: You need to enable System Restore before your system is in trouble, not after. (Do it now, while things are running smoothly. That way it will 'record' data while the system is in a good state that you can use to restore a malfunctioning system later.)

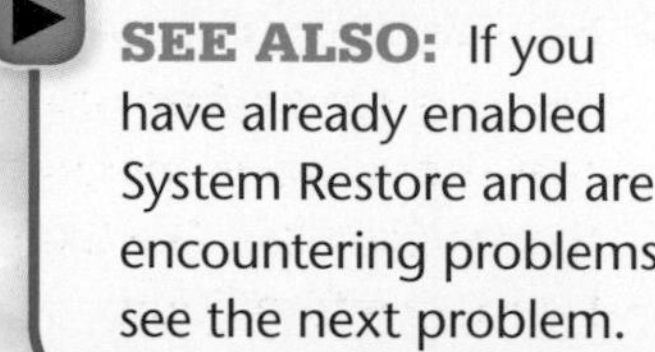

SEE ALSO: If you have already enabled System Restore and are encountering problems, see the next problem.

Problem 4: How do I use System Restore?

One day, it's fine. The next day, not so good. Maybe it was something it ate in the form of a program that had been loaded or software (driver) that had been loaded for an external device, such as a printer. With Windows you can restore the settings of your laptop to an earlier date.

1. Open the Control Panel.
2. Click on the System and Maintenance link.
3. Click Backup and Restore Center.
4. In the Tasks panel, click on the Repair Windows using System Restore link.

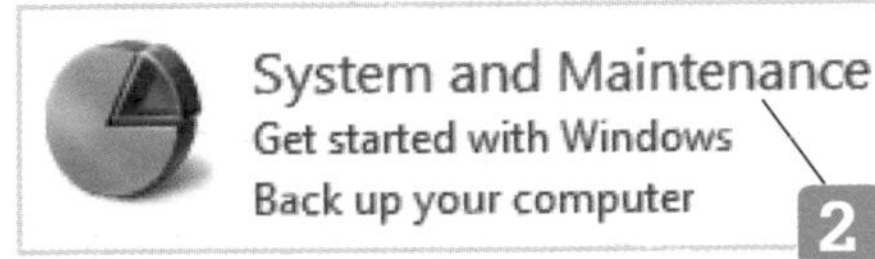

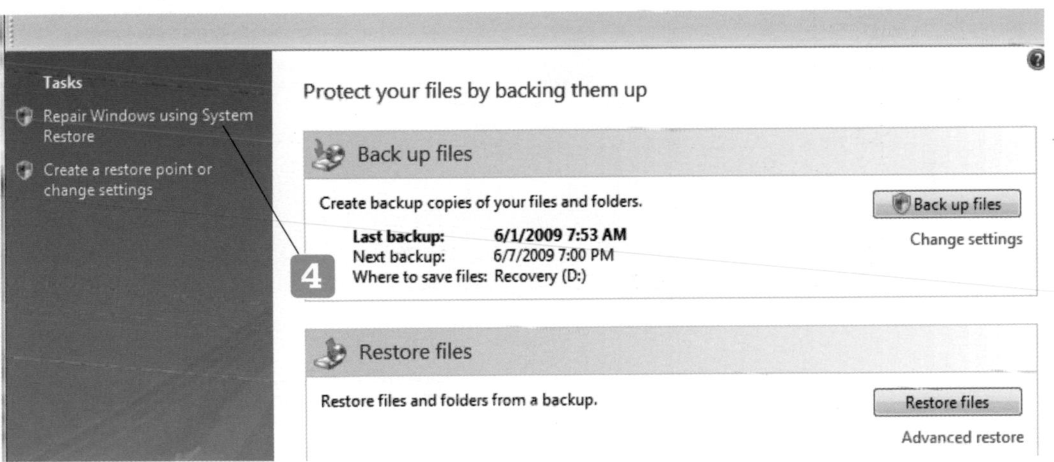

SEE ALSO: In order to restore your files, System Restore needs to have taken a snapshot of your operating system at some time in the past. See the previous problem for more information.

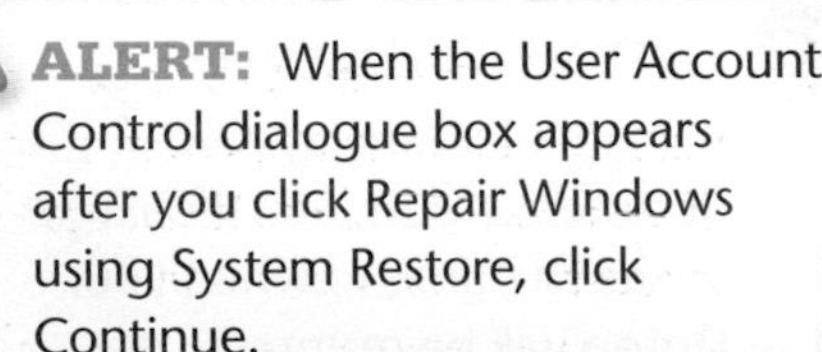

ALERT: When the User Account Control dialogue box appears after you click Repair Windows using System Restore, click Continue.

5 The System Restore window has options for when you want your laptop restored to. Click on the Recommended restore button to undo the most recent changes made to your laptop.

6 Click on the Next button.

7 Click on the Finish button.

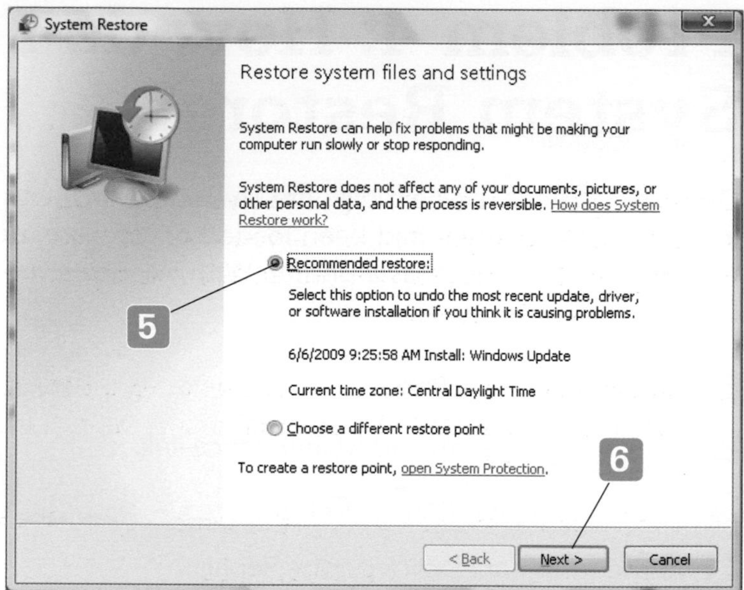

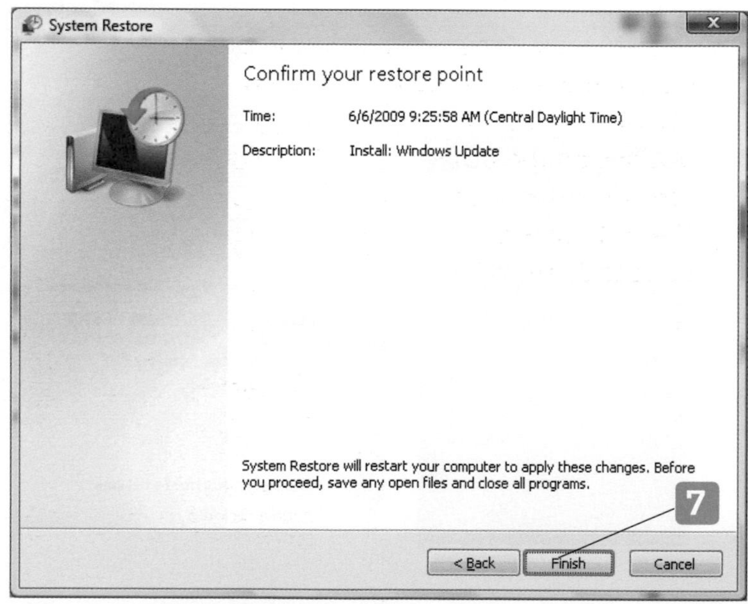

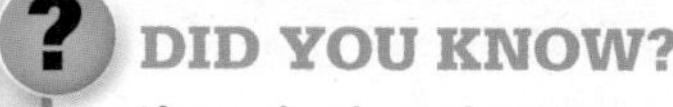

DID YOU KNOW?

If you look at the System Restore window, you'll be able to see the time to when your laptop will be restored.

ALERT: Always start with the most recent System Restore point to see if this fixes the problem. If not, use a more distant restore point.

Problem 5: How do I adjust my external mouse?

Connecting an external mouse will solve your difficulties when using a touchpad. At least, that's what you think. But you might still end up with a mouse that moves strangely or stops moving altogether. You can adjust your mouse behaviour to make it more user-friendly, however.

1. Plug in an external mouse and see whether it behaves in the same way as your track pad or pointer stick. If the external mouse works well, the problem lies with your laptop's hardware.
2. If the external mouse behaves the same way, click Start and choose Control Panel.
3. Click Mouse under the Hardware and Sound heading.

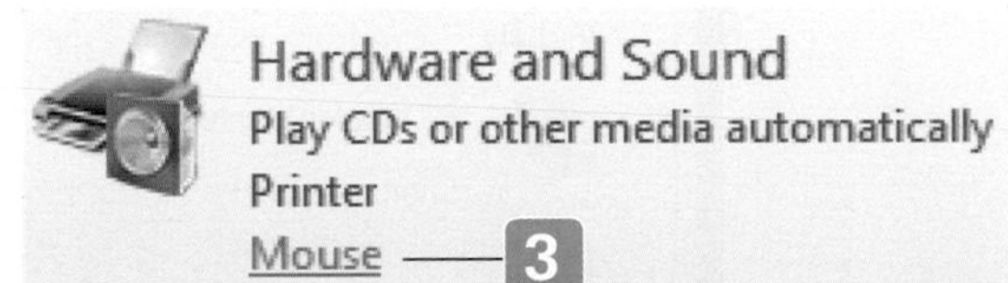

4. In the Mouse Properties dialogue box, ensure that the ClickLock feature is disabled. Skim the options on the other tabs to ensure that the settings are correct there too.

5 If step 4 doesn't solve the problem, click Pointer Options and adjust the pointer speed and other settings to change how the pointer works.

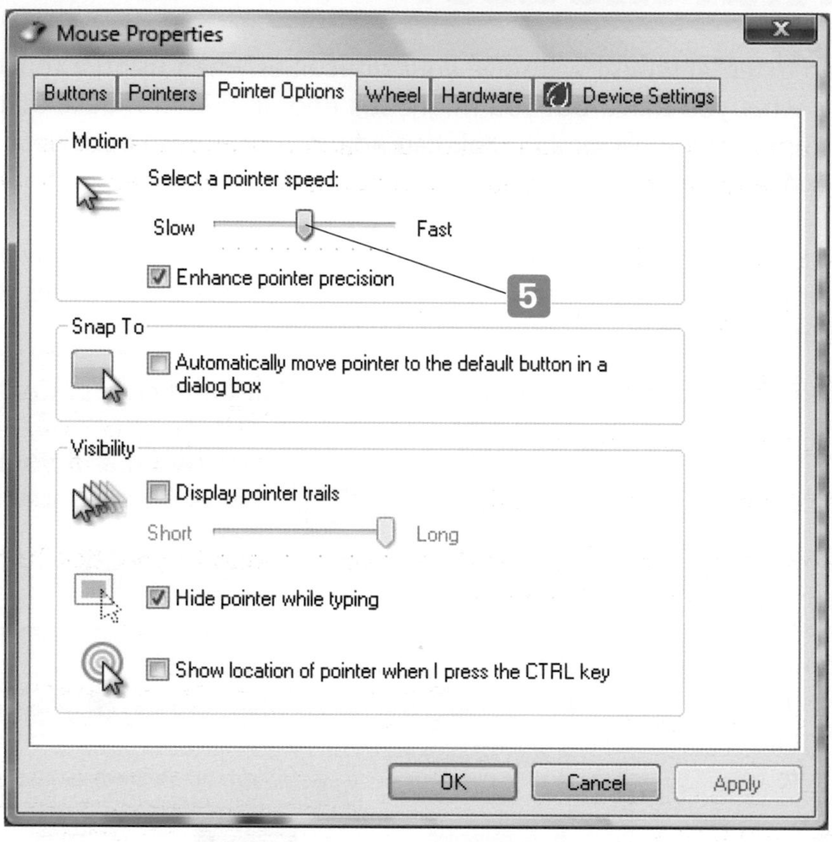

ALERT: If you think the problem is in the hardware, the next step is to call a qualified repair person or your manufacturer. It is officially out of your league.

Problem 6: I have vision problems. How can I make my laptop easier to use?

If you have vision problems, you can make your laptop contents easier to see. If you are blind, you or a friend can optimise your computer so it can be used without a display.

1. Open the Control Panel.
2. Click Ease of Access.
3. Click Ease of Access Center.

3 Ease of Access Center
Let Windows suggest settings
Change how your mouse works

4. Click Make the computer easier to see.
5. Click one of the High Contrast options.
6. To have your computer read text and descriptions aloud to you, tick Turn on Narrator or Turn on Audio Description.

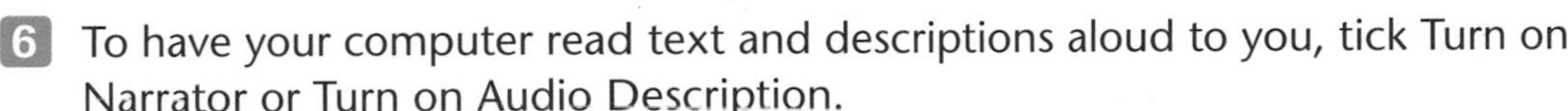

7. Click Save.
8. To make objects on your monitor appear larger without having to change screen resolution, click Change the size of text and icons.
9. To activate an interactive magnifying glass on screen, click Turn on Magnifier.

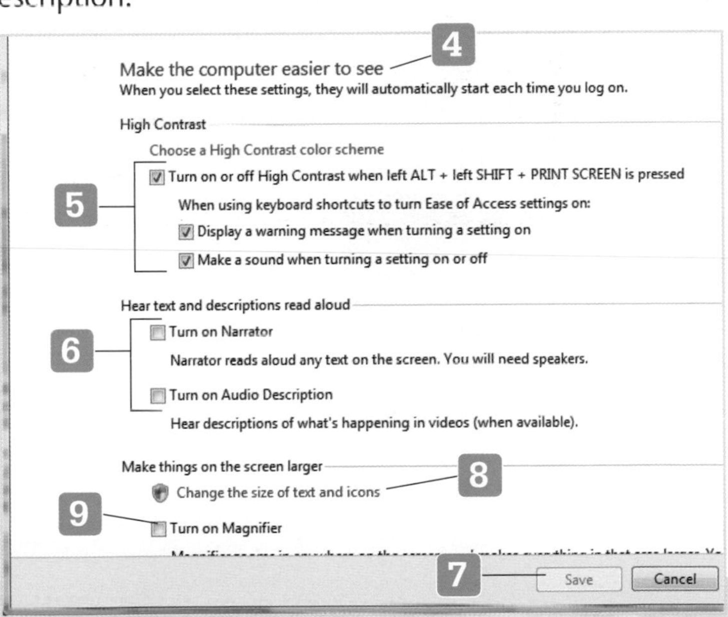

DID YOU KNOW?

When you choose one of the vision enhancements, they will start automatically each time you log on to Windows. You will have to deselect them from the Make the computer easier to see screen if you want to disable them.

10 If you clicked Change the size of text and icons, click Larger scale to make text bigger.

11 Click OK.

12 If you clicked Turn on Magnifier, the Magnifier appears immediately at the top of your screen. Move the mouse arrow around the screen, and the contents appear above.

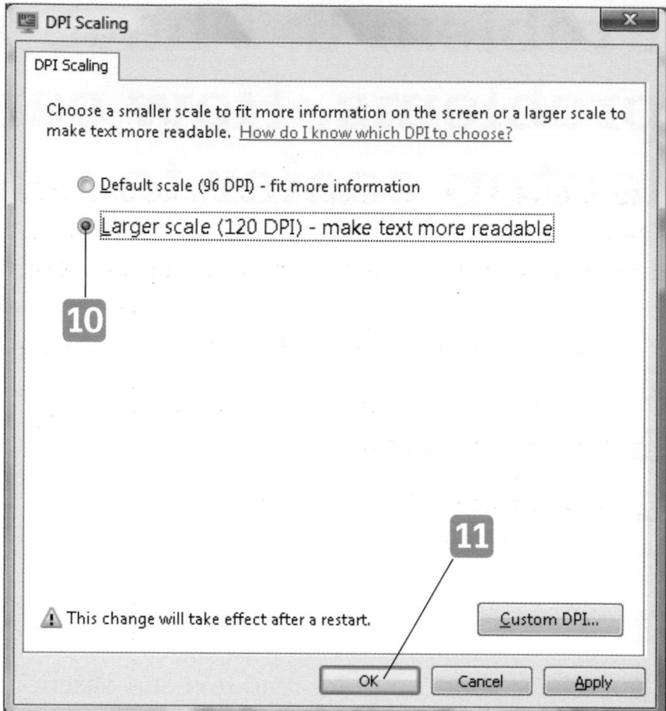

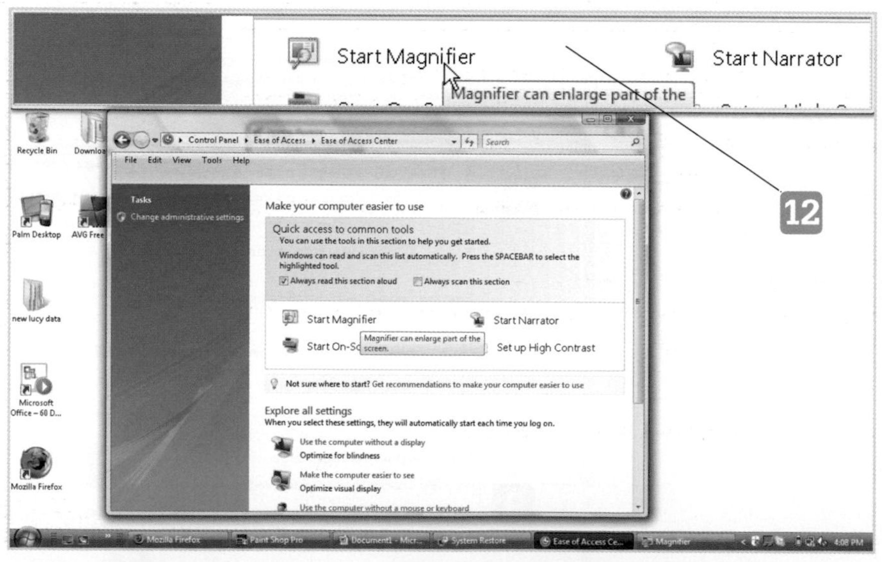

ALERT: You need to restart your computer for the larger text size to appear. However, the Magnifier appears immediately without requiring a restart.

HOT TIP: Click Custom DPI to enter a number larger than 120 DPI (dots per inch) if you need text to be even bigger than 'Larger scale'.

Problem 7: I can't use a mouse or keyboard. What can I do?

The Ease of Access Center also provides options for using alternative input devices other than a mouse or keyboard. If you have trouble typing, you can activate an on-screen keyboard and then select keys using a joystick or other device.

1. Open the Ease of Access Center.
2. Click Use the computer without a mouse or keyboard.
3. Tick the box next to Use On-Screen Keyboard.
4. Click Save.

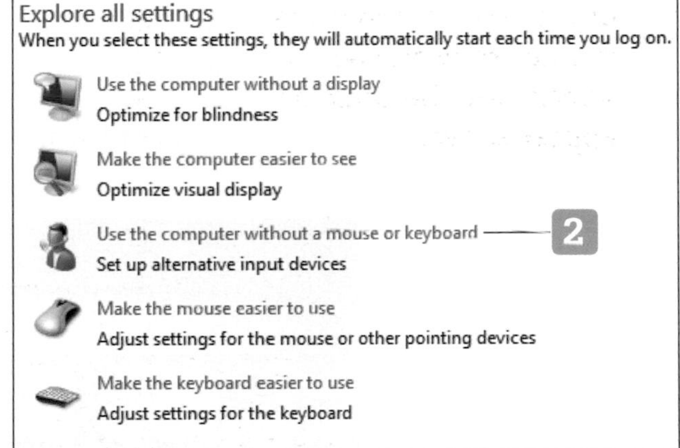

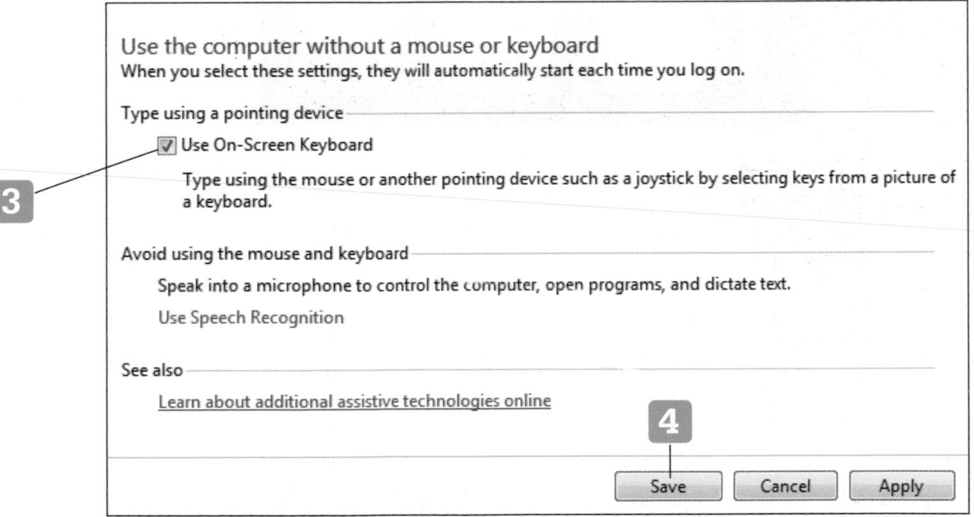

DID YOU KNOW?

Windows also lets you do speech recognition: instead of typing characters, you can speak into a microphone to open programs or enter text. Click the Use Speech Recognition link on the screen labelled Use the computer without a mouse or keyboard.

Problem 8: How do I start my laptop in Safe Mode?

If your laptop doesn't boot up correctly, it could be that an update or program you installed is causing problems. You can use Safe Mode to remove any programs you recently installed to see whether the problem is fixed.

1. Restart by holding down the power button until your laptop shuts down, wait a minute, and then press it again.
2. Before you see the Windows logo or the progress bar at the bottom of the screen, press and hold the F8 key.

3. From the menu that appears, select Last Known Good Configuration to see whether your computer begins running normally.
4. If Step 3 fails, repeat Steps 1 and 2.
5. Select Safe Mode. Log into your laptop, if possible.
6. Use Safe Mode to explore your system and remove files or programs that may be causing a problem.

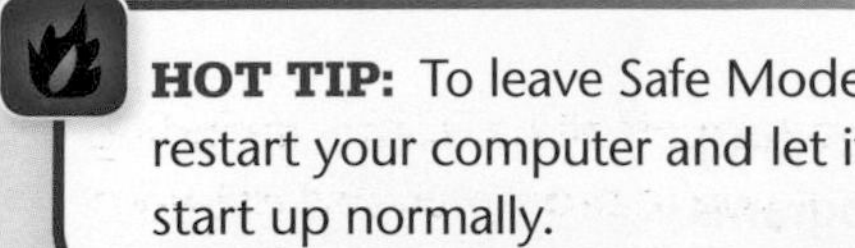

HOT TIP: To leave Safe Mode, restart your computer and let it start up normally.

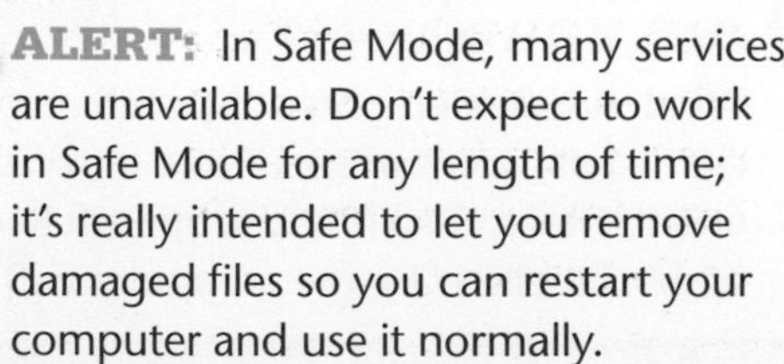

ALERT: In Safe Mode, many services are unavailable. Don't expect to work in Safe Mode for any length of time; it's really intended to let you remove damaged files so you can restart your computer and use it normally.

Problem 9: How do I reconnect to the Internet?

Sooner or later, you'll probably encounter problems connecting to the Internet. Before you call your Internet Service Provider's support staff, there are some tried-and-trusted approaches you should take first.

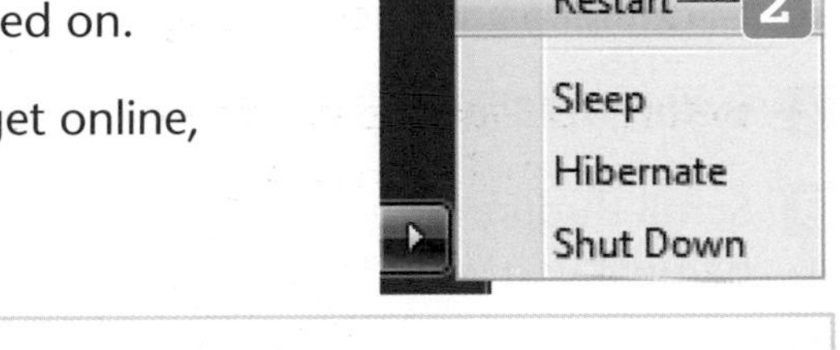

1. Make sure your modem, router, cables and other hardware are properly connected, plugged in and turned on.
2. If your laptop uses a wireless connection to get online, restart your computer.
3. Open the Network and Sharing Center.
4. Click the red X.
5. Perform the steps presented in the Windows Network Diagnostics dialogue box.

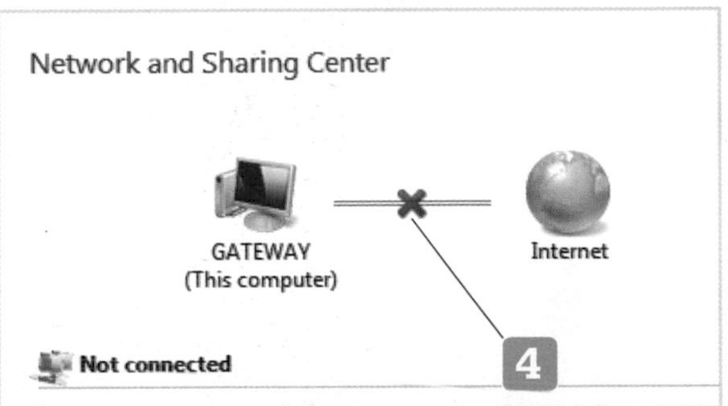

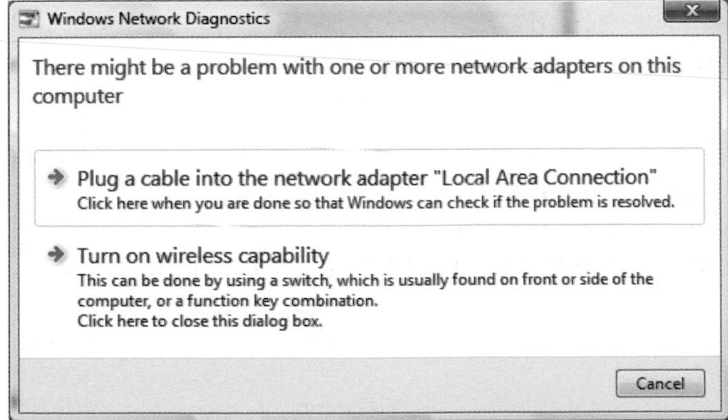

ALERT: When restarting a cable or satellite modem, you need to turn it off completely first. That involves removing any batteries.

DID YOU KNOW?

You need to turn off all hardware, including the laptop, if you're prompted to reset your broadband or satellite connection. Restarting should be done in the following order: cable/satellite/DSL modem, router, laptops.

Problem 10: How do I remove programs I don't want?

Conventional wisdom dictates that if an article of clothing has hung in your wardrobe for more than a year without being worn, it should be given away. The same principle applies to your laptop. If you haven't used an application in a long time, you can safely remove it because you probably never will.

1. Click Start, and then click Control Panel.
2. In Control Panel, click Uninstall a program.
3. Scroll through the list. Click a program name if you want to uninstall it.
4. Click Uninstall or Change.
5. Follow the prompts to uninstall the program.

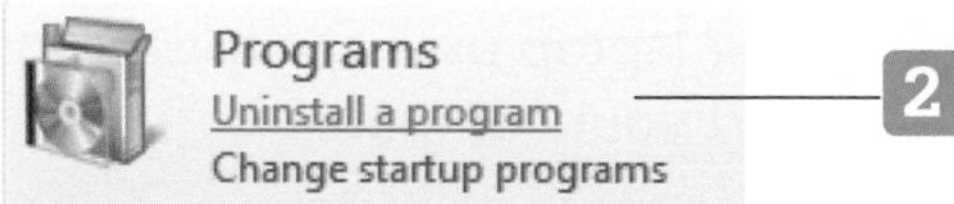

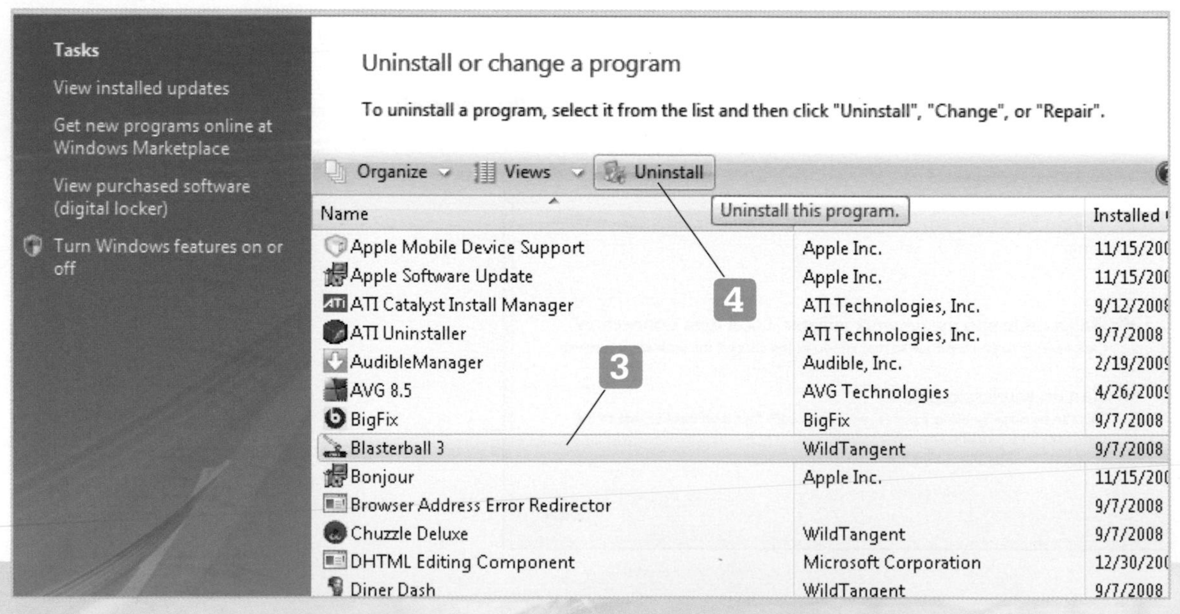

DID YOU KNOW?

Your laptop may have come with programs that you don't need. Manufacturers also add applications that you don't want, such as office suites or games. If you don't use it, lose it.